KT-467-861

# CONTENTS

# ACKNOWLEDGEMENTS

So many people contributed to this book that to mention them all would require a whole new battle with Green Books over the word count! But warm thanks are due to Helen, Philip and Max in Stroud; Andy, Linda and Lucy in Sheffield; Mischa, Julia and Flo in Brighton; Sophy in Cornwall; Chris and Richard in Lincoln and to scores of others, many of them mentioned by name in these pages, who generously gave time, energy, tea and cakes in support of this endeavour. I am in your debt.

Special thanks also to the contributors who listened to my impossibly detailed requests followed by a stipulation to use no more than 400 words! In most cases they wisely ignored me.

Thanks to Ben for explaining the intricacies of 'Survey Monkey' and to Transition activists all over the world who responded to a survey circulated by the Transition Network. I'm sorry I couldn't use more of your inspiring stories.

I'm sure Rob Hopkins would fit the bill for the famous song by Ian Dury And The Blockheads, *There Ain't Half Been Some Clever Bastards*. Thanks Rob for all your insightful comments from start to finish of this project.

Archimedes said: "give me a firm place to stand and I'll move the world." Totnes is now my firm place, so thanks to everyone who has made me so welcome and all those, here and elsewhere, who are slowly but surely moving the world.

Finally, of course, many thanks to Amanda Cuthbert and all the team at Green Books.

My love and thanks to 'Isabella Sol' and to all our children.
May we all live in homes with sunshine and soul.

In memory of Kevin Gately, who might have written a book
but never got the chance.

# INTRODUCTION

In *The Pattern of English Building*, his seminal review of vernacular English construction techniques and the wide range of building materials that have defined English architecture – from flint and chalk to clay, oak and straw – Alec Clifton-Taylor wrote:

> "all these different materials imposed architectural forms appropriate to their character and, despite the many visual improprieties of the last century and a quarter, the pattern is still remarkably complete. It was the great difficulty of transporting heavy materials which led all but the most affluent until the end of the eighteenth century to build with the materials that were most readily available near the site, even when not very durable."[1]

In a world that lacked the hydrocarbon punch that today bestows the ability, which we take for granted, to move mountains, people in a wide diversity of locations developed forms of construction that reflected local materials, the local climate and other cultural influences particular to that place. From Devon's curvaceous cob cottages to the limestone roofs of Dorset; from the intricate timber framing of Suffolk to the granite-walled homes of Leicestershire, it was the materials that defined the forms of building

– leading also to a wide range of artisans and craftspeople: masons, ironmongers, lime kiln-keepers, thatchers and so on.

Over the past hundred years, during what one might call 'The Age of Cheap Oil', the process of building shelter has, like most other aspects of our lives, become increasingly industrialised. A recent study by British Gas[2] found that houses built during the 1960s were built to such shockingly poor standards of energy efficiency that they performed worse than the Tudor homes of the 1500s. In an oral history interview I did in Totnes, Devon, a man who grew up in the town in the 1960s recalled his grandmother, with whom he and his mother lived, keenly moving out of an old house that was a converted cider press.

> "She just wanted modern. She wanted electric fires, electric cookers, electric everything. She wanted automatic this, that and everything. So we moved, at my grandmother's insistence, from this wonderful rambling old building . . . to a brand-new house, typical of its time. Wooden-framed, single-glazed windows, open fire for a chimney which she quickly replaced with an electric fire ("I'm not having any more of that dirty coal business"). The winters were

actually colder than in the previous house. You'd wake up in the morning, and your breath would have condensed on the window, frozen on the inside. Inside it was cold, outside it was cold. Eventually my mother paid for an electric fire to be put in so you could reach out of the bed and turn it on. Electricity was cheap in those days."

These days our challenges in terms of shelter are different from those of the 1960s. We no longer live in a world of cheap and abundant energy. Promises of 'electricity too cheap to meter' have been and gone, and the climate change caused by our burning of fossil fuels is an increasingly urgent issue. It is clear that the target of avoiding a 2°C rise in greenhouse gas emissions is being overtaken by reality: feedbacks not expected for 50-100 years are already under way – the melting of Arctic ice, the release of methane from the seabed, the melting of permafrost, the disappearance of glaciers; the list goes on . . . This is all happening just because of a 0.8°C rise in the levels of $CO_2$ in our atmosphere since fossil-fuel burning began in earnest. The urgent need is not only to reduce emissions, but to seek to phase them out altogether by 2030.

Over the past four years, the rapidly growing Transition movement has argued that climate change cannot be looked at in isolation from the imminent peaking in world oil production, with the resultant price volatility and interruptions to supply. This realisation has mobilised thousands of communities around the world to start planning for life beyond cheap energy – to see the end of the age of cheap energy and the need for urgent decarbonisation not as a disaster but as an opportunity; a once-in-a-lifetime opportunity to rethink basic assumptions. Transition Initiatives can now be found in villages, islands, cities, districts, boroughs, universities and schools around the world.

They focus on the practicalities of relocalisation, offering a creative process of engagement and awareness-raising that seeks to involve the community in designing a new, and more appropriate, way forward. The impact of Transition thinking is starting to emerge in the most unexpected places. A report in 2010 from Lloyds Insurance and Chatham House[3] argued, as Transition has for the past four years, that peak oil needs to be looked at alongside climate change, and the following quote from that report could have been taken straight from a Transition publication such as this book:

> "Energy security is now inseparable from the transition to a low-carbon economy, and businesses plans should prepare for this new reality. Security of supply and emissions-reduction objectives should be addressed equally, as prioritising one over the other will increase the risk of stranded investments or requirements for expensive retrofitting."

Just as they have in all other aspects of our lives, cheap fossil fuels have come to underpin the way in which we build our homes. In the same way that it has been argued that our current food system means that we are, in effect, as Dale Allen Pfeiffer put it, 'eating oil', such is the embodied energy in new buildings that it could be argued that we now live in buildings made from oil too.

In the same way that, across the world, the Transition movement is arguing for seeing peak oil and climate change as two sides of one coin, Chris Bird's book represents an important shift in the debates around what the housing of the future will be like. Much of the literature on green building focuses on new build using local and/or natural materials – what is often termed 'natural building' – as self-builders discover the possibilities presented by materials such as cob, straw bales, hemp and so on. I have been involved in a number of natural building projects, and have taught straw-bale, cob, cordwood and hemp/lime construction courses. These are all wonderfully democratic materials; anyone can get the hang of them and use them to create individual spaces that feel so different from our everyday idea of what a house should feel like.

The point Chris makes in this book, however, is that the decisions about housing we need to make will bring together the challenges we face today (peak oil, climate change, the need vastly to reduce our energy consumption) with the challenges faced in the past (the need to rediscover local building materials). Much of what is known as 'green building' sources its materials from far and wide – sheep's-wool insulation from Germany; lime from France; shingles from Canada. Like a delicious but distantly sourced organic meal, this represents an approach that is highly vulnerable to volatile energy prices.

The core argument of *Local Sustainable Homes* is that housing ourselves can be, and needs to be, about far more than simply having a roof over our heads. The model today is one of homes designed for us, built from high-embodied-energy materials, with a high carbon footprint; materials sourced wherever in the world they can be found cheapest; and the property purchased in a way that saddles us with a debt we then spend many years struggling to pay off. How would it be if, instead, we were more involved with our homes' design, if our choice of materials meant that it became possible for local businesses to emerge to provide them, if the construction process worked in such a way that people could be trained to engage with construction for the first time, and if the homes were built in such a way as to require no space heating at all? We could, by building 'sustainable homes',

produce buildings that lock up more carbon than they produce, that have a local distinctiveness, and that stimulate the local economy rather than leaching from it.

Of course, it is not all just about new buildings. Of Britain's approximately 24 million homes, at least 87 per cent are projected to still be in use by 2050. Retrofitting existing homes saves 15 times more $CO_2$ than demolishing and rebuilding them. Over the past 30 years we have also used our housing stock to introduce the ruinous idea that our houses will increase in value for ever, and that we can use them as a cash-dispensing machine. In the UK, and especially in Ireland, this has led to a huge problem of overpriced, energy-inefficient housing that nobody can afford, and historically unprecedented indebtedness. Alongside energy efficiency and local materials, it is clear that we also need to find new models for how we 'do' housing – such as cohousing, housing cooperatives and so on. Many such models are explored within these pages. As the implications of the bursting of the debt 'bubble' continue to unravel, the owner–occupier model will become increasingly difficult to sustain, and we will need to look at a variety of ways in which we may house ourselves.

Possibly the greatest challenge, however, is tackling the low energy efficiency of our housing. The UK has some of the worst housing stock in Europe in terms of energy efficiency. How to retrofit buildings of such wildly different types? Many innovative schemes are under way, and Chris explores some of these here.

The question this book addresses, ultimately, is: What is a 'local house'? In ten years' time, might it be possible that the building standards require that new buildings be constructed using almost entirely local materials, but built to very high energy-efficiency standards, and that the existing housing stock be made vastly more energy-efficient, again using mostly local materials? While little is yet happening in terms of the use of local materials for retrofits, one very exciting development, under construction as I write, is the building of two 'local Passivhauses' in Wales. These use largely local materials (over 90 per cent local for one of them), and are built to the Passivhaus standard, requiring no space heating at all. Their construction involves the seeking of local materials, the training of local builders, the recycling of local newspaper (for insulation) and the engagement of local window-makers to manufacture high-performance windows from local timber. It is a project that is beginning to model the future of construction in such a way that the future comes into distinct focus.

The challenge, though, as Gill Seyfang of UAE puts it,[4] is "scaling up the existing small-scale, one-off housing projects to industrial mass-production". Housing ourselves, and reducing the energy consumption of our existing homes, if done well, could become one of the key drivers of the regeneration of our local economies. These challenging times demand that we think smart, and that is just what Chris Bird does within these pages.

Rob Hopkins, September 2010

# CHAPTER 1
# WHAT IS SUSTAINABLE HOUSING?

*"Have nothing in your home that you do not know to be sustainable or believe to be energy-efficient."* With apologies to William Morris

You could do worse than look in the Oxford English Dictionary for a definition of sustainable housing. 'Sustainable' – 'able to be sustained or upheld at a particular level without causing damage to the environment or depletion of resources' and 'house' – 'a building for human habitation'.

I don't have a problem with the definitions but, in my dictionary at least, they are 768 pages apart – a reflection of how separate the two concepts are in the real world. Our homes are just not sustainable. In the UK almost 30 per cent of all energy use is in domestic buildings, so our houses are responsible for over a quarter of all greenhouse gas emissions. A breakdown reveals that 28 per cent is used for space heating, 22 per cent for water heating, 10 per cent for cooking and 40 per cent for lighting and appliances. As summer temperatures rise, energy savings from improved insulation could be more than offset by increased use of domestic air conditioning.

But these figures underestimate the impact of housing because they don't include the construction of buildings, infrastructure or demolition. Building shelter is estimated to use 16 per cent of the world's freshwater supply, 25 per cent of timber and 40 per cent of fossil fuels and manufactured materials. The housing industry contributes around 50 per cent of all pollution in the world, with cement alone responsible for 8 per cent of total greenhouse gases.[1] And house building is a very wasteful industry. Around 20 per cent of all construction waste in the UK is caused by over-ordering materials that are then sent to landfill.

> "For every new house built, one is thrown away!"[2]
>
> Katy Jackson

## Why do we need sustainable housing?

So housing makes a big contribution to greenhouse gas emissions and hence to climate change, and for that reason alone has to change. As Paul King, Chief Executive of the Green Building Council, says: "Our homes and buildings should be in the front line in the battle against climate change, rising fuel prices and energy security."[3]

But there's more. As we reach peak oil, it becomes increasingly difficult to continue building and using our houses in the same old way. Look around your home. What can you find that doesn't depend on cheap oil or other fossil fuels for its extraction, processing, manufacture, synthesis, transport or installation? Not much. Bricks and clay tiles are fired in kilns heated by gas or electricity (itself likely to be generated from burning coal, oil or gas). Cement and plasters are also energy-hungry materials. Plastics use energy in their production and oil as a raw material, and metals, another non-renewable resource, require enormous amounts of energy for mining, extraction and fabrication. Even natural materials such as stone and timber are likely to be transported hundreds or even thousands of miles.

There are also good social reasons why we need sustainable housing. In a typical winter, around 25,000 people die in the UK because they can't afford to keep warm in their own homes. As many as 4.4 million British homes, 20 per cent of our total housing stock, fail to provide adequate thermal comfort – and this figure is rising as fuel prices increase. Millions of people live in fuel poverty, defined as spending more than 10 per cent of household income on fuel for space heating, and this is increasing alongside fuel prices. Average household gas bills in the UK rose by over 100 per cent between 2003 and 2008, and electricity bills rose by 70 per cent.

Poorer people tend to live in less energy-efficient houses but actually have smaller carbon footprints than those in 'Middle England'. A study of household carbon emissions by postcode showed that middle-class areas, such as Rickmansworth and Gerrard's Cross, were the worst polluters, with more than 36 tonnes per household, while less affluent communities in Stockton-on-Tees, Newcastle and London were responsible for less than 15 tonnes per household.[4] Although travel and consumerism are responsible for much of this difference, larger houses are a significant part of the problem. The Intergovernmental Panel on Climate

## Housing in crisis

According to Shelter, the leading charity for the homeless, less building, increasing demand and rising costs have created an affordability crisis. Large numbers of people are priced out of buying or even renting a home. The problem is particularly acute for young people on low salaries, with public-sector workers effectively priced out of London or the South East. In England:

- Nearly 80,000 households were found by local authorities to be homeless in 2008/09.
- There were almost 1.8 million households on local authority housing waiting lists in April 2008.
- At the end of June 2009, 60,230 homeless households were living in temporary accommodation.
- More than half a million households live in overcrowded conditions.

Poor housing wastes more than just energy and resources. According to 'The Real Cost of Poor Housing', a report from the Building Research Establishment, it also costs £600 million a year in healthcare.[5]

Change (IPCC) suggests, probably optimistically, that we must reduce household carbon emissions to around 2 tonnes to limit global warming to 2 degrees Celsius. An average household in India has a carbon footprint of just 1 tonne. Poorer households, without any choice, have a head start when it comes to reducing carbon emissions.

## Why are we in this mess?

Enough facts and figures! You get the picture. Housing makes a big contribution to greenhouse gas emissions and we need to do something about it. But before we rush into action let's consider why we're in such a mess.

The architect and author James Wines blames, among others, the great modernist pioneer Le Corbusier. In 1923 Le Corbusier, in homage to a new wave of industrialism, proclaimed: "There exists a new spirit! Industry, overwhelming us like a flood which rolls towards its destined end, has furnished us with new tools adapted to this new epoch, animated by the new spirit." A spirit that, Wines argues, is now "tarnished and discredited in the face of current environmental realities."[6]

Le Corbusier can hardly be blamed for the arrogant attempts to control and dominate nature that are central to modern industrial societies, but, by embracing this spirit and founding an architectural movement that sees houses as 'machines for living in', he did contribute to our current situation. Wines suggests:

> "dumping all of the ego-motivated excesses associated with most architecture of the Twentieth century in favour of a more socially responsible and environmentally integrated approach . . . to progress from ego-centric to eco-centric."[7]

So what would architecture that put ecology ahead of ego look like? Part of the answer can be found in the natural building movement.

## Natural building

In the past few decades the eco-centric approach has progressed under the title of 'natural building'. Crucial to this are decisions about how, where and why to build, as well as about the choice of natural materials.

Natural building emphasises low-tech methods, broad rather than specialist skills, respect for the local environment and regional traditions. It encourages self-build, not just as a way for owner–occupiers to save money but also because of the psychological benefits of hands-on building with natural materials. Natural building involves systems and materials that emphasise sustainability by focusing on durability and the use of minimally processed, plentiful, renewable and salvaged materials to produce healthy living environments. It tends to rely on human labour more than on technology, and it varies with local ecology, geology and climate, the character of the site and the needs and personalities of the builders and users.

If we limit ourselves to local and natural materials, won't that make our houses boring? Certainly not. Some of our most beautiful houses are built with a limited palette of materials from the area. Picasso puts it nicely:

> "Forcing yourself to use restricted means is the sort of restraint that liberates inventing. It obliges you to make a kind of progress you can not even imagine in advance."[8]

Eco-housing pioneers were inspired by Schumacher's *Small is Beautiful*, the self-sufficiency movement associated with John Seymour and the 'natural' homes showcased by the Centre for Alternative Technology to build for personal and planetary health.

In his influential book about our consumer society, *Affluenza*,[9] Oliver Tickell identifies a strong association between self-esteem and housing. Bigger homes, frequent remodelling and obsessive DIY for little real benefit are symptoms of our addiction to consuming as a way to boost our sense of self-worth. Housing is just another part of our consumer culture; but natural building can be the antidote.

Step into any good bookshop and you'll find dozens of books about natural building. Straw, cob, rammed earth, timber frame, lime, hemp and earthships all have passionate advocates, some of whom you'll meet in this book. In recent years the use of natural and sustainable materials has started to penetrate the retrofit market. Wool, woven hemp and recycled newsprint insulation are widely available. The big DIY stores promote 'Earthwool' loft insulation made from recycled plastic bottles and have a range of 'environmentally friendly' products to make our homes and gardens more sustainable. Of course, a lot of this is 'greenwash' – do we really need fountains and garden lights powered by solar energy? – but it does reflect a growing awareness of natural materials and the need to reduce the damage our homes do to the environment.

## What makes housing sustainable?

If we take a narrow definition of sustainability, then we can end up talking about houses that cope with the challenges of climate change and peak oil while actually contributing to these problems; homes that might be wonderful places to live in but part of the problem rather than viable solutions. A home that runs entirely on renewable energy but requires enormous quantities of materials and energy to build is not

## Inspired by nature

Nature can provide the inspiration as well as the materials for building. Antoni Gaudi and Frank Lloyd Wright looked to nature for inspiration long before words such as 'ecology' were in common use. Gaudi studied the intricate structures of leaves, flower stems and tree trunks as models for the structural systems used in his buildings. Visiting his Sagrada Familia in Barcelona is like walking beneath a forest canopy. Wright was influenced by geology and seasonal change. His iconic 'Falling Water' illustrates how a house can be an extension of its environment and use materials drawn from the local area.

William Morris and the Arts and Crafts movement celebrated natural forms and materials in building design, and more than a hundred years later buildings are still inspired by nature. In Zimbabwe the high-rise Eastgate Building is designed to mimic the way that tower-building termites in Africa construct their mounds and use passive ventilation to maintain a constant temperature. The building uses less than 10 per cent of the energy used in conventional buildings. (See the case study at www.biomimicryinstitute.org.)

The Eastgate building in Zimbabwe mimics the passive air circulation used in termite mounds.
Photograph: Michael Pearce / Aga Khan Trust for Culture

sustainable. So we need a holistic understanding of sustainable homes that encompasses the total impact of housing on our planet.

This is a big ask, but anything less is really avoiding the problem. If we consider energy use in a finished building but ignore 'embodied energy' – the energy used in the materials or in construction techniques – then we'll have a false idea of the carbon footprint of that property. If natural materials are transported long distances, then the true environmental impact may be higher than if synthetic local materials are used. Even a home built with sustainable and local materials that runs on little or zero energy may be unsustainable if it fails to encourage environmentally friendly behaviour, is sited a long way from employment opportunities, doesn't form part of a viable community or has an adverse effect on biodiversity, the water cycle or the availability of land.

Even what a house looks like can affect its sustainability. We might disagree with Germaine Greer when she says that "new homes are universally ugly, and eco-homes are the most horrible of the lot",[10] but if her point is that aesthetics are an aspect of sustainability then she is right. Homes and communities that speak to people in a language we instinctively understand and feel comfortable with are homes and communities that work. When Christopher Alexander and his colleagues, writing in *A Pattern Language*,[11] articulate the deeply rooted patterns in rooms and houses, streets and neighbourhoods, towns and cities that help our built environment to function, they identify the words and structure of a language we recognise but have forgotten how to speak. Sustainable homes just feel right, even if we can't always explain why.

## The twelve commandments of sustainable housing

1. **Aim for low or zero net energy use** or even net energy production, achieved through the rational use of insulation, passive solar design, thermal mass and renewable energy generation. Location is an important consideration, as some sites may not be suitable for renewable energy. For a sheltered north-facing slope with no potential for hydro-generation and a rocky substrate unsuitable for ground source heat pumps, then grid electricity from a green supplier may be better.

Once the energy needed in the day-to-day life of a building has been minimised, the energy used in construction becomes a bigger proportion of overall energy use – so make careful choices about materials. Natural materials include rock, gravel, sand, clay, straw and other plant fibres such as hemp, timber, wool and recycled materials. Of course, all waste during construction should be minimised. (See Table 1 and Figure 1, pages 17 & 18.)

2. **Avoid resource depletion.** You'll know about peak oil from the introduction to this book, but building materials such as copper, aluminium, zinc and lead are also becoming scarce.

3. **Don't build unless you have to.** It's better to retrofit or refurbish existing buildings. If you must build, then small really is beautiful. Larger buildings use more energy and materials and take up more land, which could be used to grow food.

4. **Avoid toxic materials.** These are harmful to people and the environment during production, installation and throughout the life of a building. PVC (polyvinyl chloride) is versatile and widely used in buildings but causes pollution during manufacture and disposal. Alternatives such as polybutylene and polyethylene

have a lower impact and are recyclable. There are also safer alternatives to synthetic paints, plasters and furnishing materials.

5. **Use water efficiently.** Harvest rainwater, recycle grey water, include drainage systems that avoid or mitigate the risks of flooding and use sustainable sewage systems such as compost toilets and reed-bed systems.

6. **Homes should be built to last: easily maintained and adaptable.** This means anticipating changing household needs, family structures and the impacts of climate change. We need to build homes to last a lifetime and more!

7. **Building materials should be suitable for recycling or reclamation** when a property is demolished, or reconfigured to meet changing requirements.

8. **Housing should be in harmony with the environment and have a positive impact on biodiversity.** Green roofs and walls are a good example. Individual and shared gardens and food-growing areas provide communal spaces and food, and promote biodiversity.

## Relative worth of construction materials assessed against a range of 'Bau-Biologie' sustainability criteria

| CRITERIA | A | B | C | D | E | F | G | H | I | J | K | L | M | N | O | P | Average score |
|---|---|---|---|---|---|---|---|---|---|---|---|---|---|---|---|---|---|
| **MATERIAL** | | | | | | | | | | | | | | | | | |
| Timber (solid wood) | 3 | 3 | 3 | 3 | 3 | 3 | 3 | 3 | 3 | 3 | 3 | 3 | 3 | 3 | 2 | 3 | **2.9** |
| Earth (clay) | 3 | 3 | 3 | 3 | 3 | 3 | 2 | 3 | 3 | 3 | 3 | 3 | 3 | 3 | 3 | 3 | **2.9** |
| Straw (natural fibres) | 3 | 3 | 3 | 3 | 3 | 3 | 3 | 3 | 3 | 3 | 3 | 3 | 3 | 3 | 2 | 3 | **2.9** |
| Stone | 3 | 3 | 3 | 2 | 3 | 3 | 2 | 3 | 3 | 2 | 1 | 2 | 2 | 3 | 3 | - | **2.5** |
| Lime mortar/plaster | 2 | 2 | 3 | 1 | 3 | 3 | 2 | 2 | - | 3 | 3 | 3 | 2 | 3 | 3 | - | **2.5** |
| Brick (fired) | 2 | 3 | 3 | 1 | 2 | 3 | 2 | 3 | 3 | 2 | 1 | 2 | 2 | 3 | 3 | - | **2.3** |
| Plywood/particle board | 2 | 1 | 2 | 2 | 3 | 3 | 3 | 3 | - | 1 | 2 | 3 | 2 | 0 | 1 | - | **2.0** |
| Glass | 0 | 1 | 1 | 0 | 3 | 0 | 0 | 0 | - | 0 | 0 | 3 | 0 | 3 | 3 | - | **1.0** |
| Fibreglass | 0 | 0 | 0 | 0 | 3 | 1 | 3 | 3 | - | 1 | 0 | 2 | - | 0 | 0 | 0 | **0.9** |
| Polystyrene | 0 | 0 | 0 | 0 | 3 | 0 | 3 | 3 | 0 | 1 | 0 | 3 | 0 | 0 | 1 | 0 | **0.9** |
| Concrete (reinforced) | 1 | 0 | 1 | 0 | 1 | 1 | 2 | 1 | 0 | 0 | 0 | 0 | 3 | 3 | 0 | | **0.8** |
| PVC products | 0 | 0 | 0 | 0 | 3 | 0 | 1 | 2 | 0 | 0 | 0 | 3 | 0 | 0 | 0 | - | **0.6** |
| Synthetic glue | 0 | 0 | 0 | 0 | 3 | 0 | - | - | - | 0 | 0 | 3 | 0 | 0 | 0 | - | **0.5** |
| Vapour barriers (foil or plastic) | 0 | 0 | 0 | 0 | 3 | 0 | - | - | 0 | 0 | 0 | - | 0 | 0 | 1 | - | **0.3** |

**3 = very desirable, flawless**
**2 = desirable, few shortcomings**
**1 = marginally desirable, some shortcomings**
**0 = undesirable**
**– = not applicable, no scientific data available**

A = Natural origin
B = Biological / ecological health
C = Resource renewability
D = Embodied energy
E = Radioactivity
F = Electrical properties
G = Thermal properties
H = Acoustic properties

I = Natural radiation permeability
J = Breathability
K = Hygroscopicity
L = Moisture content / drying potential
M = Absorption / regeneration
N = Toxic vapours
O = Odour
P = Biological stress

Table 1. Based on the Bau-Biologie system used by Harvestbuild Associates.

9. **Housing should be part of communities** that meet all our needs for employment, shopping, social life, education, arts and being in touch with nature. Community is an essential ingredient of sustainability. Alongside the development of natural building there have been social innovations such as housing cooperatives, cohousing, intentional communities, communes, all manner of collective self-building groups and many other models that promote fruitful interaction between neighbours.

Homes and neighbourhoods where people feel unsafe are not sustainable, but neither are communities where security is promoted through locked gates, security guards and burglar alarms. In sustainable communities people leave their doors unlocked.

10. **Homes should appeal to the eye and feel good to be in.** Many of the features that characterise such homes are identified in *A Pattern Language* by Christopher Alexander, who studied successful buildings and

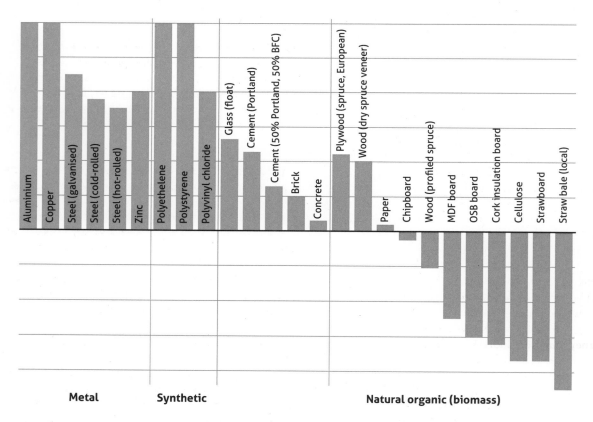

Figure 1. Net CO$_2$ emissions in kg resulting from the production of 1kg of various building materials. Research by Richard McMath, with additional information from Jakub Wihan. Jakub Wihan, MSc Architecture thesis (2007), 'Humidity in Straw Bale Walls and its Effect on the Decomposition of Straw', available at www.jakubwihan.com/pdf/thesis.pdf

lists their key features. However, far from tying us to the past, Alexander suggests that buildings that feel good "are adapted, deeply, to land and to people . . . for it is not style that makes a building living or dead, but the freshness of its responses to its surroundings."[12]

11. **Housing should be affordable.** Unless the rich can find a different planet to live on, then sustainable housing has to be a right not a privilege.

12. **Location. Location. Location.** Houses should be located so as to minimise environmental impact and, in the UK, oriented to make optimal use of passive solar gain while avoiding cold winds.

## Models we can learn from

So is this book limited to examples that tick all the sustainability boxes outlined above? No! Models don't have to be perfect to hold valuable lessons. Psychologists suggest that the 'good enough' parent is better than the so-called 'perfect' parent, who meets the child's every need and thus prevents him or her from learning to cope with problems. Perfect examples of housing would seem so difficult to emulate that we'd be put off before we even started.

So here we take a look at examples of sustainable housing that are going in the right direction, rather than holding up a few pristine examples that may have reached some imaginary goal. Perhaps we'll learn more from people who have just started the journey than from individuals or communities further along the path. There won't be one 'perfect' solution, but we almost certainly do have all the answers we need. We don't need to discover a 'magic bullet' or invest billions in developing new technologies or smart materials to solve our housing problems. Everything we need to make our homes sustainable is already here. We know how to build houses that are

Green roofs provide insulation, reduce rainwater run-off and look beautiful. Photograph: Tim and Kate Birley

warm in winter and cool in summer without consuming unsustainable quantities of energy. We have a rich heritage of vernacular buildings, constructed from locally available materials, that just needs to be rediscovered. We also know what makes a community work and we know what makes us happy.

### Ideological barriers

Good examples abound but are ignored because 'that's not what we normally do' or because they don't make a profit. Is it possible to spread lessons from the 'green niches' of sustainable building to the eco-developers and mainstream builders? Dr Gill Seyfang, a researcher at the University of East Anglia, points out that the overlap between these areas is usually around just one aspect of sustainability: low carbon.[13] How can we encourage, lead and even force the mainstream to adopt sustainability in the wider sense?

Green niches can be powerful examples, but their value is limited because 'green pioneers' and communities from which sustainable housing initiatives spring usually have an ideological basis that rejects and conflicts with the mainstream. Sustainable ideas and practices are not ideologically neutral, and this makes it difficult to transfer them to a mainstream with fundamentally different values. And modifying

## Story from Nicaragua

In 1986 I travelled with a group of health workers through Nicaragua. The Reagan-inspired 'Contra' war against the elected Sandinista government was seriously damaging the economy, and many people, although much better off than under the Somoza dictatorship, still lived in poverty.

I have many powerful memories of that trip, but one of the most abiding is a visit to a small rural community near the border with Costa Rica. A campesino showed us his fields and explained how he was trying to reduce his dependency on harmful pesticides. Then he took us to his home, a single room shared with his wife and their three young children. The simple timber frame supported a thatched roof, and the walls were a rough mix of stones and dried mud. The mud had shrunk as it dried and the walls were filled with cracks: perfect hiding places for the Triatoma 'assassin bugs', which creep out at night to feed on human blood and carry the single-celled parasite that causes Trypanosomiasis. Even today, around 20,000 people die every year from this preventable but difficult-to-treat disease.

The single room was about fifteen feet by eight; dark and blackened by soot from the open fire on which they cooked. The earth floor was the same level as the ground outside and undoubtedly became a quagmire when it rained. A rickety bed occupied one end of the room and the children slept in hammocks slung at night. It was hard to imagine more basic living conditions.

We talked for a while about the difficulties of farming, about how things had changed since the revolution and the elections, about the availability of healthcare and education and, of course, about the war. Then someone asked what else was needed that would really make a difference to these people's quality of life. We expected the answer to be about their home. Surely they wanted a larger house with brick walls and a solid floor, a better roof, more rooms, a proper kitchen and perhaps electricity?

The farmer led us down a path to the well shared by the community of perhaps a dozen families. He explained that heavy rain caused the river to rise, overflow into the well and contaminate it with organisms causing diarrhoea and parasitic infections. What they needed in order to improve their lives was a safe supply of drinking water. Their housing, he said, was not a problem.

I tell this story to make a point about expectations, perceptions and reality. The Nicaraguan family was used to a certain standard of housing and expected little better. But the reality was that better housing would have improved their health and not just their comfort. In Britain and the rest of the developed world, however, many of us take for granted a standard of housing way beyond what we need in order to live healthy lives. We live in unsustainable homes that are costing the Earth, and the price is being paid by the campesinos of Nicaragua and poor people everywhere through climate change and resource depletion.

Now I am not suggesting that we all start living in mud huts – although I do know a few buildings made of little more than earth and straw that most people would be very happy to occupy – but bigger houses are not always better, more bathrooms don't mean we'll be cleaner, and a comfortable home is made by the way we welcome guests and not by how much we spend on it.

Nicaraguan family in their cramped mud-and-thatch house.
Photograph: Chris Bird

sustainability to make it acceptable risks throwing out the baby with the bath water.

This suggests that sustainable housing can flourish only in a society with different values and priorities. What would our homes look like if the economic goal was to increase gross national happiness rather than gross national product? Surely we would evaluate our homes according to the criteria outlined on pages 16-19 rather than by price, equity, en suite bathrooms or appearance in glossy magazines.

The characteristics of sustainable consumption developed since the 1980s by the 'New Economics' movement have been usefully applied to sustainable housing. Localisation, reduced ecological footprint and community-building clearly overlap with the 'twelve commandments' criteria described earlier, but two further characteristics directly challenge the very basis of capitalism. The 'New Economics' vision suggests that we build our homes collectively and create a new infrastructure, wherein people are empowered to create their own affordable and sustainable homes. Does this make capitalism redundant, and how would the building industry respond? While some parts of the construction industry may be happy to adopt aspects of green building and sell us their own version of an eco-home, they may be less enthusiastic about writing themselves out of the script altogether.

## Construction, contraction and convergence

What is contraction and convergence, and what does it mean for housing? The Global Commons Institute proposes a framework for a global reduction in carbon emissions while simultaneously moving towards greater equity and social justice. The framework, known as 'contraction and convergence', consists of reducing overall emissions of greenhouse

gases to a safe level (contraction), while every country eventually brings emissions per capita to a level that is equal for all countries (convergence). In Britain, this means reducing our current per-capita emissions of about 12 tonnes down to 1.5 tonnes. Some countries with low per capita emissions might initially be entitled to a rise in their carbon rations and could sell their surplus to richer countries. Once all countries achieve an equal level of emissions – 2030 is the target suggested by the Global Commons Institute – then the carbon ration for all countries would continue to fall to an agreed safe level.

'Contraction and convergence' represents a break from the vicious cycle where the affluent industrialised world reaps benefits from fossil fuels while the developing world pays a disproportionate share of the cost in terms of climate change. In its place stands a virtuous circle where everyone benefits from reducing fossil fuel dependency. Based as it is on a philosophy of equal shares within a global limit, the framework could usher in a new era of global justice.

So what does this mean for housing in the UK and other industrialised countries? If we take Britain as an example, a fall from 12 tonnes to 1.5 tonnes – an 85-per-cent cut in carbon emissions applied equally across the entire range of human activity – means an 85-per-cent cut in carbon emissions from the construction and occupation of our homes. In fact, there are some human activities that are more difficult to 'decarbonise' than housing, such as transport , agriculture and certainly flying, so housing must make a bigger contribution. Zero-carbon housing is not out of the question.

Contraction and convergence was mentioned in the 2006 Yearbook of the Association for Environment Conscious Building (now the Sustainable Building

Association), and the article touched on the implications for housing.

"Bearing in mind the embedded energy in the existing building stock, the balance between demolition and refurbishment will be dramatically altered."[14]

Levels of consumption in the developed world, and by elites in developing nations, are possible only because of the unequal distribution of resources between rich and poor. We are living beyond our means and 'stealing' from energy stores of the past, from our children's future by degrading the environment they will inherit, and from poor people everywhere (see Figure 2). This applies to housing as much as to any other human activity and must be reversed through a process of contraction and convergence.

## Retrofit or new build?

Imagine yourself walking around your community in the year 2050. Lots of things will have changed, but it's a pretty safe bet that around 80 per cent of the houses you can see have already been built in 2010. We don't have the time, money, materials or energy to demolish the homes we have and start from scratch with wonderful new homes, even if they were extremely low-carbon. Nor would we want to destroy our architectural heritage, regional variations or the sense of place that develops over centuries. Making

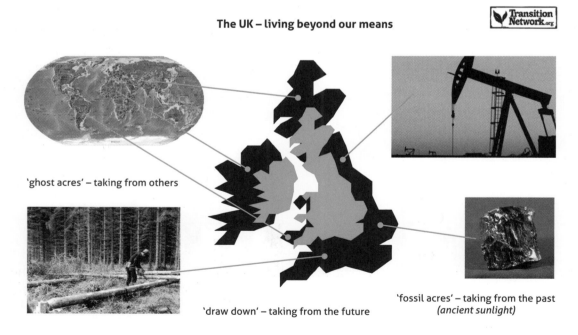

**The UK – living beyond our means**

Transition Network.org

'ghost acres' – taking from others

'draw down' – taking from the future

'fossil acres' – taking from the past
*(ancient sunlight)*

Figure 2. We sustain our present levels of consumption by stealing from the past (fossil fuels), the present (people in less developed countries) and the future (our children, who will inherit an impoverished world). © Naresh Giangrande

existing homes greener is vital. Of course that doesn't mean we can ignore new build, and the three million homes envisaged by the Department of Communities and Local Government by 2020 should be at least carbon-neutral. Figure 3 shows just how much energy conventional building materials have already consumed compared with low-embodied-energy materials such as timber. Why waste it through unnecessary demolition and rebuilding?

## Conclusions

- Our homes have an unacceptably large and unsustainable ecological footprint and don't meet the basic needs of a large and growing number of people.

- Sustainable homes have many features, but these vary with location, available materials and who builds and lives there. There is no single perfect example.

- We can't be purists and we must learn from all the faltering and imperfect examples, as well as from models where the faults are not so obvious.

- Unless we look at a full life-cycle analysis, we risk making problems worse.

- We don't have much time!

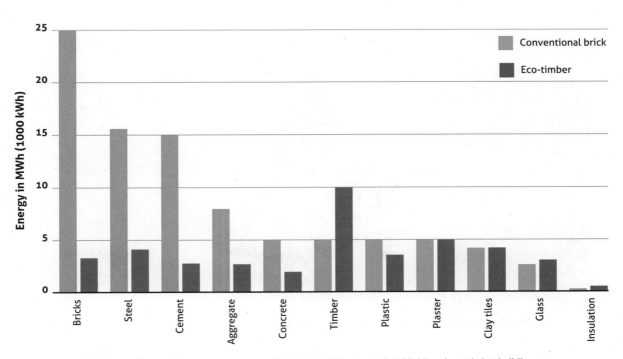

Figure 3. This chart shows the embodied energy in various materials for conventional brick and eco-timber buildings.
© Centre for Alternative Technology

# CHAPTER 2
# MAKING THE CASE FOR CHANGE

*"If your home isn't part of the solution then it must be part of the problem."*

With apologies to Eldridge Cleaver

Wouldn't it be great if all you had to do was explain to people about the problems of climate change and peak oil, and they changed their behaviour, retrofitted their homes and started living sustainable lives? No chance. One of the strengths of the Transition movement (see Introduction) is our appreciation of just how many psychological barriers to change there are.

*The Transition Handbook*[1] by Rob Hopkins makes an analogy between our addiction to unsustainable lifestyles, subsidised by cheap oil, and other dependencies, such as addiction to drugs, alcohol or gambling. Lessons learned from helping people to overcome addiction to alcohol or tobacco are valuable in promoting the changes we need in our housing. Rob Hopkins uses the 'Stages of Change model' developed by the psychologist and author of *Addiction and Change*, Carlo DiClemente[2] (see Figure 4), which shows people at different levels of readiness to change. There is no point in trying to persuade someone to insulate their loft if they haven't even started to think about issues such as climate change and rising energy prices. Some people may be ready to change but are unsure about what to do, while others may have started to change and lost momentum. It's quite possible for one person to be at different stages for

different changes. For example, someone might be prepared to block draughts but not to consider renewable energy.

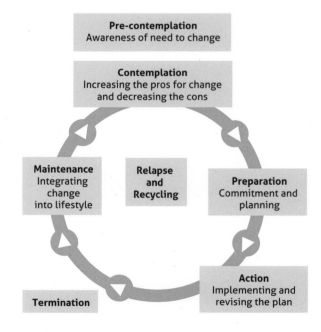

Figure 4. The Stages of Change model. (After DiClemente, 2003.)

Rob explains this in more detail in *The Transition Handbook*, but the important thing to remember is that change is incremental and different initiatives can help people along at different stages. In practice, most interventions impact on people in a variety of ways. Seeing *The Age of Stupid*, a powerful film about racing towards catastrophic climate change, may jolt some from the pre-contemplation stage. For others, the film reinforces an existing awareness and commitment to action.

This chapter looks at how campaigns and initiatives try to break down the psychological barriers to change.

## Friends of the Earth Energy Challenge

In 2007 Friends of the Earth Scotland took retrofitting to the heart of government and got the public thinking about the problem.[3] They challenged five Members of the Scottish Parliament (MSPs) to reduce the carbon emissions from their homes over one year. The MSP who made the greatest reduction would be the winner. The Energy Saving Trust provided National Home Energy Ratings at the start and end of the challenge, specific advice on improvements and smart monitors to measure electricity use. Scottish & Southern Energy commissioned thermal images of each home, to show where heat was leaking out.

The MSPs started from very different baselines and faced a range of different problems. A bit like in the real world!

**Rob Gibson** (SNP) already had an energy-efficient home with a $CO_2$ output of just 32.4kg per m² per annum. It was difficult for Gibson to make further cuts, but he plans to install solar panels and a wood-burning stove.

**Jim Hume** (Liberal Democrat) cut emissions from 80.4 to 75.9, reflecting the fact that he lives in a solid-walled rural home with no gas supply, which puts it firmly in the 'hard to treat' category. Plans to top up loft insulation and install a solar panel were delayed by a shortage of willing contractors, but Hume is pressing ahead with a 6kW wind turbine. It's good to know that at least one senior MSP is now familiar with some of the obstacles to energy efficiency.

**Mary Scanlon** (Conservative) had a baseline of 44.6 and reduced it to 43.5 by changing light bulbs and installing reflective material behind radiators. Changing her old gas boiler and running a shower with hot water from the boiler would have cut around 25 per cent.

**Jack McConnell** (Labour) failed to make any savings because building work delayed his plans for draught-proofing and underfloor insulation.

It would have been embarrassing for **Robin Harper** (Scottish Green Party) if he hadn't won. Harper cut his emissions from 72 to 42.3 by adding more loft insulation, fitting secondary glazing and installing a condensing boiler. But why wait for a challenge from FoE to take these fairly obvious measures?

Through this campaign, Friends of the Earth generated media coverage for the not-so-sexy subject of home energy efficiency, and some MSPs have since become effective 'energy champions'. Home energy efficiency and renewable energy have moved up the political agenda in Scotland, with greater awareness of obstacles in the planning and support systems. Furthermore, the thermal imaging surveys high-lighted the poor enforcement of building standards, and the difficulties experienced by some MSPs in getting work done demonstrated the skills shortage in some areas.

Maybe we should all be issuing such challenges to get the issues raised in county, district, town and even parish councils throughout the UK.

## Psychological barriers to change

A few years ago Transition Town Totnes visited a variety of homes with Rob Scott-McLeod from the Building Research Establishment. Rob explained how to improve energy efficiency in properties ranging from modern-built to several hundred years old.

We visited a 1950s home and clambered up into the loft to discover about 30mm of compressed and ineffective mineral wool insulation. The house owner was away, but we did know a couple of things about him. First, he was an active supporter of the Transition movement and must have known about the importance of loft insulation. Second, we all believed he could afford to install effective insulation if he chose to do so.

In the absence of the homeowner we discussed what the problem could be. What was stopping someone from dealing with a simple problem with a simple solution? Some sort of psychological block?

Rosemary Randall, a psychotherapist in Cambridge, came to the same conclusion but went on to develop 'Carbon Conversations' to tackle the problem.

"There are three aspects to tackling climate change," says Randall. "We can use *technology* and government *policies* to bring about change, but we also need *individuals* to make behavioural changes. I see these as three legs of a stool, and if one leg is missing the stool falls over." Individuals are aware of the problems and usually understand the simple steps needed – but they don't take those steps. So Randall developed a series of conversations, held over six

sessions, to encourage behavioural change. And it works! "People typically reduce their carbon footprint by around 10 per cent after completing the course and make plans for a further 20-50-per-cent cut in the next three to five years," claims Randall. Over 300 people completed 'Carbon Conversations' by August 2009, and Randall was asked to explain the idea in Manchester, where the International Festival and the *Guardian* invited scientists, engineers, campaigners and members of the public to submit their climate-saving ideas. 'Carbon Conversations' reached a shortlist of the most promising – which ranged from algae mopping up carbon to cloud-seeding and hydrogen fuel.

## Green Doctors

Is part of the answer to have heroic 'green doctors' dashing in to 'cure' our energy problems? Ground-work, a charity that describes itself as 'building sustainable communities in areas of need through joint environmental action', started the 'Green Doctor' project in Leicester.[4]

During the three-year pilot project, Green Doctors visited nearly 800 low-income households, where they installed technical measures such as low-energy light bulbs, hot-water-tank jackets and draught excluders. They also supplied water-saving bags for flush toilets, composters and bird boxes. Perhaps more importantly, the 'doctors' had the time to help householders apply for loft insulation and central heating, as well as to give advice tailored to individual needs. No charges were made for the visits or any of the measures installed.

A simple balance sheet of the project does not look particularly impressive when seen against the scale of the problem. Over three years nearly 7,000 measures

## Carbon Conversations

### Rosemary Randall, psychotherapist and a founder of Cambridge Carbon Footprints

As a psychotherapist, understanding how or why people change is central. I've tried to bring some of this knowledge to my work on climate change, exploring the reasons why many people find the problem hard to acknowledge, why they neglect to act and why – when they do act – they find themselves anxious, guilty or upset. Climate change is enormously distressing. It's painful to take on what it means and painful to make the personal changes that action requires. It's both a systemic, global problem and a deeply personal one, involving the ordinary acts of everyday life.

For the average UK citizen with an ordinary 12-tonne-emission life, going beyond token changes is difficult because our use of resources is tied up, not just with practical issues, but with our sense of ourselves – our identity, values, desires and status. Who am I if I'm not the chap with the fast car? Who am I if I no longer shop for a new outfit each Saturday? Can I bear the sense of guilt, loss and despair that truly engaging with climate change will bring?

If people are to make serious changes to their lifestyles they need support. They need space to explore what is involved for themselves, their families and their aspirations. They need time to work through the conflicts between desire and reality; conscience and social pressure; status and need. We need both to normalise the expression of complex and difficult emotions and establish new social norms that make it seem ordinary to live a truly low-carbon life.

In the 'Carbon Conversations' groups I established in Cambridge, we do this by weaving together discussions of practicalities with discussions of how people feel and what change means personally. For example, we approach the need to reduce household emissions by 80 per cent by exploring what makes a home a home. The statements that come up again and again are to do with comfort, security, safety, a sense of belonging and privacy. It's clear that making changes to the home has

A Carbon Conversation Group gets down to work in Cambridge. Photograph: Rosemary Randall

the potential to threaten this basic building block of personal security. Take reactions to one of the frequently cited 'low-hanging fruit': turning the thermostat down to 18°C. It ought to be a no-brainer, but for one person it brought up associations of her bitterly cold childhood house, where chilblains marked the onset of winter and the chill brought a sense of neglect and despair that she could ever be warm again. One comfort of her adult life was the power to be warm as toast. Someone else in the group also experienced cold houses in childhood, but for him it became a mark of his resilience and independence to brave the freezing bathroom and wear a hat to breakfast. For a third person a 21°C house was central to her sexual identity – she feels at her most confident floating round the house in T-shirt and underwear. Dressing for 18°C would make her feel a frump.

When stories like these are listened to, shared and explored, people can work through the conflicts and feel supported and proud of the changes they make. If we can normalise the expression of emotion, acknowledge the losses and work through the conflicts we face, I believe we stand a better chance of truly creating the low-carbon society we need.

**See http://cambridgecarbonfootprint.org/action/carbon-conversations/national-carbon-conversations**

were installed, mainly low-energy bulbs and radiator panels, with estimated average savings of around 0.68 tonnes of $CO_2$ per household per annum – around 13 per cent of the heating and electricity costs for a typical household.

But just looking at a few technical measures and energy outcomes ignores valuable lessons. Green Doctors make only two visits a day, typically lasting between 45 minutes and several hours. This enables them to establish a rapport with householders, find out what the householder cares about, and understand the situation from his or her individual perspective. This creates trust and the opportunity to encourage lasting behaviour change. Essential prerequisites for this are having time to listen, being non-judgemental and providing convincing and relevant advice.

The luxury of time means that Green Doctors can install energy-saving measures and then talk to householders about energy and the environment in a way tailored to their own interests and knowledge. Energy companies have cut the costs of meter reading by relying on estimates, customer readings and external meters. Direct contact with householders has declined dramatically. Green Doctors reverse this process giving the opportunity for encounters like these:

> "A Green Doctor was talking to a resident who complained about being warm and got up to open a window. It turned out that she did not understand the controls and the central heating was permanently on and had been for over a year!"

> "The Green Doctor found a radiator in a box room that was very hot and discovered that the householder didn't understand thermostatic radiator valves."

> "In several cases old people had been sent low-energy bulbs but were unable to fit them."

Simple problems with simple solutions, ignored because nobody had the time to discover and deal with them. The value of this work has been recognised and Green Doctors now operate in many inner-city areas.

The choice of 'Green Doctors' as a name for the staff was a conscious attempt to anchor a fuel-poverty project in the language of two sectors: environment and health. 'Doctor' implies the intervention of a person with the expertise to 'cure' the problem. Groundwork considers this a useful metaphor for a home visit, since it doesn't require any interest in environmental issues and is readily understood by people from diverse social and cultural backgrounds.

Green Doctors use publicity designed to catch the attention of householders and journalists, who identify the project with stereotypical heroic medics dashing to the rescue, playing to the drama of popular TV programmes such as *Casualty* and *ER*. Of course, the downside of this approach is that it can relegate householders to a passive role. The challenge is for Green Doctors to go beyond this and work *with* rather than *for* householders. Only in this way does change persist when the doctor departs.

## Energy advice and action

A number of projects support people who are ready to act but are unsure about what to do. An important feature of these projects is that, alongside the advice, there's the encouragement that comes from knowing you are not alone. Other people are insulating their lofts and tackling the draughts, so, even if you are not actually doing it alongside them, you are still part of a group.

## Household Energy Service

Light Foot Household Energy Service (HES) was one of ten finalists in the Big Green Challenge. This competition was launched by NESTA (National Endowment for Science, Technology and the Arts), which was concerned that the onus for a 'miracle cure' to solve climate change rests too heavily on science and technology when individuals and community groups also have solutions:

"Energy efficiency is not simply a technical problem, and it doesn't need anything shiny to make it happen. It just needs people to act. $CO_2$ emissions can be dramatically cut through decisions made in the home. HES guide people through this process. We give advice and support where it is needed. Everyone knows it makes sense to reduce energy use . . . you only have to look at your latest fuel bills."

Adam Kennerley, Chief Executive at Light Foot

So what makes HES special? For a start, it operates only in collaboration with existing community networks, acknowledges that changing to a low-carbon lifestyle is a gradual process, and understands that change begins with the information on which we base our decisions. The process begins with a household energy survey, which is processed by a professional Energy Officer. Each participating household then receives a tailored energy report and carbon footprint. HES continues to support participants by helping to arrange loft insulation, advising on energy-saving appliances and renewables, updating grant information and organising bulk purchases.

The free service started in Bishop's Castle in 2005, where HES aims to involve 40 per cent of households and reduce their carbon emissions by a minimum of 7 per cent – a total of 580 tonnes of $CO_2$. The long-term aim is to partner the town as it reduces its emissions by 85 per cent by 2050. HES also works in Clun, Montgomery, Newtown, Knighton, Bucknell and Presteigne.

## Meadows Ozone

Meadows Ozone, another Big Green Challenge finalist, is a community-owned energy services company based in the Meadows area of Nottingham. By providing local people with advice and interest-free green loans, it aims to combat fuel poverty at the same time as reducing carbon emissions. Many local people have already benefitted from free energy audits and access to free or discounted loft and cavity wall insulation.

The Meadows is an area of high deprivation and many local people are affected by debt and fuel poverty. To tackle these issues, Meadows Ozone developed an interest-free green loan scheme in partnership with a local credit union. The loans help homeowners and tenants to make energy-saving improvements to their homes.

A key factor in local people's acceptance of the project is the fact that Meadows Ozone is based at the offices of the Meadows Partnership Trust, which is well respected within the community. The team also accepts that success in addressing local needs requires members of the community to play an active role, so they can develop a network of 'green champions' to raise awareness throughout the community. Green champions complete a day's training in energy efficiency and behaviour change, delivered free of charge by National Energy Action.

"Local residents have used green loans to install double glazing, solar panels and cavity wall insulation and to upgrade their home appliances to 'A' rated equipment . . . We're also working with a resident who's applied for a loan to install a wind turbine on their property . . . and having local ambassadors shows other people in the community that this is a genuinely local initiative and helps to break down the barriers sometimes experienced by organisations coming from outside the area."

Ian Nicholson, Energy Advisor

## Hyde Farm CAN

www.hydefarm.org.uk

Obama can, so why not Hyde Farm? Hyde Farm Climate Action Network consists of over 150 households living on the Hyde Farm Estate in Balham, South London, who want to reduce their contribution to climate change. The area is a lively community of 1,800 households, mainly Edwardian houses and flats in a conservation area, with around 4,000 residents. These hard-to-treat houses make it challenging to reduce household emissions, but by working together as a community the network is finding creative and cost-effective ways to take action on climate change.

The network, which is inspired by the Transition movement and has informal links with Transition Town Brixton, describes itself as welcoming, informal, fun and supportive. Activities include annual open evenings that mix education with a social event. Over 200 people attended the 2009 event, which featured stalls from the Energy Saving Trust, Green Homes Concierge Service, a local contractor specialising

in draught-proofing and sash-window restoration, plumbing and electrical contractors, a solar supplier, a Waste and Resources Action Programme recycling advisor, Women's Environmental Network Carbon Counters, Food Up Front, local crafts from recycled materials and more.

The network's draught-busting events really demonstrate the value of action. They are held in the homes of local residents and showcase techniques developed by local people to insulate the Edwardian homes typical of the area. They also sell draught-proofing and insulation materials at reduced prices and share experience with other community groups with a similar housing stock.

## Thermal imaging in Oxfordshire

A picture paints a thousand words, so the Environment Group in Brightwell-cum-Sotwell, a parish with fewer than 600 homes in South Oxfordshire, uses thermal images rather than words to demonstrate heat loss.

Thermal imaging cameras show temperature rather than colour. Images are best recorded after dusk and when there is at least a 10-degree temperature difference between inside and outside. Areas where a lot of heat is lost from buildings – uninsulated roofs and single-glazed windows for example – normally show up as red, orange or yellow, while thermally efficient areas where less heat is lost appear in dark blue.

In November 2007 the group wrote a 'Thermal Imaging Proposal' that persuaded South Oxfordshire District Council to purchase a thermal imaging camera for loan to community groups. Six members of the group learned to use the camera and by March 2008 gathered nearly 500 images from over 60 village dwellings of different ages and types. They also investigated the thermal efficiency of the primary school and of the village hall. Detailed information on construction, building materials and other factors was recorded for each building and used to interpret the images.

Each household receives a report with images and suggestions for improving insulation. The report comes with a 'Brief Guide to Energy Saving' prepared by the Environment Group, with help from the Thames Valley Energy Centre and the Energy Saving Trust.

Results of the thermal surveys have been displayed at various local meetings and at the primary school's 'Eco Day'. In 2009 the project won a £500 award in a competition organised by Oxfordshire ClimateX-change. It is now doing follow-up work to discover what action householders have taken.

## Peak Oil in Bristol

In 2009 Bristol City Council and the Green Capital Momentum Group set up a Peak Oil Task Force and produced a report on the evidence for peak oil, its potential impact on Bristol, and what actions could be taken. The report focuses primarily on city infrastructure for transport, energy, food, services and jobs, and mentions the need to make better use of existing housing stock and to develop 'walkable' neighbourhoods. It's a valuable example of how to develop fruitful partnerships to get the climate change / peak oil message across. Transition Bristol played a key role.

## Conclusions

- We can't ignore the psychological and social barriers to change, and interventions, campaigns and projects must accept that people have different levels of consciousness and willingness to change.

- Practical change and psychological change complement each other.

- Credibility is vital, so it is important to work with established groups where possible.

- It's also important to work with both individuals and whole cities, and at every level between.

## Bristol's Peak Oil Report

**Dr Angela Raffle, Consultant in Public Health and Transition activist**

Rushing in with 'you have to make this change because I say so' is unlikely to succeed if people haven't yet grasped the information that tells you that change is necessary. So information needs to get to the right people, in the right way, in a format that will last, and with pointers to what action is needed next. Bristol's Peak Oil Report[5] started this process in a very powerful way.

So how did it happen? Transition Bristol was instrumental, but only by working carefully and flexibly with others.

Key interventions were as follows.

• Ensuring that Transition Bristol had a seat on the Green Capital Momentum Group – set up by the Bristol Partnership to drive 'green' changes (every City has to have a Partnership, it's a forum where public, private and voluntary organisations meet).

• Raising Peak Oil in a constructive way at every opportunity. There is a difficult balancing act between irritating people enough to make them do what you want, and irritating them in a way that means they just want to get rid of you.

• Using a charismatic and knowledgeable expert, Daniel Lerch of the Post Carbon Institute, to run a seminar for key people. This has to be someone who knows their stuff and has the skills to connect with people intellectually.

• Helping set up the Peak Oil Task Force and supporting Simone Osborn, who produced the report. Inez Aponte, from Transition Bristol, wrote the scenarios that bring the report alive, enabling readers to step into the future.

Building a positive future for Bristol after

# Peak Oil

the bristol partnership

BRISTOL GREEN CAPITAL
INSPIRING CHANGE

The Bristol Peak Oil Report aims to build a positive future for Bristol after peak oil.

We now have to publicise and promote the report in every way possible; turn the ideas into plans, and the plans into actions . . .

# CHAPTER 3

# SUSTAINABLE HOUSING IN TOTNES

*"Totnes is where, when you go there, they have to let you in."*

**With apologies to Robert Frost**

## Introducing Totnes

Totnes, a town of around 8,500 people in South Devon, straddles the river Dart about halfway between Dartmouth on the coast and Dartmoor to the north. The Dartington Hall Trust and Schumacher College are nearby and the town has long benefitted from the influx of radical and alternative thinking associated with these institutions.

In 2006 Rob Hopkins, Naresh Giangrande and a core of local people concerned about climate change and peak oil began the work that eventually led to the launch of Transition Town Totnes (TTT). The Transition idea spread like a benevolent virus around the planet and now seems such an obvious response to the problems we face that, if it hadn't happened in Totnes, then it would certainly have developed elsewhere.

But Totnes is where it did happen, so what progress has the town made in making housing more sustainable?

## So what's happening in Totnes?

Transition Town Totnes has initiated a number of exciting sustainable housing projects. 'Transition Streets' involves education, energy efficiency, renewable energy and a large installation of solar photovoltaic (PV) panels on a civic building. 'Transition Homes' is a development of truly affordable low-carbon buildings that model how we can live in a post-oil world. There are also developments around cohousing and lots of smaller projects, but potentially the most significant of all is the redevelopment of a derelict industrial site for a mixture of housing and employment. All this and more are integrated into the ambitious 'Energy Descent Action Plan'[1] for Totnes, covering the next 20 years. We will return to these initiatives later, but first, in order to understand how they came about, we need to look at the origins of the theme and project groups behind them.

## The Building and Housing Group

Formed after an 'open space' event, the Building and Housing Group established a reputation for successful public meetings, with speakers and films on natural building, energy efficiency and renewable energy. With the exception of the architect Bill Dunster, who designed the radical Beddington Zero Energy Development (BedZED), all the speakers came from the local area – a great tribute to the skills and experience available right on Totnes's doorstep.

Alongside these meetings were visits to local houses to examine the possibilities for improving energy efficiency in a range of different properties, and two 'eco-tours' of nearby Dartington to visit new build and refurbished 'eco-homes'. The second eco-tour attracted 75 people – a big group to show around your home!

Towards the end of 2009 the group decided to focus on practical activities rather than public talks, more energy went into the Transition Homes project, and in June 2010 people had the chance to sample a variety of natural building techniques and materials over a 'taster' weekend.

These and other events attract a range of people to the group. Architects rub shoulders with carpenters, experienced builders share stories with DIY enthusiasts, and self-builders make the tea alongside people who build only in their dreams. And out of this mix comes ideas.

## Transition Homes

In 2008 a couple of people came up with the idea of low-cost but extremely well-insulated homes as a solution to the shortage of affordable homes. This developed into the Transition Homes project, a development of affordable low-carbon homes generating most of their own energy, harvesting and recycling water and using compost toilets. Part of the site for the development will be devoted to growing food, and parking will be limited to space for disabled or shared cars. Construction methods and materials will be a model for how we must build in a post-oil world.

A sub-group met fortnightly to consider designs, while another sub-group explored possible sites, legal structures and planning issues. With hindsight, this separation may have been a mistake, as differing 'visions' developed for what the project was all about. A few people dropped out and the project was put on hold for a few months while a shared understanding of what 'Transition Homes' really are was established.

The root of this problem starts with a major obstacle that most projects like Transition Homes face – the high cost of land. If you want to build affordable homes you need land at affordable prices. This excludes land with, or likely to be granted, planning consent for market housing. That leaves rural exception sites (see pages 158-9), where land costs are much lower but the local authority requires 100 per cent of the homes to be affordable. There may be exceptions where some 'intermediate affordable' homes are allowed for sale or shared ownership.

This creates a potential problem because 'Transition living' is about lots more than just the home. There's no point in building low-carbon sustainable homes if the people who occupy them don't commit to low-carbon sustainable living. So how could the project develop a model of affordable and sustainable homes and ensure that they are occupied by people prepared to make the necessary behaviour change? Part of the answer is that the design of the homes will put off many people who are already unwilling to change their lifestyles. Compost toilets are not to everybody's taste! Agreeing to a 'Resident's Charter' for sustainable living will also help. But this is an experiment and there are bound to be problems, conflicts and disagreements. The challenge is to learn from them.

By the middle of 2010 the project was well established. Negotiations were under way with the Dartington Hall Trust and other landowners, several meetings had taken place with councillors, planning officers and local residents, and a Community Land Trust was established to ensure that the homes remain affordable in perpetuity. Information on progress is available at www.totnes.transitionnetwork.org.

## Natural buildings

Totnes and the neighbouring village of Dartington have some great examples of 'eco-homes'. One example is a stunning straw-bale house in a superb location, looking down over Totnes, built by Jim Carfrae and completed in 2006.[2] The build was financially viable because Jim and his partner Kate bought the plot and gained permission to build three homes instead of just one. Selling the additional homes helped to finance their innovative straw-bale home.

## Mud King

In 2008 Jim and Kate Carfrae hosted an evening with Bruce King, Director of the California-based Ecological Building Network, founder of the Green Building Press and author of three books on building with earth and straw, who was visiting Devon to see its wealth of earth buildings. King opens his website with a quote from Henry Thoreau, the pioneering environmentalist:

> "What is the point of having a good house if you don't have a decent planet to put it on?"[3]

### Transition Homes – key features

- Zero-energy homes
- Built with sustainable local materials
- Affordable
- Integrated with food production
- Not dependent on external sewage systems
- Experimental communities to develop a model for living sustainably beyond cheap fossil fuels
- Learning centres for sustainable energy, building, food and waste reduction, reuse and recycling

Bruce King takes that quote to heart and aims to reconcile the human need for good housing with the planet's need for sustainable buildings. For many years King and his colleagues have been at the centre of efforts in the US to give straw bale, rammed earth and other sustainable building methods a (dare I say) solid foundation. Quoting the World Watch Institute, King points out that:

> "Buildings account for one-fourth of the world's wood harvest, two-fifths of its material and energy usage, and one-sixth of its fresh water usage. These demands will be exacerbated as population growth compels us to multiply the total number of buildings on the planet over the next generation. We clearly must find a way to provide safe and decent shelter for all without ravishing the global ecosystem."

"About a year ago," says King, "I read a paper by Rob Hopkins on peak oil that really convinced me that this is a key problem, and I now talk about 'building beyond oil'." In a recent article King quotes another iconic American to illustrate the problem:

> "We have become great because of the lavish use of our resources . . . But the time has come to inquire seriously what will happen when our forests are gone, when the coal, the iron, the oil and the gas are exhausted."
> President Theodore Roosevelt (1908)

The evening's discussion is free-ranging. One minute King is explaining how the Romans built such enduring structures; the next he is talking about building homes from surplus shipping containers or working with venture capitalists hoping to make 'gazillions of dollars' from developing plant-based spray-on insulating materials.

He is certainly no purist and sees a limited role for straw-bale or earth buildings in the developed world. "I spoke at a meeting in Hong Kong recently," he says. "It's the most densely populated place on the planet. A 20-storey building would be a small project. What does sustainable building mean in that type of environment? A living roof would be pointless because it's such a small part of the building, so maybe we should be thinking about living walls."

Discussing earth buildings, King says: "You have to be either very rich or very poor to build with earth. Either rich enough to take the time off to build such a home or poor enough to live in a community where people

This thatched cob cottage is being built in Dartington, while the owners live in the adjacent mobile home. Photograph: Paul Barclay

still work collectively on earth buildings." But he agrees that the future must be about rebuilding local economies and communities where such collaboration thrives. "It has to be that way," he says.

The conversation covers hempcrete, rammed-earth building (King calls this a 'poster child', meaning it can be beautiful but very expensive), alternatives to oil for pipework and electrical insulation, bamboo – and the crucial importance of skilled building workers.

The room is rich with possibilities that are visible only when you move away from reliance on cheap fossil fuels to provide the energy and materials for building and, as with Transition itself, buildings of the future become an attractive option rather than just an unwelcome necessity.

I like the quotes that pepper King's website and make no apologies for ending with another:

"As for the future, your task is not to foresee it, but to enable it."
Antoine de Saint Exupéry, *Citadelle* (1948)

## Cob Cottage

www.barclayscobhouse.blogspot.com

Paul and Ivana Barclay are rebuilding history. Their thatched cob cottage in Dartington wouldn't look out of place in an ancient Devon village. The materials may be traditional, but this is a new building and, by incorporating underfloor heating and renewable energy, it embraces a modern understanding of energy conservation and sustainable technologies.

During three years of building Paul and Ivana opened their doors to schoolchildren, neighbours and visitors from afar. Hundreds of people have been inspired by

their reinvention of the Devon vernacular, but what made them choose this path?

Paul, whose background is computing rather than cob, went to a talk by master cob builder Kevin McCabe (see page 187). He was inspired, worked with Kevin for a few months to gain experience, and bought a plot where he and Ivana could live alongside the build. Ivana produced a design for the kidney-shaped house, which nestles comfortably in the curve of the lane. "Ivana designed the house around our needs as a family," says Paul, "then we had technical help with drawings and from Barry Honeysett, a structural engineer experienced in cob." The design was acceptable to planning and building control officers, and early in 2007 the couple started to build. The cob walls rose quickly and by November the thatched roof was in place. Waiting for the cob to dry and shrink before rendering walls and fitting windows and doors is one of the disadvantages of the material, and a typical build time is at least 15 months.

Inside there are no dead corners, a cob stairway winds up around the chimney and the walls curve pleasingly into the oak-lintelled windows. This is a 'hand-sculpted house', full of shapes difficult to achieve in concrete blocks or timber.

## Retrofits

Two homes in Dartington show what can be achieved to reduce the carbon footprint of typical 1960s detached houses.

## Energy from the sun . . .

Richard and Heidi Orrell have insulated, blocked draughts, installed double glazing and reduced heat loss through improved flooring. They had the gas supply disconnected and fitted wood-burning stoves with back boilers connected to their radiators. While neighbours wash cars at the weekend, Richard is busy with a chainsaw and axe, laying in a supply of logs for the winter.

Solar water-heating panels and a first phase on PV panels were installed in 2004, followed by more PV panels in 2008, making a total of around 3.5kWp (kilowatt-peak). Richard, who works for the Met Office in Exeter, told a TTT eco-tour: "We aim to make this a carbon-neutral house."

In 2009 their home was accepted into the 'Old Home Superhome' network, but what really makes Richard and Heidi such good examples is not the retrofit of their home but the way they live their lives. In their garden you'll find vegetables and fruit trees. They sometimes use a car belonging to friends and are members of the 'Moor Cars' car club, but most of the time they cycle or use public transport. Since I've known them they've taken family holidays in the Alps, Lapland and Scotland but never used a plane.

## . . . and from the ground

In the same road, Gerald and Lucia Cox have installed solar PV and solar thermal panels, but they've also

The Transition Town Totnes Eco-Tour stops to look at Richard and Heidi Orrell's retrofit of their 1960s home. Photograph: Chris Bird

added a ground source heat pump. Space limitations dictated a vertical system, so they bored 45 metres down to a constant groundwater supply. Solar-powered pumps bring up water at a temperature of 12°C, from which heat is extracted and used for space heating through their central heating system.

## Sawmill and Building Hub

Another regular stop on the TTT eco-tour was Paul MacDonald's massive straw-bale sawmill, which makes full use of the sound-proofing qualities of straw bales as well as of their thermal benefits. Paul, one of the founders of the TTT Building and Housing Group, started the mill as a 'no-waste' business, in collaboration with the Dartington Hall Trust's Landscope Project. Local timber was milled and the 'waste' used as firewood, as bedding for animals or as a medium for growing gourmet mushrooms such as shiitake and oyster. There were also plans to use a process of wood gasification to generate both heat and electricity, with charcoal as a by-product.

It was hoped that the project would grow beyond the original concept into a 'hub' for sustainable building enterprises, including architects, builders, suppliers and possibly a centre for the reclamation and reuse of building materials. Unfortunately the whole enterprise went bust in May 2010, partly due to cash-flow problems and partly as a result of the general decline in construction.

## Totnes Sustainable Construction Ltd

In 2009 seven members of the TTT Building and Housing Group established Totnes Sustainable Construction (TSC) as a non-profit-making company limited by guarantee. The aims are sustainable design, construction and refurbishment, with an emphasis on real affordability. Although the company has no formal link with the Transition movement, Rob Hopkins is one of the seven directors, all of whom are long-standing TTT activists. Since it is a company limited by guarantee, any profit must be ploughed back into development and growth and cannot be paid as dividends.

> "We prioritise the use of local and sustainable materials and want to build in an aesthetically pleasing as well as environmentally friendly way. We want to pioneer building in a way that meets the challenges of climate change, peak oil and people's aspirations for a different way of life."
>
> Chris Noakes, TSC Chair

Good employment practice is another objective listed in the company's memorandum of association, and TSC Ltd undertakes to promote the well-being of employees and subcontractors through work that is satisfying, safe and useful.

## Transition Streets

In December 2009 Transition Town Totnes was successful in its bid for £625,000 for a project called 'Transition Streets'. The successful bid rested on the foundations of two other TTT projects: the Energy Descent Action Plan and Transition Together (TTog). Like 'Carbon Conversations' (see page 27), the 'Transition Together' project helps groups of people overcome the psychological barriers as well as some of the practical obstacles to sustainability. The project grew out of 'Home Groups', set up with support from the 'Heart and Soul' group within Transition Town Totnes, which brought people together as self-help groups.

TTog forms small, social groups of friends, neighbours and colleagues and then supports them in taking a number of effective, practical, money-saving and carbon-reducing steps. A workbook helps each person to build an action plan to improve household energy efficiency, minimise water use, reduce waste (and consumption) and explore local transport and food. It also helps people understand what's behind rising energy prices and climate change and what this means for them, their family and their local community.

© Transition Streets

By the middle of 2009, with funding from the Calouste-Gulbenkian Foundation and Big Green Challenge Plus, the Transition Together project had three successful pilot groups and began rolling out the programme nationally, to ten other locations through the Transition Network.

In September 2009 the Department of Energy and Climate Change (DECC) announced a 'Low Carbon Communities Challenge', with up to £500,000 available for up to 20 community energy projects. The deadline for applications was incredibly tight but, after several brainstorming sessions and a lot of hard work from a small group that wrote the application, the Transition

A Transition Streets group at their first meeting. Photograph: Lou Brown

## Transition Together: one participant's perspective

### Carole Whitty

Our estate is approximately 20 years old. It overlooks a green lane in which nestle the secrets of thousands of years of living. Each year the lane grows nature's survival packs under the shade of its ancient oaks, and foragers gather fruit and wisdom from the hedgerows.

The estate sits comfortably at the side of the lane. At first sight the houses resemble some kind of film set. Each has a unique shape, size and character and yet is united by the architect's design and stone colours. It looks friendly, but busy lives meant that greetings were often just fleeting acknowledgements as cars and wrapped-up people passed by, and life was just a whirlwind of work, children, sleep and little else. We knew our immediate neighbours and spent time together when occasion allowed, but knew no-one else.

So when a leaflet dropped on our doormat asking if we wanted to be part of a pilot project called 'Transition Together', we were curious and went along to find out more. We were presented with a folder of excellent materials on how to reduce our carbon footprint and quickly established a way to work through them as a group. We had such a clear purpose and focus that we soon forgot we didn't really know each other, and had an extremely warm and welcoming first meeting.

As time passed we did get to know and care about each other and how the group works. If you need something, are in trouble or just need a chat, one of us will be there. We know what we have in common and what we don't, and now have enough interest in each other's ideas and opinions to continue meeting long after the last page of the resource book has been turned.

So what happened to our individual and collective carbon footprint? There are two enormous benefits of working with others in your own street on this agenda. One is proximity to each other and the other is that we share the same house characteristics. We share our energy issues and potential solutions and finally managed, with bottoms in the air, to find our stopcocks and water meters! There was a healthy element of peer pressure, and as time went on our commitment to make a difference deepened. We measured our results as part of the pilot's evaluation and had all saved carbon and money and continue to do so!

Transition Together works on several levels:

- Just reading the course materials will almost certainly help you make changes as an individual.

- Working as a neighbourhood group makes the solutions easier to find, and curiosity about what you are doing spreads to others in the road.

- Getting to know your neighbours makes your road look and feel different, with a greater sense of place and belonging.

- On a larger scale, the programme provides a model for tackling peak oil and climate change but also for dealing with issues such as building community resilience.

So our beautiful, enduring, ancient Green lane reminds us daily of the urgent need to find enduring modern answers to the challenges of today and the future. In our humble way, through our Transition Together programme, we are on the case!

**See www.transitiontogether.org.uk**

Streets bid (cheekily asking for an extra £125,000) was ready.

The project, outlined overleaf, illustrates one of the big problems with this type of government competition.

DECC's terms stipulated that the money had to be spent by March 2010, and the only way to do that in such a short period of time was to support photovoltaic installations. Fortunately the TTog model enabled the project to use discounted PV as a 'carrot' to attract people to the programme and to carry out other energy-efficiency measures.

## How it works

Round One of Transition Streets involves over 150 households in 18 groups, which reflect a cross-section of the community. There are four stages to the project.

- Stage 1. Behaviour change promoted by groups of residents working through the TTog programme.

- Stage 2. Energy efficiency through implementing measures recommended by a home energy audit. Project partners, including the Energy Saving Trust, Devon Association for Renewable Energy and South Hams District Council, assist with this stage.

- Stage 3. Discounted PV systems installed on suitable homes, where residents complete stages 1 and 2. Transition Streets assists low-income households with additional grants and low-interest loans, to ensure that systems are installed in a representative cross-section of households. Data are collected on energy consumption and generation to evaluate the benefits of all three stages of the project.

- Stage 4. Community awareness is increased by helping to finance a retrofit of Totnes Civic Hall. This building is central to life in the town and, in partnership with Totnes Town Council, the hall has been fitted with 14kWp of PV panels. A public digital display shows how much energy is being generated and carbon saved. In addition, an 'Open Streets' event showcases some of the upgraded houses, to illustrate what the project has achieved.

Copland Meadows Transition Together Group, ready to post the first petitions in their campaign for solar photovoltaics. Photograph: Lou Brown

As PV systems are installed, money comes back into the project, enabling subsequent rounds of spending under far less time pressure than the initial cycle. Additional funds from other sources may enable the project to expand. The ambitious target is to involve 10 per cent of the town's 3,500 homes, with the expectation that half of those involved will take up the opportunity of subsidised PV systems.

## Cosy Devon

The Cosy Devon scheme, administered by Energy Action Devon (the local face of the Energy Saving Trust), offers free and heavily discounted loft and cavity-wall insulation. Cosy Devon works with local project partners, including Transition Town Totnes, who refer households for insulation measures.

Thousands of households in Devon qualify for free insulation but fail to apply. Perhaps people see the adverts and remember the old saying, 'If it sounds too good to be true it probably is.' But the benefits are real. People aged 70 or over, or people on any one of a long list of benefits, are eligible for free insulation, and local groups such as TTT are better placed for getting that message across than any number of adverts in newspapers or on television.

Transition supporters Mary Popham and Nikky Evans visited hundreds of households in Totnes to explain how they could benefit from Cosy Devon, and scores of them had free insulation as a result.

## Live, work and play – the Atmos Project

In 2008 the Dairy Crest factory, the largest employer in Totnes, closed with the loss of over 160 jobs. In just a few months a local group developed ambitious plans to redevelop the site to create 500 new jobs, 40 homes and community space including a gallery / arts venue, restaurants and green spaces. Their first victory was to prevent the owners from demolishing a historic building, part of Brunel's visionary but ill fated 'Atmospheric Railway', hence the title for the project.

The Atmos vision is to:

- be a unique, contemporary, globally significant, carbon-neutral development

- be an inspiring place to live, work, learn and relax

- be part-owned and managed as a community enterprise closely aligned to the emerging response to peak oil

- complement and improve the prosperity of other organisations in the area by attracting new investment, new talent and new customers

- establish a meaningful connection with the historic town

- use environmentally responsible materials and building forms

- develop ways of coping with the flood risk that can be used by other brownfield sites facing similar flood risks.

Operating under the umbrella of the Totnes Development Trust, the Atmos group developed a detailed business case and designs for the site, which included an innovative response to flood risk from the adjacent River Dart. By February 2010 the group had raised and spent around £25,000 in developing plans and a business case for the site, and local architects and designers had done a lot of *pro bono* work. The project has support from the Regional Development Association, Devon County Council and Totnes Town Council, and the Dartington Hall Trust. Unfortunately, Dairy Crest has an eye on the financial bottom line rather than on the long-term prosperity of the town and, at the time of writing, has so far declined to accept

Initial designs for a mixed housing and employment redevelopment of the Dairy Crest site in Totnes. © Dave Chapman

Atmos as the preferred bidder and to work closely with them. South Hams District Council, although supportive of the project, is unwilling to use compulsory purchase powers to acquire the site.

## Cohousing

A small group of Totnes residents has for nearly 15 years been trying to establish a cohousing community. (For more on cohousing see Chapter 5.) By working with a local developer the group may have succeeded at last – see box opposite.

## Energy Descent

The Tones and District Energy Descent Action Plan (EDAP), which includes input from over 500 people involved in dozens of development meetings, visioning and drafting sessions, sets out a plan to build a more resilient and cohesive Totnes to face the future.

The community was 'invited to dream how the future could be and then work out the practical pathways to get there'. And dream they did.

The comprehensive plan gives a detailed timeline, a 'positive story', taking us to 2030 – describing what might happen and how to monitor progress. The following are a few extracts from the section on building and housing.

## Pathways across the timeline:

### 2016-20

**Individuals**
- Many people are retrofitting their homes with heatwave add-ons: pergolas with vines, porches and shutters are giving the area a Mediterranean appearance. Larger gutters and huge water butts are also very visible.

## Cohousing at Baltic Wharf

**Laura Keeley, Totnes Cohousing Group**

Totnes Cohousing Group was started in 1996 by people interested in living in a friendly and cooperative neighbourhood. In this area of South Devon building land is at a premium and very expensive.Our search for somewhere to build about 30 highly sustainable dwellings and a common house leaves us, on the rare occasions when land becomes available, competing with established developers.

About two years ago we started discussions with TQ9, a group planning to develop its five-hectare riverside site at Baltic Wharf for a mix of uses, including housing. We asked it to include cohousing as part of its proposals and we met with a positive response. Since then we have found TQ9 ready to involve us in the cohousing layout and in many aspects of the housing design. A cohousing design sub-group has regular meetings with the architect, for the members to familiarise themselves with building design issues and also to explain these to the rest of the group, so we can make informed decisions. Other sub-groups are responsible for fundraising, liaising with the local authority and an interested housing association, publicity and press, membership, group development and problem solving. Like the rest of the development, we aim to make affordable homes part of the cohousing community.

We have been lucky to find a solicitor to work pro bono on our initial legal agreement with TQ9, and Max Comfort at Stroud Cohousing provides support and advice for nominal expenses. If we are successful, this will be the first cohousing included in a commercial building development. The advantage is that we don't have to spend time and money doing the development work ourselves. The disadvantage is that the houses will inevitably cost more, and we don't have complete control over everything. We rely on a good working relationship with the owners, the developers and the architect. Hopefully the outcome will be one more example of cohousing in the UK.

The current plans are for tightly clustered terraced housing with narrow car-free streets, a small car park beyond the common house at the entrance to our neighbourhood, and a community kitchen garden and orchard off to one side. We have agreed to limit our allocated car parking to about 18 spaces, to encourage car sharing or a car pool. Outline planning for the whole development will be resubmitted by the end of 2010, being closely followed by a detailed application for phase one – which includes us. We continue to be in consultation with the architect and TQ9 about building materials and methods, levels of insulation, renewable heat and power options, affordability . . . there is lots to do!

- People are generally much fitter: hod-carriers, carpenters and builders all prefer the natural and often lighter materials they are using for new builds and retrofits.

### Community
- Totnes and District now features five working slate quarries and ten small lime kilns, as well as eight new sawmills. Oak and sweet chestnut shingles are now commonplace.

- As the local buildings infrastructure grows, with more sawmills, well-managed woods and so on, building becomes a more seasonal process. Timber has to be ordered in advance, and materials such as cob, clay plasters and lime can only be used during the spring and summer months.

## 2021-25

**Individuals**

- All 18-year-olds complete their education feeling confident that they could help to build a house. They have been trained, during their school years, in the range of natural building techniques, and much life and beauty has been breathed into their sterile classrooms through their practical workshops.

## 2026-30

**Individuals**

- A survey shows that 100% of householders can tell a casual enquirer the depth of the insulation in their loft and walls and under the floor. Many of them put it there too.

- The survey also reveals that 30% of the local community live in buildings with some shared or communal space occupied by people to whom they are not directly related. Most agree they prefer to live this way.

**Community**

- Many young people spend their gap year staying in the area, but getting involved in a natural house-building process. They volunteer, and live and work as part of a team for nine months, during which time they build a house or shelter and learn all the relevant skills by doing so.

- Alan Sugar's new series 'The Baleprentice' puts ten novice natural builders on to a building site with the brief to build him a straw-bale retirement cottage. Each week he weeds out and throws off the site the member of the team who is pulling his or her weight the least.

**Policy-makers and service providers**

- SHDC [South Hams District Council] publishes its latest guidance on building and planning, and for the first time barely mention the word 'cement', as this has become a very expensive and rare material.

## And who implements this plan?

"If we wait for government to act it will be too late. If we try and do it all on our own it will be too little. But by organizing with friends, neighbours and our community, it may be just enough, and it may be just in time. We urge you to be brave, cast aside your fears and shyness, and enjoy the ride."[4]

Jacqi Hodgson

## Conclusions

- Build on what works – Transition Streets grew from Transition Together Groups, which were based on Home Groups.

- Learn from others and be prepared to change the format of events as they grow.

- Tap into local resources, such as people who have refurbished their homes or built with natural materials.

- Be ambitious – Atmos, Transition Homes and plans for cohousing as part of a major brownfield development are big ideas.

# CHAPTER 4

# REFURBISHMENT AND RETROFIT

*"Uninsulated property is energy theft."* With apologies to Pierre Proudhon

## Why bother with existing homes?

In 2008 the UK's total greenhouse gas emissions were equivalent to 628 million tonnes of carbon dioxide. Thirteen per cent of this total, around 84 million tonnes, was attributed to emissions from homes. But these figures hide some unpleasant realities.

First, while emissions from almost every other sector decreased, mainly due to economic decline, emissions from the residential sector increased by 3.1 per cent. Second, electricity suppliers are responsible for 220 million tonnes of the total, and if we apportion this to the end users we find that in 2007 (the most recent year for which figures are available) homes were actually responsible for 26 per cent of emissions. Add to this the emissions from construction, demolition and dealing with household waste, and the figure rises to around 30 per cent, an average of 5-6 tonnes for each residence.

Approximately a third of this, over 10 per cent of the national total, could be saved by relatively simple energy-efficiency measures. Fifty-five million tonnes of $CO_2$ emissions could be saved by insulating our homes more effectively. When we consider the fact that around 80 per cent of the homes we'll be living in by 2050 have already been built, the central role of refurbishing the existing housing stock becomes clear. Even if every house built between now and 2050 is zero-carbon then, unless we also tackle the carbon emissions from the homes already built, the residential emissions total falls by only 40 million tonnes. Refurbishment and retrofit of existing homes is vital.

## Home truths

The first time it really hit me that all homes would have to become zero-carbon was during a seminar on low-carbon existing homes. The hall was packed with architects and designers; big developers and small eco-builders; council officers and environmental activists. The green and the not-so-green all focused on one of the first slides in a presentation by Brenda Boardman from the Environmental Change Institute at Oxford University.

"I'm giving you the bad news first," said Brenda as she explained the slide. Meeting the target of an 80-per-cent cut by 2050 suggests that housing would be cut from 30 per cent to around 6 per cent of total emissions to fulfil its share. But no, that's not how it works. Cutting carbon in areas such as transport,

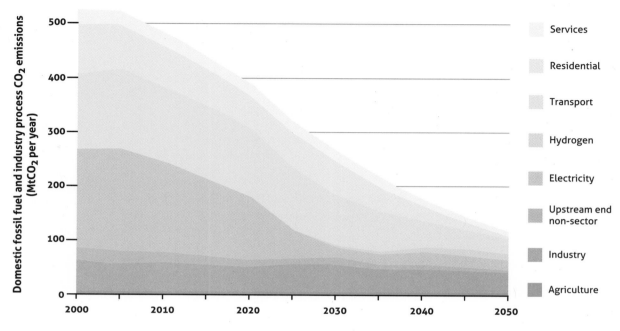

Figure 5. $CO_2$ emissions from various UK sectors showing reductions required to meet 2050 targets. Note that residential emissions must decline to almost zero. © UK Committee on Climate Change

industry and agriculture is much more difficult, so housing has to cut more . . . and faster! The band representing housing on the graph in Figure 5 dwindles rapidly as the years pass and almost disappears well before 2050. Housing must become virtually energy-neutral even before the 2050 deadline.

Around the room heads shook and delegates muttered. It wasn't necessary to read lips to know they were saying it was impossible.

"Now for the good news," said Brenda with a confident smile. "We have all the technology and skills we need to make housing carbon-neutral. It can be done."

Boardman's next slides showed the abysmal state of housing in the UK.

Standard Assessment Procedure (SAP) scores assess the energy efficiency of houses. The scale runs from 0 to 120 and a zero-carbon house would score 100. Any score above 100 shows a carbon-negative home, producing more energy from renewables than it uses. Houses that use more energy for space and water heating, lighting and appliances have low scores. When comparing houses of similar size, the lower the SAP score, the higher the carbon emissions are.

SAP scores are usually translated into ratings: A for the most efficient homes down to G for the least efficient. Figure 6 illustrates the distribution of the UK housing stock and shows very few homes in the A and B categories but large numbers in the heat-leaking G, F and E categories. In terms of $CO_2$, the most inefficient 10 per cent of UK houses emit 13 tonnes per year each.

Even the best 10 per cent are responsible for an average of 3 tonnes per year.

In 2005 the average SAP score was 45. By 2050 it must be increased to more than 90. Anything less and the large contribution expected from housing towards an 80-per-cent emissions cut would not be achieved. In fact, even these levels of cuts may be inadequate. The UK government's Committee on Climate Change suggests that a cut of 90 per cent may be necessary, and there are persuasive arguments for reducing rather than just stabilising atmospheric $CO_2$ levels.

## What does this really mean?

It is clear from these figures that we are burning fossil fuels and letting most of the energy leak out of our homes and blow away in the wind. We are also using far too much energy for domestic appliances. In fact, space heating has become more efficient in recent years, but these savings are more than offset by increases in energy-hungry appliances such as plasma television screens, tumble dryers, dishwashers and computers. In the UK the Energy Saving Trust suggests that by 2020 electronics will use 45 per cent of electricity in the home. We don't have the space in this

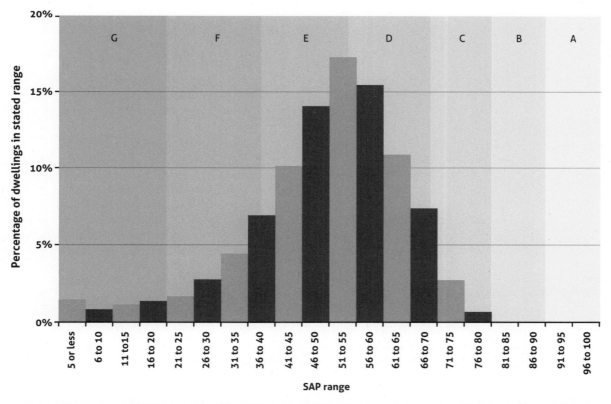

Figure 6. Distribution of UK housing stock by SAP rating and categories. Category G is extremely poor while Category A is good. Note the virtual absence of homes in categories A and B! © Brenda Boardman

book to consider energy use through appliances, but for more information take a look at *Time to Eat the Dog?* by Robert and Brenda Vale.[1]

But what about the other side of the coin? What about renewables? We mustn't forget that all the technologies used to generate heat and electricity come with their own environmental costs and are not a substitute for reducing consumption. A draft response to government proposals for a renewable heat incentive from the Sustainable Building Association (AECB)[2] argues that many renewable technologies can be more damaging than burning fossil fuels, and in 2010 George Monbiot sparked a heated debate by suggesting that feed-in-tariffs for solar photovoltaics undermine more effective carbon reduction strategies.

## People making a difference

Do you remember those suggestive car stickers that were common a few years ago? 'Cavers do it underground' and 'Surfers do it in the sea', but usually catchier than that? Well, I can't remember any along the lines of 'Insulators do it in the loft' or 'I've been stuffing cavities' (actually, just forget that last one, it's awful!) The point I'm trying to make is that eco-renovation isn't really very sexy. Or is it? Trawl through the web and you find a large number of sites where people are 'doing it in the loft' and . . . well, lots of other things. What's more, these websites are getting a lot of visitors. Perhaps the times are changing.

### A Lesson from Lewes

www.evelyneacoproject.co.uk

When Julia Waterlow in Lewes bought a house to let she had far more in mind than just an investment. She wanted to upgrade an ordinary semi-detached house to good environmental standards and simultaneously provide a practical example of what is possible at a reasonable cost. She wasn't aiming for a high-tech zero-carbon home, just a bread-and-butter model of what could be achieved on a limited budget. Alongside the refurbishment Julia built a website, to explain what she did and why (see left).

From the start Julia established clear aims and principles. She wanted the house's occupants to use as little fossil fuel as possible yet have a comfortable and convenient lifestyle. This included encouraging tenants to live in a sustainable way by providing advice on energy-saving behaviour. It was particularly important to help other landlords or property investors, as well as owner-occupiers, make decisions about what steps they could take to improve their houses. Among the principles Julia followed were:

- Use sustainable materials as much as possible.

- Reuse materials or find second-hand materials that will do the job.

- When using new items, they should be the most environmentally friendly.

- Don't be too influenced by smartness or fashion – materials and items should just be clean, fresh and usable

- Take time and don't rush into decisions

- Accept that there will be compromises owing to time and money.

- Keep costs down as far as possible and ensure a reasonable payback on expenditure.

- Record the extra cost of using sustainable materials.

- Record why decisions and options were made and taken.

The result is an authentic, warts-and-all, account of an eco-renovation. Want to know what type of wall insulation to fit? Julia has been there. Which is the most eco-friendly loft insulation? Look at the pros and cons that Julia considered before making her decision. You don't have to follow the same path but you can learn from her journey.

## The Yellow House

www.theyellowhouse.org.uk

George and Annie Marshall's inspiring website (see above) says: "We took a very ordinary English terraced 1930s house and set out on a limited budget to turn it into our dream eco-house: comfortable, clean, healthy, beautiful and a model for low impact living."

Many of you will know about this 'virulent' yellow house. No, it's not the yellow house shared by Vincent Van Gogh and Paul Gauguin in the South of France, it's on a council estate in Oxford! It's been featured on television and regularly opens to the public during Oxfordshire Eco Open House events.

The Marshall's website outlines their principles of ecological design and ideas about green living, and you can tour the house room by room to see what they've done and how they did it. You can also search the site by topic: heating, insulation or water, for example. Hyperlinks make it easy to follow something that grabs your interest or to find suppliers and other sources of information.

## Nottingham Eco-Home

www.msarch.co.uk/ecohome

Penney Poyzer and Gil Schalom spent ten years and over £30,000 on an eco-refit of their Victorian villa in Nottingham. Penney, who is active in Transition Nottingham and known as the 'Queen of Green' since her BBC television series 'No waste like home', meticulously documented the transformation and has a video tour of the property on YouTube – and on a BBC website (link from website above) you can take a 360-degree virtual tour of every room.

## From Little Acorns . . .

www.3acorns.co.uk

Donnachadh McCarthy studied anatomy, became a ballet dancer, lived with the Yanomami Indians in the Amazon Rainforest and then settled down to become an environmental activist. His 1840's Victorian terraced house in Camberwell, South London, is a marvel. Donnachadh installed so much insulation and so many renewable energy and waste-saving measures that in 2006/7 his home, '3 Acorns', had a carbon footprint of minus 114kg – in contrast to the UK average of 6 tonnes (6,000kg). He uses just 28 litres of mains water a day, in contrast to the London average of 160 litres, and produces virtually no domestic waste. In fact, because Donnachadh collects waste wood for his wood burner, he is actually a net importer of waste.

In 1997 Donnachadh's house was the first private home in London to export solar electricity from the roof to London Electricity, and during 2006/7 the 1.2kW-rated system exported about 20 per cent more electricity to the national grid than he imported. A wind turbine installed in 2005 has not been a success, however – the system cost £2,800 but produced just 16kWh in a whole year – about £1.60 off the electricity bill! '3 Acorns' also has solar water heating, a super efficient gas heater and rainwater harvesting.

Donnachadh has a positive environmental impact way beyond the example of his own home. '3 Acorns

Eco-Audits' provide environmental auditing to businesses, charities, families and individuals, and he has also published *Saving the Planet without Costing the Earth – 500 simple steps to a greener lifestyle* and *Easy Eco-auditing – How to make your home and workplace planet-friendly*. There's also a DVD, *Greening a Business – the eco-auditor calls*. Donnachadh is a columnist for *The Independent* and regularly appears on television and radio.

Donnachadh McCarthy may be something of a celebrity, but '3 Acorns' is a model that most of us can follow. Over 70 per cent of the energy-saving suggestions in *Saving the Planet* cost nothing.

## CarbonLite refurbishment

Andrew Simmonds, Chief Executive of the Sustainable Building Association (AECB), found himself living in a 150-year-old cottage with carbon emissions of around 13 tonnes per year and a young family to keep warm. For Andrew this was the perfect opportunity to apply the AECB CarbonLite programme (see page 162) to the refurbishment of his own home, with a target of reducing emissions by around 85 per cent, close to Passivhaus standards (see pages 163-4).

This remarkable refurbishment is now part of the Old Home Superhome network (see page 53) and a case study for the European Passive House Network and the Energy Saving Trust. The builders, Eco-DC, demonstrated the necessary skills to achieve the high build quality vital for this level of refurbishment and also managed to work with the family of five *in situ*! A detailed report can be found in *Green Building* magazine.[3]

### ... and lots more

There are scores if not hundreds of other websites where people document their retrofits so we can learn from their successes and failures. In fact, you don't even have to have a real home, as Katie Taylor, a web designer, demonstrates with her 'vertual' house ('vert' being 'green' in French) – see www.vertualhouse.co.uk. No problem, unless people substitute environmentally friendly homes in SIMS, 'Living Villages' and other cyberspace communities for energy saving in the real world!

## Using the experts

Want to refurbish your home but don't know where to start? In 2008 Ecos Renew was established to facilitate the sustainable refurbishment of existing buildings. It's part of Ecos Trust, an educational charity that promotes sustainable housing. The Trust set up Ecos Homes in 2002, to build sustainable homes for sale on the open market – developments at Great Bow Yard and Stawell received numerous 'green building' national and regional awards, so they have good credentials – but also recognised the importance of refurbishing existing homes.

Ecos Renew provides a flexible service that includes independent assessments, detailed design, obtaining consents, project management, building works and installation of low-carbon technologies. Manager Jim Cornick says: "there is a real roadblock at the stage where a householder has received a general energy / carbon assessment report (such as from Energy Saving Trust) and then faces the task of getting detailed independent advice and assistance to generate designs, specifications and costs for the work and its implementation.' This is where Ecos Renew fills a gap.

Ecos assessment surveys start at £280 for a small terraced property and increase to about £350 for a four / five-bedroom detached house. This figure could be smaller if there's already an EST report or several similar properties that could be surveyed together.

## The customer's view

Sally Lever, a member of Transition Wells, used Ecos Renew when deciding how to eco-renovate her house:

"Ecos Renew came to the house to do a survey and produced a pretty comprehensive report. This included explanations of what they were looking for, why particular measures were important and their relative effectiveness in saving energy, improving quality of life, etc. We briefed them beforehand and explained the areas that were of most concern and interest to us. They charged us £280.

As a result, my partner and I have put together our household energy descent plan! And we've started implementing it. We've already put in extra insulation and draught-proofing, researched a new heating system and given more thought to how we use the house.

We'd got so far with researching our eco-renovation efforts ourselves – we're both fairly knowledgeable on sustainability matters and are ex-engineers so we understand some of the physics – but still found it useful to ask very specific questions of those who've actually built sustainable homes. It boosted our confidence around some spending decisions and probably saved us money on expensive but less effective energy-saving measures.'

## Survival of the retrofittest

Various collections and networks gather the fittest of the retrofits and make the stories available to a wider audience. Perhaps the most valuable is the 'Old Home Superhome' network, set up by John Doggart at the Sustainable Energy Academy (SEA).

## Old Home Superhome

The Sustainable Energy Academy, a charity founded in 1982, "promotes education and action to reduce the carbon footprint of buildings and communities". It has a national impact through its network of exemplar, energy-efficient homes, which are accessible to the public. It's an ambitious project that aims to have over 200 homes involved within five years.

In April 2009 there were 50 properties in the network, with information about the work undertaken, companies used and energy saved. Access is through open days and video 'fly-throughs' where householders conduct a tour. It's also possible to contact properties via email through the SEA website, www.sustainable-energyacademy.org.uk.

Camden Superhome owner Sarah Harrison, the first person to join the Old Home Superhome project, says:

"I've made an 82-per-cent carbon saving to my Victorian house and now I've helped hundreds of people renovate their homes through having my home open, something I would never have done without SEA. The great thing is that they organise the publicity and make sure people turn up on the day you have the open house."

Not all of the properties in the network are real homes. The Leicester EcoHouse, for example, is a show home that demonstrates hundreds of environmental features and ideas (see www.gwll.org.uk/ecohouse). Set up and managed by Groundwork Leicester & Leicestershire, with financial support from Leicester City Council, the EcoHouse reopened in February 2000, after a major expansion and refurbishment funded by the National Lottery, the European Union

## Grand Designs campaign for refurbishment

Kevin McCloud, the Grand Designer himself, is an influential figure in UK building. So when McCloud launched the Grand Designs 'Great British Refurb Campaign' with the support of the UK Green Building Council, the Energy Saving Trust and the Worldwide Fund for Nature (WWF) it was a positive development.

McCloud describes the campaign as "partly about grant aid, partly about tax and partly about getting the skills and accredited workers . . . and getting informed policy into government white papers is a key part of the campaign."[4]

The campaign website has case studies, regular news updates and advice about how to retrofit homes. There's nothing particularly original about the campaign or the website, but McCloud has a profile within building similar to that held by Jeremy Clarkson (*Homo petrolensis*) in the motor industry. You are as likely to find him addressing the Conservative Party Conference as opening an eco-refurbishment exemplar home in Manchester. Actually he's done both on the same day!

See www.greatbritishrefurb.co.uk

holders agreed and the first 'Oxfordshire Open Eco-Houses' was born.

There were various drivers behind this event. First, little attention is paid to the energy efficiency of existing homes, in comparison with that of new build. Second, people want to see things with their own eyes and talk directly to people they can trust rather than 'experts' or company reps selling a product. Third, showcasing eco-homes helps to make eco-renovation desirable and aspirational. Finally, bringing together householders creates a foundation for future activities, a local network of retrofitters such as 40% House or Old Home Superhome.

The first Oxfordshire event, in November 2007, included 18 houses and attracted over a thousand visitors. Each house offered a detailed fact sheet, free low-energy light bulbs in exchange for completed feedback forms, and tours led by householders with support from volunteers. Lessons were learned, the event was a great success and a 28-page 'Step by step guide' to running similar events is now available (see http://coinet.org.uk/download/EcovationPackFinal.pdf or call 01865 403334). These steps include the following.

- Initial idea
- Contacting eco-renovators
- Securing funding
- Information from and for householders
- Publicity design/printing
- Getting volunteers
- Boxes of information and material for householders
- The weekend
- Evaluation

and more than 100 businesses. Over 100,000 visitors have benefitted from the introductory video, audio guides, touch-screen computers and interactive displays.

## The Open Eco-House idea

In August 2007 the Climate Outreach Information Network (COIN) and ClimateXchange, both based in Oxfordshire, asked householders who had done significant eco-renovations if they would open their houses to the public across one weekend. The house-

Similar events took place in 2008 and 2009 under the title 'Ecovation', which also runs the Oxford Ideal

Green Home Show and compiles a directory of local eco-renovation suppliers and professionals. There are also eco-kitchen workshops for people interested in making sustainable adaptations to the most carbon-intensive room in our homes.

## Imitation

Imitation is the sincerest form of flattery, and similar 'Eco Open House' events followed in Stroud (see page 138), Brighton (see page 88), Lewes (see page 91), London (see page 56), Norfolk, Llanidloes, Leicester and elsewhere. Between 2007 and 2010 more than 10,000 people have visited several hundred different eco-properties during Open House weekends. Visitor numbers are highest where events are 'piggy-backed' on to established programmes such as 'Heritage Open Days' and 'Open House London', who also provides insurance cover.

## Open Homes and Gardens

www.mendipenvironment.org.uk

Mendip Open Green Homes and Gardens is different from other Eco Open House events. Gardens are included, a number of geographically separate communities are covered and the 2009 event lasted four days.

The majority of homes were located in and around the towns of Glastonbury and Frome, where there are successful Transition Initiatives and more awareness of sustainability issues, but there were also open homes in rural areas and villages. The project was initiated by Transition Glastonbury's Low Impact Buildings Group and Mendip Environment Community Interest Company, who worked with Wedmore Green Group, Sustainable Frome and Somerset County Council's Renewable Energy Advice Officer.

The event benefitted from the involvement of Kevin McCloud, who visited two of the featured homes in the presence of the local press.

The total cost of the project was over £10,000, which came from Mendip Strategic Partnership, Somerset County Council, Wessex Water, the Sustainable Energy Academy and two local businesses, Solarsense-UK (a local solar energy company) and Wiggly Wigglers, which produces sustainable garden items.

Over 400 people made an average of nearly four visits each to the 27 open homes, and a detailed analysis of the event, with suggestions for improvements, is available from Mendip Open Green Homes and Gardens.[5]

## Open House Safari

When Torridge Action Group 4 Sustainability organised an Open House event in rural North Devon, its members agreed that it was madness to have people driving all over the countryside in cars to look at energy saving in houses. So the group arranged for minibuses to transport visitors from a 'base camp' on eight half-day tours and called it the 'Powerhouse Energy Safari'. It even estimated the environmental footprint of the event and offset the carbon.

Ben Brangwyn, the Transition Network Coordinator, who spoke at the 'base camp' event, says:

> "The day was really informative and lively with a minimal carbon footprint. It felt very engaging and companionable to be travelling with like-minded people learning about renewable energy installations and sustainable buildings.

## Social Learning Theory

Open House events make sense as a very obvious way for people to learn, but there is a solid theoretical basis for such behaviour modification. Psychologist Albert Bandura developed a social learning theory which suggests that people learn from one another through observation, imitation and modelling. The theory has been called a bridge between behaviourist and cognitive learning theories, because it encompasses attention, memory and motivation. Behaviour is explained in terms of interaction between cognitive, behavioural and environmental influences.

"Most human behavior is learned observationally through modeling: from observing others, one forms an idea of how new behaviors are performed, and on later occasions this coded information serves as a guide for action."[6]

Many eco-renovation activities come about through a specific opportunity, e.g. moving house or replacing a bathroom. That's when the 'coded information serves as a guide for action', and can tip the scales in favour of sustainable materials and low-carbon technologies.

Jo Hamilton and Gavin Killip, researchers at the Environmental Change Institute at the University of Oxford, who are involved in organising the Oxford Eco-Home Open Days (see page 54), assessed the impact and limits of learning from such events. They agree that social learning addresses some of the barriers and negative perceptions associated with eco-renovation and suggest that we learn most effectively from models that are attractive to us or influential for us, such as our parents (at a certain age), celebrities, people who are successful or powerful, or people who are simply like us. However, the researchers also refer to the 'value-action gap', where behaviour doesn't always match or follow values, and recognise that not all the changes in behaviour result from learning-based experience.

Hamilton and Killip, despite being enthusiastic about Open House events, conclude that further research is needed to assess how "visitors process the information and experience, and what they do as a result". They also accept that the order and consistency needed to conduct such research could threaten the greatest strength of these events: "the power of real-life experience and the telling of a 'story' by an ordinary citizen about their own home."[7]

Actually seeing what others had done not only inspired me, it made me feel it's possible to do something similar in my own home."

## Open House London

www.londonopenhouse.org

In 2009 Open House London showcased many new and renovated eco-buildings. Nearly 50 buildings carry the green dot that marks them as 'Green Exemplars'. From a small terraced house in Camberwell to the iconic BedZED development in Sutton; from the

Camden Council zero-carbon refurbishment of a Victorian house to an eco-friendly new build squeezed into the eight-foot gap between neighbouring buildings – old and new, affordable, expensive and very expensive, Green London, alongside the not-so-green majority of the city, is open to all.

'Coolly, madly, greenly' is how Open House London brands its environmentally friendly slant. As well as listing a large selection of green buildings, it collaborates with *Sustain* magazine and the UK Green Building Council to produce a green building guide; and *Sponge*, a network of young professionals interested in sustainability, arranges a tour of green buildings in the Regent's Park and Portobello area.

The event highlights good examples but also real problems in making sustainable housing an everyday reality. Architect Peter Smith shows me around an affordable housing development in Hackney and admits that the project falls far below achievable standards of energy efficiency. "By the time this development is finished it will already be four years out of date," says Peter. "It reaches Eco Homes Very Good – perhaps equivalent to Code for Sustainable Homes Level 3 – while adjacent buildings under construction across the road will achieve level 4 or 5." And because this development is for a housing association, it is built to a higher standard than a private development would be required to meet. I'm reminded of a comment from Mischa Hewitt, Project Manager for the Brighton Earthship (see Chapter 6), who told me, "today's new build is tomorrow's retrofit".

## A haus in Hackney?

A short bus journey away from the Hackney housing development described above lies what is described in the Open House guide as an "extreme low-carbon refurbishment of an 1840s terraced house in a conservation area. Insulation, airtightness, mechanical ventilation and heat recovery (MVHR), solar thermal and triple glazing reduce emissions by 80 per cent", with ambitions of meeting Passivhaus standards.

A long queue winds down the road, where expensive cars are parked alongside bikes chained to lamp posts and trees. This house is obviously attracting more visitors than the worthy but unsexy affordable housing.

'1840s' means solid walls and 'conservation area' means no external insulation permitted. The solution is 15-20mm of high-performance insulation on the inside of the front and back walls. To compensate for the loss of space, the house is extended at the back, which involved complex and expensive dismantling and reconstruction. A fact sheet suggests that carbon emissions, excluding electrical appliances, will fall from six tonnes per year to just over one tonne after the refurbishment. But how many tonnes have gone into the build? And how much has it cost?[8]

A four-bedroom house for sale in the same road, in 'highly regarded De Beauvoir Town', is priced at just under £1 million. Remember that we are still in Hackney, where levels of social deprivation and unemployment are among the highest in the country; where crumbling blocks of flats, often hopefully called 'mansions', house a population with one of the highest levels of tuberculosis in the UK.

In nearby Waltham Forest, the William Morris Gallery has an exhibition about *News from Nowhere*, Morris's imagined journey in a utopian future. If Morris were alive today, I imagine he would have said: "have nothing in your houses that you do not know to be environmentally friendly or believe to be sustainable". The gallery occupies the enormous house where Morris was born and lived until 1854, but we remember Morris not for the wealth into which he was born but as an artist, designer and socialist pioneer. He may not have commented on sustainable housing but he was an early campaigner against pollution and poor building standards, and said:

> "[T]he material surroundings of my life should be pleasant, generous, and beautiful; that I know is a large claim, but this I will say about it, that if it cannot be satisfied, if every civilized community cannot provide such surroundings for all its members, I do not want the world to go on."[9]

Eco-refurbishments costing hundreds of thousands alongside thousands of neglected homes that haemorrhage heat and energy while failing to meet even the government's unambitious plans to raise all social housing to 'Decent Homes' standard (see page 164) should offend us just as Morris was offended by such injustice. The 1840s retrofit may provide valuable lessons but these must be applied to all homes, not just those of the rich.

## Greening the streets

Transition Horncastle, in Lincolnshire, won funding from the British Gas Green Streets project for energy saving and for renewable energy technologies, to be used in four 'early years' community buildings and 32 households. It's not just the under-fives who benefit from the community buildings, as they are also used by around 1,300 other people. Horncastle also plans to engage the wider community by providing energy-saving guidance and advice and by building awareness of energy-saving measures in young children. Gearoid Lane, Director of Communities and New Energy at British Gas, said: "We chose Transition Town Horncastle Green Babies and Toddlers project because of their sheer level of dynamism and desire to improve the lives of the people of Horncastle."

Transition Horncastle is one of 14 projects to share the £2 million Green Streets fund. In 2011 the projects go head-to-head in a number of challenges to reduce energy use, generate local energy and increase support amongst members of their own community. Progress will be monitored for a year by the Institute for Public Policy Research, and the project chosen as Britain's greenest community stands to win a further £100,000 in funding from British Gas.

Other Green Streets communities include the following.

- The village of Casterton in Cumbria, which plans to install a biomass system in a local school and measures such as insulation for solid walls in local 'hard to treat' homes.

- The Bradford Bandits BMX Racing Club, which will install a wind turbine to power floodlights at Peel Park BMX track and help to educate local residents and install energy-efficiency measures in their homes.

- Hyde Farm Climate Action Network, which will work with the local school to install solar PV panels on the roof to reduce the school's energy use by 20 per cent and inspire the pupils and parents. It will continue to educate its network of 200 households on energy efficiency.

- Climate Friendly Bradford upon Avon, which is turning a wide range of local homes into demonstration projects for green energy and insulation.

Members of Transition Horncastle celebrate their Green Streets award. Photograph: Transition Horncastle

## Low-carbon communities

The next logical step from retrofitting your home as part of a supportive network is doing it as part of a community. Targets for reducing carbon emissions from your home can be extrapolated to neighbourhoods, villages, towns and even cities. The feeling that you are the only person making changes is overcome, as change becomes the social norm. There's even some healthy competition as communities strive to become the first to justify a 'carbon neutral' prefix.

### Carbon-neutral Ashton Hayes

www.goingcarbonneutral.co.uk

Towards the end of 2005 Garry Charnock and other residents in Ashton Hayes near Chester came up with the idea of making their village the first carbon-neutral community in the UK. They put the idea to the Parish Council, which stipulated that a public meeting should be held to discuss the matter.

The launch meeting was held on a bitterly cold evening in January 2006, but over 400 people (75 per cent of village adults) attended to support what has since become a successful and frequently emulated model for community action on climate change. Since 2006, Ashton Hayes, a well-knit community of 350 homes and about 1,000 people, has cut carbon dioxide emissions by 23 per cent. Initiatives include reducing travel and planting 14,000 trees, but making homes more sustainable is a key part of the process. Some residents have cut their energy bills by 50 per cent by improving insulation and changing their behaviour.

The project benefits from a high profile, grants, awards, extensive media coverage and support from the University of Chester, but its success rests on a pool of between 30 and 50 volunteers and on a very high level of community support. As part of his MSc in Climate Change and Sustainable Development, local resident Ged Edwards carried out a survey and found that an astonishing 99 per cent of households are engaged in environmentally friendly behaviour.[10] Motivations include environmental concern, moral responsibility, saving money, encouragement from friends and family, being part of the community-based programme and pride in Ashton Hayes.

Ashton Hayes, a community with carbon-neutral ambitions.
Photograph: Carbon Neutral Ashton Hayes

Barriers to further change are chiefly lack of time, other pressing demands and, to a small degree, the cost of larger capital items. Not surprisingly, the retired are doing more than employed people. Thirty-five per cent of people became more actively involved in village life through the project – a significant benefit even without the reduction in $CO_2$ emissions. This is a view echoed by Tracey Todhunter in *Sustained* magazine:

"No doubt we would continue to thrive if we abandoned our goal of carbon neutrality, but take away our Time Bank, gardening club, ballet classes and football team and the situation would be very different. Rather than be seen as an 'eco-pioneer' I'd prefer to be known as the kind of person who willingly waters her neighbour's plants when they're on holiday, finds time for a cup of tea with the elderly gentleman across the street or collects a prescription for a friend in need. Find the communities where these kinds of things are commonplace and you'll probably find a low-carbon community; certainly one that could make rapid reductions if it chose to. This growth in low-carbon communities isn't just about the planet: it's about people. When we have respect and tolerance for our neighbours, care for the environment follows naturally."[11]

Tracey Todhunter, freelance writer and former part-time Policy and Campaigns Manager for the Low Carbon Communities Network

In 2009 the project was selected to lead Zerofootprint's 'Villages without borders' project, which uses software tools to help communities record, measure and share their carbon emission data and provides guidance on ways to lower a community's carbon footprint. Zerofootprint is an award-winning Canadian not-for-

## The 'Big Rules'

Ashton Hayes believes one of its best decisions was to adopt some 'Big Rules' – many of which will be familiar to those in the Transition movement – to keep the project team on the same path and avoid conflicts in the village. These are as follows.

- Our project is owned by Ashton Hayes Parish Council.
- Our aims are two-fold:
  - to help Ashton Hayes become carbon-neutral
  - to share our experiences and inspire others.
- We see this as a journey towards carbon neutrality and do not know when we will get there.
- It is a non-political 'grassroots' project.
- We are a non-confrontational group.
- We recognise that human activity is contributing to major climate change but do not apportion blame or point the finger at anyone.
- We welcome everyone to join in and support our aims.
- We do not focus on the threats of climate change, more on the benefits of taking action.

profit organisation dedicated to helping communities go green.

Ashton Hayes has provided support to over 100 other communities trying to reduce their carbon footprints, has a 'toolkit' and three films about its experience, and in 2009 was twinned with Notteroy, a town of 20,000 people that aims to become the first carbon-neutral community in Norway. And all of this happened before it won a £500,000 grant from the Department of Energy and Climate Change's Low Carbon Communities Challenge in January 2010.

## Sustainable Blacon

www.sustainableblacon.org.uk

Blacon is a township of around 16,000 people in Chester, not far from Ashton Hayes. But this is an urban community that once contained one of the largest council estates in Europe, now owned by the Chester and District Housing Trust. Here there are tower blocks and fuel poverty and social deprivation – but, in common with Ashton Hayes, there is also a strong community identity.

'Sustainable Blacon' is based on regeneration work undertaken since 1999 and on the successful ways in which local people worked to improve life here. Reggie Jones, one of the three Labour councillors who represent the area, says: "It's a special community with a huge community spirit and a sense of belonging. There's a strong feeling of together and a desire to improve the image of Blacon."

Blacon Community Trust set up Sustainable Blacon Ltd to take forward the area's plans for a secure future for Blacon. The people in charge are local residents, representatives from Chester and District Housing Trust and Cheshire West and Chester Council, and advisers from energy, green spaces and urban design backgrounds.

Household energy is a key theme for Sustainable Blacon, which supports schemes enabling residents to insulate their homes. Through a partnership with British Gas and with Chester and District Housing Trust, they are upgrading houses as one of British Gas's ten UK Flagship Areas for its Community Energy Saving Programme. The Trust also plans to demonstrate low-carbon technologies on a large scale in Blacon, with smart meters and renewable energy.

In December 2010 it was also successful in the Low Carbon Communities Challenge, and will be spending more than £500,000 on refurbishing two demonstration houses and on giving access to advice and practical support to 16,000 residents.

Judi Sellwood, Blacon Community Trust Manager, says:

> "This is an engaged community working with people at the cutting edge of renewable energy technologies. It's also a deprived community, so if we can make it happen here we can make it happen anywhere."

### Low Carbon Communities Network

The Low Carbon Communities Network encourages low-carbon and zero-carbon technologies and lifestyles at a community level by offering mutual support, materials and infrastructure to make communities more effective and efficient in collective action, and lobbying for a low-carbon future. In 2009 the network had a successful conference, with scores of communities represented. Figure 7, overleaf, illustrates the choice facing us and which options the network favours.

## Refit West – a role for business?

www.forumforthefuture.org/projects/refit-west

Forum for the Future is an independent, non-profit-making organisation promoting sustainable development. It believes that working with mainstream partner organisations, such as Cadbury, Marks & Spencers, Vodafone and AkzoNobel, encourages them towards a sustainable future. The organisation was founded in 1996 by, among others, Jonathon Porritt and Sara Parkin.

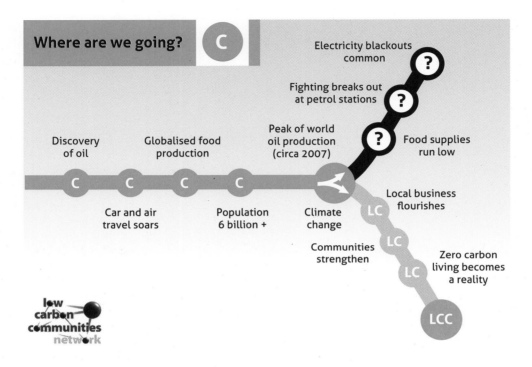

**Where are we going?** C

Electricity blackouts
common ?

Fighting breaks out
at petrol stations ?

Peak of world
oil production
(circa 2007) ?

Food supplies
run low

Discovery
of oil C

Globalised food
production C

C

C

Local business
flourishes LC

Car and air
travel soars

Population
6 billion + 

Climate
change

LC

Communities
strengthen

LC

Zero carbon
living becomes
a reality

LC

low
carbon
communities
network

LCC

Figure 7. The Low Carbon Communities Network offers two responses to climate change and peak oil.
Which looks the best option to you? © Low Carbon Communities Network

A typical 'Forum' project is Refit West, a Bristol-based initiative that tackles the refurbishment of private housing – something that has so far really taken place only at the level of individual homes. The private sector accounts for 93 per cent of Bristol's housing and represents a significant part of the carbon challenge. Refit West aims to retrofit 1,000 homes in Bristol by the end of 2011.

Arup and Rok, major building companies and partners for this project, developed a model to demonstrate the carbon and cost savings that could be achieved by retrofitting generic types that broadly represent the housing stock of Bristol. The method encompasses developing baseline house types, selecting the most appropriate refit options available, modelling the energy and carbon savings, and feeding in cost estimates.

Four packages of measures were applied to the different generic house types.

**Package 1**
Energy-saving lighting
- Draught-proofing
- Roof insulation
- Cavity-wall insulation

**Package 2**
- New windows
- New boiler and controls

**Package 3**
- Internal wall insulation
- Floor insulation

**Package 4**
- External wall insulation
- Floor insulation
- Solar thermal panels
- Solar PV panels

Users of the model enter the numbers of each house type to be upgraded, the refit measures already in place and the package of measures to be installed. The model then calculates the SAP rating, $CO_2$ reduction and cost per house (or group of houses), as well as a cost per kilogram of $CO_2$. For groups of houses, a 'clustered' (within walking distance) or 'dispersed' scenario can be selected. Contractors can make considerable savings where they work from one base and share equipment and skills.

Refurbishment of social housing where large numbers of homes are treated within specific neighbourhoods has considerable economies of scale. This model allows these savings to be calculated for private housing. The best value for money is achieved by implementing Package 1 on 50 or more clustered Victorian three-bed semis. $CO_2$ savings cost just £0.38 per kilogram, but are limited to reducing emissions by around 25 per cent. Installing extensive retrofit measures on clusters of over 20 homes can produce savings of over 55 per cent and reduce emissions by around 75 per cent, at a cost of about £2.00 per kilogram of $CO_2$.

So how can the economies of scale achieved with social housing be extended to private housing? Kirklees and Sheffield have achieved this by offering free loft and cavity-wall insulation to all householders, but the costs of extending this to full retrofits could be prohibitive.

Financial incentives and 'pay as you save' schemes may help by allowing householders to finance energy-efficiency measures from future savings on energy costs or from feed-in-tariffs. Community cohesion is another key factor. The ability of neighbours collectively to seek quotes for the refurbishment of whole streets and communities may depend on community infrastructures already present. Or, better, community cohesion may be an added benefit, where neighbourhood groups are brought together for collective retrofit schemes by some outside intervention.

## Retrofit for the future

In February 2010 the government announced awards totalling £17 million to a wide range of projects retrofitting social housing. The 'Retrofit for the Future' programme is funding 87 projects across the UK from the first round of 190 projects, which received £20,000 each to support feasibility studies.[12] The 87 'finalists' receive an average of £140,000 to carry out retrofits on social houses and to demonstrate cuts in carbon emissions. Many of the projects will attempt to retrofit homes to Passivhaus standards (see pages 163-4).

Each house will be monitored for two years after refurbishment, to assess the value of energy-saving measures and the potential to roll out solutions in a cost-effective manner.

## Do we need to think about payback times?

In their detailed and thought-provoking *Time to Eat the Dog – A real guide to sustainable living*,[14] Robert and Brenda Vale consider the issue of payback times for home improvements such as insulation or installing a solar water heater. People don't think about payback when they fit a luxury kitchen or buy a new car, so why, they ask, should it be important when making our homes more energy-efficient?

Using examples of fitted kitchens on the website of a New Zealand installer, the Vales point out that the difference between the cost of a deluxe kitchen (£6,100) and a premium kitchen (£10,500) could pay for a solar water heater. Ask a kitchen installer about payback times and you'll get a blank look. "This is a deluxe kitchen," they'll say. "It will make cooking more enjoyable, make your life easier, impress your friends and add value to your home. Why worry about payback times?"

In contrast, when we look at energy-efficiency measures and renewables, there are so many calculations about payback times that it's hard to see the wood for the trees. Sticking with the example of a solar water heater, New Zealand's Energy Efficiency and Conservation Authority calculates the payback time on a system that saves 3,000kWh of electricity a year as 9.2 years – which no doubt leads many people to shake their heads and spend their money on sensible items like a new kitchen or a better car.

Rob Hopkins had solar panels installed on his roof a few years ago and wrote about the issue of payback times in Transition Culture, his regular blog exploring 'the head, heart and hands of energy descent'. Here's an extract.

> "The question I find myself asked though when I tell people about it is "but what is the payback on them?" Now I have to say honestly that I have no idea, I haven't sat down and worked it out, but what intrigues me is the nature of that question.
>
> It is not a question we ask when someone buys a new TV, a car, an iPod, mobile phone, a swimming pool, a boat, a sofa, new carpets, a DVD player, a jacuzzi, a fitted kitchen, a new cooker, a motorbike, timber decking for the garden, a new conservatory, a caravan, a new fridge, a holiday, a computer, a printer, a double bass, a new chest of drawers or a painting.
>
> Somehow all these things are OK because we want them, we think they will make us happier, or because we feel we need them. When it comes to solar panels those criteria no longer apply. Odd that. I am buying them because they will increase the resilience of my family, reduce

our footprint and make us less oil-vulnerable, but ultimately it is actually because I want them, in exactly the same way that people want the things on the list above.

I have no idea of the payback (although I guess I am assuming that there will be one). I suppose for me I see them as being essential, whereas most of the other things on the list aren't. Will rising oil prices move people in the same direction, or will such things be seen more and more as an unaffordable luxury? I suppose it depends to what extent people want them, and what we can do to help generate that . . ."[15]

Now, I had solar panels installed at about the same time, as part of the 'Solar Challenge' project run by Transition Town Totnes. The difference was that I did ask about payback times. I asked the question of four different installers, who each quoted figures for at least two different systems, and the answers varied enormously. The only constant was the suspicion with which I treated these answers. At the time I asked because I wanted to get the best value for money, but now I think there is a more important reason why payback times should be considered.

The cost of an item is ultimately a reflection of the energy that goes into producing that item. So the cost of a solar panel should reflect the total amount of energy used in its construction. This is called 'embodied energy' and must include energy used in collecting and processing the raw materials; building the factory where the panels are made; housing, feeding and transporting employees; distributing the product to installers; and the energy used in putting the panel on your roof . . . the list is almost endless and very difficult (not to say tedious!) to measure accurately. Of course there are other things that affect price, such as

supply and demand, or profit, but embodied energy is a major factor. It is also vital to understand the impact of feed-in tariffs for electricity generation and for the planned renewable heat incentive, which pay people for the electricity and heat they generate, and how these may encourage us toward false solutions.

Some clever people in universities have measured the embodied energy in photovoltaic (PV) systems, compared that to the energy produced by PV in different climates, and then calculated how many years it takes to 'pay back' the embodied energy used to make the PV in the first place. Engineers at the University of Bath estimate the energy payback for a typical PV system as over 16 years in the UK.[16] In sunny Northern Italy the same system would pay back the embodied energy in 7.5 years. Other researchers suggest that the Bath calculations are based on older systems and that energy payback is much quicker. A study from the University of Bologna optimistically suggests a payback of less than 2 years in an area with medium sunshine such as Northern Italy, and these figures are often quoted by companies selling PV systems. Although not quite as favourable, the Bologna figures are largely supported by research in the Netherlands suggesting an energy payback time of

## National Existing Homes Adaptation Tool (NEAT)

How well prepared are our homes for the floods, droughts, heatwaves and extreme weather events that will accompany global warming? NEAT is a tool to help you assess your home and what adaptations may be necessary. You can access the tool through www.sustainablehomes.co.uk/impact_on_climate.aspx.

## Energy efficiency and heritage buildings

### Nils White, Conservation and Design Officer, South Hams District Council

Making historic houses more energy-efficient seems consistent with their conservation and the wider green agenda – an effective way of ensuring their future use while driving down their carbon footprint – and there are a number of ways in which their performance can be improved. But in our enthusiasm to upgrade existing building stock we should not forget that many houses listed for their architectural and historic importance were virtually 'zero-carbon' in their form of construction and when used as originally intended.

In a rural county like Devon, most vernacular construction materials and techniques had a very low embodied energy compared with modern equivalents. Earth for cob walling came from around the site, and stone and slate were usually won from quarries nearby. Thatch was a local product associated with grain production, and timber was harvested sustainably (and often reused from earlier buildings). Materials producing high carbon emissions such as lime, brick, glass or metals were expensive and used sparingly. And, perhaps most significantly, these houses have lasted; often for centuries.

In everyday use, heating was provided from smallwood collected locally and, though open fires were hardly efficient, most of the time a single fire was shared by everyone in the house. In most houses, spaces were compartmentalised and easy to heat.

In the last few decades, however, there has been a tendency to transform these buildings and the way they are used. Partition walls have come down, meaning larger areas need to be heated, oil- or gas-fired central heating is the norm, with radiators in every room, and, significantly, the number of occupants has plummeted. What had been low-energy houses became veritable gas guzzlers and energy consumption per capita shot up. No wonder improving their energy efficiency is seen as imperative and, usually, there is much that can be achieved in this regard, including roof insulation, draught-proofing, secondary glazing and upgrading boilers and heating controls. There is ongoing research at a number of sites, including Devon, into lowering the energy consumption of these buildings, and in the next few years our understanding of how best to achieve this is likely to grow considerably.

However, most historic buildings function differently from modern ones – they need to 'breathe' – and inappropriate use of insulation and associated vapour barriers in walls and even floors can lead to rapid deterioration of a building's fabric, caused by moisture build-up (and this tends to involve removal of historic fabric). So, while these measures may improve energy performance in the short term, they can jeopardise the buildings' character and long-term future. Other changes, such as double glazing and solar panels, may disfigure a building while producing energy savings that are marginal or unproven. Of course, we urgently need to make fundamental changes to reduce our consumption of and dependency on oil, but sacrificing the character of the precious 1 or 2 per cent of our building stock that is listed, by using unproven measures, is not the right way to do it. It is not historic buildings that are inefficient but how we use them, and this is where changes can most easily be made.

2.7 years in Northern Italy, [17,] equivalent to about 6 years in the UK; and by British research suggesting a 4-year payback.[18]

## So why is all this important?

It's important because we are running out of time to deal with climate change, and of the fossil fuels we need to tackle the problem. We may have already reached peak oil, and groups like The 100 Months Club believe we must reduce carbon emissions in – well, by the time you read this it's a lot less than 100 months. We can't invest for long-term returns because we may not have a long term!

## Conclusions

- Existing homes are 90 per cent of the problem, so refurbishment and eco-retrofits are far more important than new build.

- We need to achieve virtually zero-carbon homes as soon as possible, so retrofits must be ambitious and thorough.

- We don't have to reinvent the wheel – whatever your home is like, the chances are there is a similar retrofit complete with details on the web that you can learn from.

- Use the national networks and establish local ones.

- Visit an Eco Open House event near you and think about organising one in your area.

- The Evelyn Eco Project is a retrofit of one house, while Ashton Hayes aim to retrofit a whole community, but they both started with an idea, and there's nothing more powerful.

## CHAPTER 5

# BUILDING TOGETHER

*"We shall insulate in the lofts, we shall insulate under the floors and in the walls, we shall insulate with growing confidence and growing strength in all our homes, we shall exclude draughts whatever the cost may be, we shall recycle in the streets, we shall install renewable energy in the towns and in the villages. We shall never surrender."* With apologies to Winston Churchill

There is probably a formula to explain the exponential relationship between the number of people involved in a project and what they can achieve. Double the number of people involved and you quadruple the chance of success before subtracting the 'too many cooks' factor – or something like that! But I doubt I could explain the empowerment that working with others leads to, any more than I can describe the wonderful feeling I always have when I watch the Amish barn-raising in *Witness*.

Anyway, thousands of people are working collectively to build low-carbon resilient communities, ranging from temporary shelters with no planning consent to sophisticated cohousing developments. Some are new build and others involve refurbishing existing buildings. Some are expensive and some are affordable to even the lowest-income groups. Many are rural but an increasing number are urban. All of them teach us something about how to make sustainable housing happen.

## Low-impact development

In 2005 Simon Dale and Jasmine Saville built a simple low-impact home in Welsh woodland and put photographs on the web to share with friends who had helped. (See www.simondale.net/house.) Before long the site was attracting 50,000 visits a day and thousands of emails from people inspired by their project. The appeal of this approach to creating sustainable homes should not be underestimated.

Simon Fairlie, founder of *Chapter 7* and editor of *The Land*, defines low-impact development (LID), with half an eye on planning officers, as "development which, by virtue of its low or benign environmental impact, may be allowed in locations where conventional development is not permitted."[1]

Low-impact dwellings range from a variety of shacks, sheds, caravans and benders to more substantial buildings such as Ben Law's house at Prickly Nut

Wood, which appealed to millions of viewers when it featured on *Grand Designs*, or the Lammas eco-terrace at Glandwr, Pembrokeshire (see pages 71-4). Many low-impact developments are, like Lammas, small communities, and even the single dwellings such as Ben Law's woodland home are likely to be built by groups of volunteers. While the buildings vary in sophistication and cost, low-impact developments generally share the following features.

- They are unique, diverse and adapted to local conditions.

- They use natural, local and recycled materials.

- They are small-scale and unobtrusive.

- They enhance biodiversity.

This simple low-impact house cost just a few thousand pounds to build. Photograph: Simon Dale

- They are usually off-grid and based on renewable resources and energy.

- They increase public access to open space.

- They generate little traffic.

- They are linked to sustainable livelihoods.

An estimated 10,000 people in the UK live in situations that loosely fit Simon Fairlie's definition, usually in small groups, and often in conflict with local planners. But, argues Fairlie, these people are slowly but surely forcing changes to the antiquated and conservative planning laws. "Such is the dead weight of English planning bureaucracy," he argues, "that you have to move a mountain to change a single comma".

Increasing numbers of people have been starting low-impact projects without applying for permission in advance. In many cases, after subsequent planning refusal by the local authority, the matter has gone to appeal, and in the majority of appeals planning inspectors are deciding that LIDs are a justifiable exception to planning policy. In England, since 1999, almost every single low-impact community that has gone to appeal – Kings Hill, Tinker's Bubble, Steward Community Woodland, Landmatters, Fivepenny Farm, Quicken Wood, Keveral Farm – has been given temporary or permanent permission.

> "It's OK living in an agricultural worker's bungalow in Wales in the summer, but each winter you become aware of just how badly they are designed and how poorly insulated. I've lived in four since 1977, and not a year has passed without me thinking about designing a house of my own that wasn't always cold and draughty; a house that faced and welcomed in the sun; a house that made sense and was fun

to live in; something that didn't cost the earth to build and didn't need a mortgage so left me free to live simply.

> "I can understand the planner's fears that if everyone were allowed free range to build what they like where they liked this country would be overrun, but yet there is something in me that revolts against a system that assumes that I and nature don't mix. At the heart of our planning laws is the unspoken assumption that people and the countryside are bad for each other."[2]

> Tony Wrench

## Why LID is important

> "Low Impact Development is a superb example of sustainability being led from the grass roots. Whilst planners and policy makers wring their hands over climate change, affordable housing and rural decline, for over a decade across the UK, LIDers have quietly got on with building a greener future from the ground up. LID is one of the few approaches offering holistic solutions to climate change, peak oil and sustainability."[3]

> Larch Maxey

Because LID uses local skills, traditions, designs and materials, it empowers those involved and contributes to a regional uniqueness and sense of place. LID housing, for example, tends to be built to very high energy-efficiency standards but also uses locally available natural and/or reclaimed materials, so the embodied energy of the building is low. LID is undoubtedly an important component of Transition.

The following examples cover a range of low-impact developments in England and Wales. Scotland has acknowledged the existence and potential of low-impact housing in its national planning guidance since 1999, and the main constraint is often land ownership. *Low Impact Development: The future in our hands*, edited by Jenny Pickerill and Larch Maxey,[4] is an excellent account and I offer no apology for mining its pages extensively.

## Lammas eco-village

www.lammas.org.uk

Imagine delivering your planning application in a wheelbarrow. It contains over 800 pages of text and 200 drawings. There are four copies of everything, as requested by the council, and all the indications from council officers during pre-application meetings are that the application will be recommended for approval. It seems that you are knocking at an open door.

Lammas campaigners deliver their planning application to Pembrokeshire County Council. Photograph: Paul Wimbush

But something isn't right. While continuing to say the application is heading for approval, planning officers avoid further meetings and then, right at the last minute, they recommend refusal and cite the lack of information that they have never asked for. The application is refused, and so begins a story that could have been written by Franz Kafka and should certainly be fiction rather than fact.

This is the story of the fight to establish the Lammas low-impact community, and, if you want to risk high blood pressure and ulcers, take a look at the community's meticulously detailed account of five years of wrangling with the bureaucrats at Pembrokeshire County Council. It's not a pleasant story, but it does have a happy ending. In August 2009 Lammas won its appeal to the Welsh Assembly and is now concentrating on sustainable living rather than sustaining the livings of council bureaucrats.

But let's go back a bit and look at why the Lammas project is so important and what lessons can be learned from the Lammas Eco Villagers' frustrating experience.

### Policy 52

In July 2006 Pembrokeshire County Council (PCC) adopted a Joint Unitary Development Plan that included Policy 52. This allows new eco-smallholdings in the open countryside on the basis that they make a positive environmental, social and economic contribution: exactly the type of low-impact development defined by Simon Fairlie.

Many of the people who founded Lammas were involved in developing Policy 52 and wrote their application specifically to meet its requirements. Of particular importance is the understanding that low-impact developments must be assessed on permaculture principles rather than on conventional agricultural criteria. This is critical, because smallholders must meet 75 per cent of their needs from the land if they are to justify planning consent. While this can be achieved in a permaculture settlement, it is far more difficult for conventional agriculture. Despite assurances that any assessment of viability would be based on permaculture principles, the council actually commissioned a standard agricultural assessment.

## More obstacles

Many other obstacles were placed in front of Lammas, leading the community to conclude in May 2009 that "Pembrokeshire County Council is blocking the progress of the Lammas project at every opportunity. What we are unable to fathom is why."

Two episodes illustrate this conclusion perfectly and give a flavour of the relationship between Lammas and the planning department. When Lammas tried to appeal against the refusal of its initial application, it was informed that the application had actually been invalid because it was not accompanied by an access statement. Since it was not a valid application, there could be no appeal. PCC had never asked for an access statement, although it should have, so the mistake was the council's. But it was Lammas that was faced with the additional cost, work and delays associated with making another application. It took the threat of High Court action to force PCC to admit its mistake and to offer to refund the planning fee.

In April 2008 Lammas arranged a review by the Design Commission for Wales, which sees it as part of its role to create a forum for dialogue between applicants and planning officers. It took a lot of effort by Lammas to persuade PCC to send a representative, but it eventually agreed. After the review, one of the Design Commission Panellists said that Lammas was 'the most inspiring project he had ever seen'. The

report sent to PCC by the Commission described Lammas as 'a significant and inspiring project' and urged the council to work with Lammas to make it happen. Unfortunately this review was not even mentioned in the officers' report to the planning committee.

Meanwhile Lammas had become a *cause célèbre*, with over 800 letters of support from all over the world in addition to backing from within Wales. Paul Wimbush, Lammas Project Coordinator, described the planning application as a test case for people's confidence in the planning system itself. Certainly the confidence of Lammas had been sorely stretched. Wimbush commented in May 2009: "Lammas's approach is most unusual in choosing to request planning permission before developing the land. To date it is an approach that has not paid off."

## Success at last!

In August 2009 Lammas finally got the go-ahead from the Welsh Assembly for a project that could help to revitalise a small part of rural Wales. Its plans, to develop an eco-village of nine smallholdings on 76 acres outside the village of Glandwr, could generate around £100,000 per year from land that previously raised just £2,500. Since the application was originally submitted, both the village school and the post office shop have closed. It is not known how many people have left the area to seek opportunities elsewhere.

Lammas plans to generate electricity from a water turbine and to grow willow and elephant grass for fuel. Families are already working the land and aim to make a living from sustainable activities such as growing worms for compost, flax to make linen shawls and willow for baskets. Smoked hams, fruit and vegetables will be sold locally. Each home, with eight acres of land, will cost around £80,000.

Trapped in red tape for seven years but the Lammas campaigners eventually broke free. Photograph: Paul Wimbush

The buildings erected on the site have a low visual impact and blend into the landscape. Largely natural materials from the locality are used, including earth, turf, timber and straw, and the buildings combine the latest in green technologies with traditional building skills. The houses incorporate sustainable technologies such as passive solar heating, rainwater harvesting and electricity generation from renewable sources such as wind, water and the sun. No mains services are used.

Cassandra Lishman, a local businesswoman and a prospective resident of the eco-village, said: "At last we can begin building our homes. We are delighted that the Welsh Assembly Government is bold enough to put their policies into practice."

But not everyone is happy. The leader of Pembrokeshire County Council, John Davies; the local Conservative MP, Stephen Crabb; Welsh Assembly Member, Paul Davis; and Fiona Phillips, Editor of the local paper all condemned the decision. "This demonstrated what we were really up against. Political prejudice based on ignorance of who we are," said Paul Wimbush, who believes that there is no problem with Policy 52, just with the politicians and bureaucrats who have to implement it.

Now, through a television series following the community as it develops, Lammas is hoping to show people that the community is not just a bunch of hippies and outsiders. "Independent film makers are talking to the Discovery Channel and BBC about a TV series and we hope this can overturn some of the prejudice against us," said Paul. Overcoming this jaundiced view of low-impact development may help people who are keen to follow in the footsteps of Lammas, as will the One Planet Development policy that Jane Davidson, Sustainability Minister in the Welsh Assembly, has introduced.

Larch Maxey, writing on bringing low-impact development into the mainstream, says:

"One of Lammas's innovative features is its commitment to working with the planning system. It is the first time an LID hamlet has sought planning permission before commencement on site. This is invaluable in moving LID towards the mainstream, as more people will consider LID if they can do so with the certainty and security that planning permission provides . . . This sets a significant challenge to the planning system, tasked with working in participatory ways with people, with a minimum of bureaucracy. It also presents challenges to

LIDers themselves to form new and innovative partnerships, working with more mainstream organisations such as Housing Associations, Local Authorities, charities, NGOs, researchers, schools, educators and enlightened building companies."[5]

Larch Maxey, researcher in sustainability and joint editor of *Low Impact Development*

## Steward Community Woodland

www.stewardwood.org

Steward Community Woodland (SCW) owns 13 hectares of mixed woodland on a steep hillside within Dartmoor National Park in Devon. At the time of writing there are twelve adults and nine children living on the site; three of the children have spent their whole lives there and one was born on the site. The project was established in 2000, to demonstrate low-impact and permaculture solutions to the many environmental challenges that humanity currently faces, in particular peak oil and climate change. Members spend their time managing the woodland, growing organic food, maintaining their low-impact dwellings and infrastructure, managing and developing renewable energy systems and welcoming visitors and volunteers to the project. Apart from a phone connection, the community lives totally off-grid and without outside services.

Shortly after moving on to the land in April 2000, SCW applied to the Dartmoor National Park Authority (DNPA) for planning permission to live at the woods and carry on its experiment in sustainable and low-impact living. The DNPA refused, so the community appealed to the Planning Inspectorate. In August 2002 it was granted a five-year temporary permission, which the DNPA attempted to overturn in the High Court. This created the bizarre situation where the DNPA faced the Treasury Solicitor – acting for the planning inspector – in front of the Judge, while representatives of the community watched from the public gallery. Without even bothering to hear arguments from the Treasury Solicitor, the Judge dismissed the case and added that the DNPA was losing sight of the policies behind the policies, as he put it; "they did not see the wood for the trees", the project was exceptional, it provided "a net gain" to the surrounding environment and community and should be allowed to slip through the rigid planning policies in the National Park. The community, as you can imagine, was delighted.

## Moor opposition

But five years later the DNPA, having learned nothing from the comments of the High Court Judge, turned down an application for the renewal of planning permission. Once again, the decision was overturned by the planning inspector, who granted permission, subject to various conditions, for the project to continue until June 2014.

Public support for the community is growing. The latest application saw 139 letters in support and just nine against. Even local objections have halved in the past five years.

One consequence of DNPA intransigence is that the community is prevented from building permanent homes that could be heated more efficiently. John Ellsworthy, his partner Son and their three children live in a structure made from local and recycled timber, with a canvas roof and scavenged windows. The house, built on the steep hillside, rests on stilts and has three levels. It's warm inside even on a cold day in December, but only because a wood-burning

stove consumes large quantities of logs. John's home is typical of the makeshift temporary buildings scattered through the woodland, and all the residents would like to build better-insulated homes.

"A few years ago I would have been more dangerous than Mr Bean with a power tool in my hand," says John, "but I did most of the work on this home for my family and that's a very empowering experience. Now I'd like the chance to build a straw-bale house that I can heat without spending so much time cutting firewood."

I'm shown around by Dan Thompson-Mills and ask what advice he would give to anyone considering this sort of low-impact lifestyle. He answers without hesitation:

> "Just do it. Just get on to the land. That's so important because it's the source of all our sustenance. We need to reverse the land clearances of the 1800s, which cut us off from the land and herded people into crowded towns and cities. People need to be able to grow food and have a spiritual link with the land. Only then can we understand the impact our consumerist lifestyles are having. At this stage we can't keep messing around. We need to get on with it and hope the authorities catch up."

## Roundhouses in Wales

www.thatroundhouse.info

Anyone acquainted with low-impact homes will have heard of Tony Wrench's Roundhouse at Brithdir Mawr in Wales. The house, a mix of cordwood and straw-bale walls with an earth roof, was built in 1997 and cost just £3,000. After several court appearances,

Tony and Faith decided to demolish it over Easter 2004 but changed their minds after demonstrations of huge public support in their defence. Pembrokeshire Coast National Park Authority attempted to get a court injunction to force demolition, but was persuaded to allow the house to stay up until Tony and Faith could re-apply under the new Low Impact Policy. Eventually, after nearly a decade of legal wrangling, temporary permission was granted in 2008. The first successful application under Pembroke-shire's Policy 52 took a battle lasting more than twice as long as the First World War! Significantly, permission was also given to build new roundhouses, visitor huts and compost toilets.

## Cohousing

I won't start with a definition of cohousing but with a story that illustrates one of its key benefits. Seven years ago Sarah Berger, an energetic 66-year-old and the oldest person in the cohousing community at Laughton Lodge in East Sussex, was diagnosed with breast cancer. The response from her neighbours was overwhelming:

> "When I came back with the news, within two minutes I had a group of six women in my sitting room opening the brandy. There were offers from people to stay the night, there was a rota to take me to chemotherapy, a rota for bringing me soup – it was amazing."

> Sarah Berger, Laughton resident

Sarah describes a community where neighbourliness has been put back into neighbourhoods, where support is available when needed; an environment many older people will remember but that is largely absent from our cities, towns and even villages.

## What is cohousing?

Cohousing balances our need for self-contained accommodation and personal space with the advantages of sharing common aims and activities with a community. Although cohousing communities originated as a means of compensating for the alienating effects of modern life, where neighbours don't recognise each other and day-to-day collaboration is minimal, they also address issues of sustainability.

The main features of cohousing communities are as follows.

- They are set up and run by their members for mutual benefit.

- Members are consciously committed to living as a community.

- Neighbourhoods are designed to encourage social contact and support among members.

- Common space facilitates shared activities such as community meals, and other amenities such as laundries, heating systems, guest rooms and transport may also be shared.

Such communities are intrinsically more sustainable than developments where people live as isolated individuals, couples or families. Shared facilities immediately result in a reduction in the resources needed. A laundry with shared machines uses far less material than machines in every household, car pools are a proven way to reduce car production and use, while the option of communal meals saves energy as well as time.

This form of housing is well established in Scandinavia, particularly in Denmark, where cohousing started in the 1960s. In Holland cohousing schemes get State funding and now form 10 per cent of all social housing. In the US there are over 100 cohousing communities, some of them established by developers who recognise a market opportunity. In Britain, however, cohousing is still in its infancy. The UK Cohousing Network, founded in 2005, lists just ten established communities and another 20 groups in the planning stage.

## So what's the problem?

A 2007 survey by the Network identified a number of obstacles to establishing new cohousing communities: high land prices; poor understanding of cohousing by local authorities; difficulty in accessing social housing grants to make cohousing affordable; a lack of capacity in groups hoping to establish new communities, which means they often have to start from scratch; and difficulties in working with housing associations, which are reluctant to allow the autonomy that is vital for cohousing communities.

The Network proposed solutions to these problems: government should give policy advice to local authorities about cohousing, planning exceptions should be made for cohousing to overcome high land prices, Section 106 agreements could make land available for exemplar cohousing projects, and there needs to be a mechanism to bring housing associations and cohousing groups together.

The first new build cohousing development in the UK was Springhill in Stroud (see pages 139-41), and this is still the only completed new build. Most are based in existing buildings, converted to become suitable for the careful balance of private and shared living that characterises cohousing.

## The Community Project – Laughton Lodge

The Community Project purchased Laughton Lodge, a small disused hospital, in 1998 and converted the main buildings into individual homes. The land, about 9 hectares, is shared communally and consists mainly of open meadow, clumps of trees, and woodland along one border. There are gardens immediately around the houses, a small pond, a vegetable patch and polytunnel, landscaped areas around the houses and a considerable amount of planting around the site, including an orchard.

One large building, Shawfield, is a common house providing a hall, a large kitchen and dining area, meeting rooms, guest rooms and an office complex. There's a workshop and tool pool in an old pump-house, and another building has been converted to provide artists' studios. Laughton Lodge is on the edge of the small village of Laughton, 15 miles from both Brighton and Eastbourne, which has some 600 inhabitants.

### How it all began

The project began with a dinner conversation among a small group of friends concerning their shared vision of a better lifestyle. After a year of looking at possibilities, visiting alternative communities and trying to decide exactly what they wanted, the group's members decided they needed to purchase a large property, and for that they would need to expand. So an advertisement was put in *The Guardian*; over 70 people responded and a few committed themselves to the project. Over the next five years, a further advert was placed; the group had an entry in *Diggers and Dreamers* and others joined through personal contact. Some dropped out along the way, but most stayed the course. Five of the original members of this group live at Laughton Lodge today, but it took six years to get there!

It took three years just to find the right property. Large properties, a beautiful old manor house for example, are extremely expensive, especially in the South East, and it became clear that a more functional institution was a better option. Laughton Lodge was ideal in many ways – large enough to accommodate everyone, with additional buildings for communal use and just enough land. Although the buildings were institutional, they had the advantage of being uniform and relatively easy to divide fairly into individual living spaces. However, the cost of converting the buildings was prohibitive and it was necessary to build four additional homes to make the project viable. This became an obstacle as the local planning policy was against new build in the area, and there were also objections from the local community, which was understandably suspicious.

It took a year to gain detailed planning consent; the builders finally started work in 1998 and families started to move into their new homes in early 1999, almost three years after first visiting Laughton Lodge. They still needed to fit kitchens, lay flooring and decorate, but the real work of learning to live as a community of over 70 people, including around 30 children, could begin.

## Financing the project

Members loaned as much as they could. Some had capital, others increased their mortgages, borrowed from friends and family, or even sold their homes. These loans acted as down-payments, although some people put in more money than their home was likely to cost.

Without a proven track record in property development it took time for the group to find additional

Residents at Laughton Lodge on one of their regular workdays.
Photographs: Sarah Berge

funding. Eventually Triodos Bank agreed to a loan, but the group never had to use this as members were starting to sell their homes and, as each phase of the work needed to be paid for, there was enough money in the project to do so.

## Lancaster Cohousing

www.lancastercohousing.org.uk

For many years Springhill in Stroud has been the shining example of what new-build cohousing can achieve. But there's a new contender, and it seems likely that Lancaster will soon be wearing the crown. After several years of searching for a site among industrial wastelands and derelict buildings, the Lancaster Cohousing Group finally struck gold and purchased a site near the village of Halton.

> "Originally, the group had been looking for a site closer to the city centre and had come together in a bid to develop an old schoolhouse. When that fell through, we searched long and hard and finally found the current site. A developer had bought it with a view to turning it into houses and light industrial units, but he went bust. We were able to buy the site, complete with two and half hectares of riverside frontage, from the receiver for an absolute song."[6]

> Chris Coates, Lancaster Cohousing founder

The south-facing site, including woodland and an old mill, overlooks the Lune, just three miles along the riverside cycle path from the centre of Lancaster. The location is beautiful, but what makes this development really exceptional are the ambitious environmental goals.

### Golden homes

Way back in 2006 the group held an 'eco-values' workshop and decided to work towards a 'community built on ecological values'. The following is an extract from the document.

> "We aim to build homes to the highest environmental standards – such as the Passivhaus or

Members of Lancaster cohousing group consider plans for the layout of their new homes. Photographs: Jon Sear

AECB Gold Standard [see pages 163-4]. This should mean they are so well-insulated that they don't need central heating, and energy bills are minimal. We will include solar water heating, wood-burners and hopefully other forms of renewable energy. The homes will have plenty of natural light and gain heat from the sun.

We will be using natural or recycled building materials with an emphasis on aesthetics and durability and avoiding PVC, formaldehyde, etc. We expect to collect rainwater from our rooftops and . . . may have a system for dealing with human waste such as a reed bed or composting.

We will think beyond the buildings in terms of environmental impacts. That might lead to a car club or organic vegetable deliveries for example. Shared facilities will mean that some things, from washing machines to lawnmowers, do not need to be owned by every household.

In all, we want to design a neighbourhood where it is very easy to live a sustainable lifestyle."[7]

These are ambitious targets. The AECB Gold Standard exceeds Passivhaus, and $CO_2$ emissions would be just 5 per cent of those of a normal UK building. There are

also plans for a biomass boiler providing heat and power for the whole site and a hydroelectric generator on the river.

An important aspect of achieving the Gold Standard is the use of efficient household appliances. While individuals will generally be free to decide what they do in their own homes, the group policy makes an exception for activities such as pouring chemicals down the sink and killing plants in a reed bed sewerage system, or for the installation of energy-inefficient appliances contrary to AECB standards. How these policies are enforced is a difficult issue, since the aim is to build a community based on trust, respect, friendship and understanding rather than on rules and regulations.

Lancaster Cohousing development sits beside the beautiful river Lune, which may have potential for generating hydroelectric power.
Photograph: Jon Sear

## Not just houses

The mill itself, on the Forge Bank side, has planning consent for mixed use, and there are plans to create an environment in which small businesses, social enterprises and community organisations may flourish. The mill and other units will accommodate a mixture of fully serviced workshops, offices and studios. Key selling points include flexible terms, a local and personal management service, shared facilities and the attractive location. The plan is for key tenants to form a cluster of sustainable business operating to a set of environmental standards reflecting the values of the cohousing development. This aspect of the project received a major boost in January 2010, when Halton Mills won a £500,000 grant from the Low Carbon Communities Challenge.

Lancaster Cohousing Group is working with Ecoarc, which first became involved in environmental design in 1986, when it worked on the Findhorn Ecovillage in Scotland. Ecoarc has a list of environmental awards as long as your arm and has already come up with a range of zero-carbon designs making use of the south-facing slope and river views. Around 30 homes, ranging from one bedroom at 40m$^2$ to four bedrooms at 104m$^2$, will be built with prices from £130,000 up to £240,000, but there may be some studio flats at lower prices. The prices seem high, but residents save through lower energy costs, car pooling, communal meals and childcare.

So how did they find the money? "We had the biggest whip-round ever," said Coates. Fifteen of the future buyers put up 30 per cent of the predicted cost of their homes to help buy the land, and the Co-operative Bank and Ecology Building Society will lend money once detailed planning consent is agreed. Twenty-one houses have already been taken and the others are likely to be snapped up, even though the 10-per-cent discount for early buyers has now gone. If all goes well building will commence in 2010, with the first residents moving in during 2012.

There are many inspiring aspects of the Lancaster development: ambitious environmental goals, recognition of the importance of community and the integration of work spaces into the project. Take a look at their website (see page 233) or their short film at www.vimeo.com/7051308.

Unfortunately, however, the homes will be unaffordable to many and prices could rise further as the desirability of cohousing, and of this development in particular, become clear. Lancaster is a pioneer and that has a cost, but the meticulous and groundbreaking work the group has done should benefit developments that follow. But are there ways of making cohousing affordable? A group in Leeds thinks so.

## Lilac not purple

www.lilac.coop

Low Impact Living Affordable Community (Lilac), which at the time of writing is on the verge of establishing a cohousing community in Leeds, started from little more than a group of friends keen to explore communal and sustainable living and an inspiring lecture on eco-villages.

"We heard Jonathan Dawson speaking about the Global Eco-Villages Network at the Schumacher North conference and set up a group to start an eco-village in Leeds. Unfortunately the task was just too big, membership of the group kept changing and we wanted to do something urban rather than rural. We decided to focus on developing a cohousing community in the heart of Leeds."

Alan Thornton, Lilac

So 'Leeds Ecovillage' was scrapped and Lilac was borne. In December 2009, three years after Dawson's lecture, Lilac was about to purchase a half-hectare brownfield site for the construction of 20 affordable and sustainable straw-bale homes. Leeds City Council, which owns the site, agreed to sell to Lilac, and a deal will be signed as soon as the group is satisfied with the outcome of site surveys. Unfortunately the council insisted on the full market price, even though the development provides much-needed affordable housing.

The purchase price, around 25 per cent of the total development costs, will be raised through deposits from the 20 purchasers and loan stock from friends and investors. Properties range from one-bedroom homes at just over £60,000 to four-bedroom houses at less than £120,000, so people with incomes as low as £15,000 may be able to join the community, which makes it far more inclusive than other new-build cohousing. Lilac has already established Lilac-MHOS Ltd, an Industrial and Provident Society which will be owned and managed by the residents, to arrange purchases through a system of Mutual Home Ownership (see page 173). This ensures that affordability is maintained in perpetuity.

Amazonails, the leading UK straw-bale building company, is involved, and using straw-bale construction will make a significant contribution to the low-carbon target. A typical house produces around 50 tonnes of $CO_2$ emissions during construction, while straw-bale houses, as well as being efficient in terms of heating, actually lock carbon into the structure.

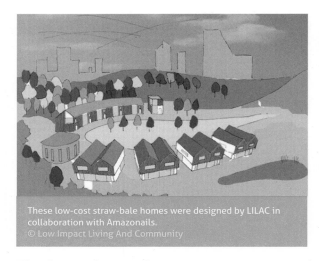

These low-cost straw-bale homes were designed by LILAC in collaboration with Amazonails.
© Low Impact Living And Community

## The future is Eco-clusters?

Cohousing in the UK may be younger and less established than in the US or elsewhere in Europe but it certainly has a big vision. In 2008, *Living Greener, Cheaper, Friendlier: The Policy Case for Eco-clusters and Cohousing*, made a convincing case for clusters of low-carbon cohousing communities as exemplars of sustainable living.[8]

The document argues for new planning policies that allow planning permission on an exception basis for sustainable, low-impact, mixed-use developments with an ecological footprint at least 40 per cent below the local average. The network argues that eco-clusters will provide replicable examples of how to reduce private car use, enable the provision of affordable and other housing and make best-practice environmental construction more financially viable. This whole-community approach to carbon reduction – including home energy, travel, food and waste disposal – accords with the approach already endorsed by the Audit Commission, which favours measuring the Local

Ecological Footprint to assess overall environmental sustainability. These benefits are in addition to enhancing mutual support, which would reduce demands by older people, one-parent families and others on public services.

The document proposes a new category for local and national planning policy – Low Impact Sustainable Settlement (LISS) – to allow exceptions to planning restrictions and development limits for schemes on suitable sites that satisfy higher environmental criteria. A LISS would have to provide independent validation that its projected ecological footprint would be at least 40 per cent below the local average. This reduction would be achieved in the following ways.

- Reduced car use. On-site work and social facilities, car pooling and other shared transport, and a commitment to walk, cycle and use public transport would reduce traffic generation to less than one-third of that of conventional communities.

- On-site working. A LISS would be required to provide work spaces on site or within 500m for at least 10 per cent of resident adults in urban locations; 20 per cent on rural sites.

- Food production. Where possible, a LISS would have land for a shared market garden. Failing this, a Green Food Plan, akin to a Green Travel Plan, would ensure that food is sourced locally and sustainably.

- Sustainability. A LISS would have to achieve Code for Sustainable Homes Level 5 (see pages 161-2) or better.

A LISS need not be large, but experience suggests that the realistic minimum size to achieve viable shared services would be around twelve units.

## The Threshold Centre

www.thresholdcentre.org.uk

An example of a LISS is the Threshold Centre in Dorset. Alan Heeks, an ex-businessman with an MBA from Harvard and one of the authors of the document on eco-clusters, set up the Threshold Centre with a group of six like-minded friends in 2004. This is a redevelopment of old farm buildings with a projected ecological footprint of 2.4 global hectares per person, less than half the local average of 5.3. The project is creating 14 cottages with cohousing use restrictions, 50 per cent being affordable through a local housing association.

Threshold aims to achieve cuts in the three main aspects of domestic carbon emissions: food, through a community market garden and local food sourcing; travel, through car pooling, on-site work and social activities to reduce car use; and domestic energy, by using shared energy systems such as biomass heating and solar PV. Houses will be Code for Sustainable Homes Level 5.

The creation of affordable social housing as part of a cohousing development is an important feature, and half of the 14 residential cohousing units will be operated by East Dorset Housing Association, a partner in the development. Although cohousing is endorsed by the Housing Corporation, now part of the Homes and Communities Agency, as a valuable new form of social housing, this is the first mixed-tenure cohousing development in the UK. During the application for planning consent the local authority expressed the view that people on the housing register would not be interested in cohousing. In fact, three times as many people on the register as there were places available expressed an interest.

As with most unconventional developments, planning consent was difficult. An initial application was refused and, in March 2008, planning officers recommended rejection of a revised application. Fortunately, councillors unanimously rejected the advice of their own officers and, subject to some conditions, voted for the application.

### Legal structure

The original Threshold Company, which owns the site, has been converted into a Community Interest Company (CIC). This makes clear its non-profit-making status, as all assets are locked and any profits must be reused for the benefit of the community. Most of the finance is structured as loans from prospective residents, but top-up loans are available from the Co-operative Bank. The company is selling long leases on residential units to repay the loans and retain ownership of the shared facilities.

The CIC is controlled by the residents, along with two external governor shareholders, the Ecos Trust and the housing association. The seven owner-occupied units are 95-per-cent shared ownership, with the CIC having a 5-per-cent share. Owners of individual units are free to sell their dwelling, but new purchasers must be acceptable to the rest of the group and accept their shared values and commitments.

The UK Cohousing Network website (www.cohousing.org.uk) is packed with information about cohousing communities in the UK and has links to similar websites around the world.

## Housing cooperatives

Cooperatives are ventures controlled by their members, where decisions are made democratically by those involved and not by outside owners. Co-ops are usually grassroots, community-based and sensitive to

## Transition Hamlets

The evolution of the British countryside produced clusters of farmsteads and work-related dwellings to form hamlets. People had an intimate association with garden produce and fruit from orchards and hedgerows. In the twentieth century psychologists concluded that there is an optimum size for communities, conducive to beneficial interaction and the formation of community bonds.

Weave these two strands together and we might conclude that 'Transition Hamlets', about two acres of homes and workshops surrounded by six or seven acres of productive land and natural woodland and linked by 'green drives', are a resilient way forward. But how to create them?

Bob Macadie, Susan Black and Susana Piohtee from Transition Hereford presented the idea to Hereford Council's Forward Planning Team. Although not included in the Local Development Framework, their ideas were well received. The project, called the South Herefordshire Area Rural Regeneration Project (SHARRP), is exploring new funding models and working with local councillors to take the idea forward.

environmental and social justice issues. They enable disadvantaged groups and communities to take control over their local environment by working together for the common good.

Housing co-ops provide housing for their members. Property is bought or leased by the co-op and rented out to members. For many people, co-ops offer a welcome chance of decent, secure and affordable accommodation. Many housing co-ops also provide facilities for other cooperatives, community projects or resource centres.

Modern co-ops date back to the nineteenth century, when working people struggled to take back some of the control that capitalism and urbanisation had taken from them. Cooperative shops gave people a choice of better quality goods and services. By the Second World War 'The Co-op' was the largest retailer in the country, and there are now cooperative initiatives in the field of finance, such as LETS schemes, credit unions, mutual guarantee societies and mutual investment societies.

Many cooperatives do not have an explicit sustainability agenda, but a radical fringe certainly does. As Dryad in Brighton (see page 91) and Fireside in Sheffield (see page 180) and show, housing cooperatives typically purchase or take over run-down properties which they renovate; they share resources through some elements of communal living and have a proactive approach to environmental issues. They are an important pathway to sustainable housing.

### Radical Routes

Radical Routes (see www.radicalroutes.org.uk) is a 'network of little fishes': cooperatives whose members are committed to working for positive social change and for "people taking control of their own housing, work, education and leisure activities. People set up co-ops to manage these activities themselves, removing the need for managers, owners, bosses or landlords."

Over 30 affiliated and associated housing cooperatives are in the Radical Routes network. Although there are no environmental criteria for membership, a survey of the groups confirms the expected commitment to sustainability. Phrases such as 'self-build ecologically sound dwellings', 'living lightly', 'ecological direct action' and 'serious eco-renovation' abound. There's even a 'bicycle breeding programme'!

Radical Routes gatherings ensure that co-ops have plenty of chances to meet and share experience and knowledge. As the network grows, these gatherings are becoming regional as well as national. There are also international meetings with similar networks in Germany and the Netherlands.

## Conclusions

- Working with others is empowering.

- Don't be afraid to break the rules – that's how we can change them.

- Change also comes from working within the system.

- Whether you work inside or outside the system, be prepared for lengthy battles with local authority planners.

- National and international networks are there to offer support.

- Just do it!

# CHAPTER 6
# SUSTAINABLE HOUSING IN BRIGHTON

*"If we don't retrofit together, we will surely freeze separately."*

**With apologies to Thomas Paine**

Brighton and Hove has a population of around 250,000, and in the 2001 census more people indicated their religion as Jedi than anywhere else in England and Wales, although I don't think Jedi are more progressive on sustainable housing than other fictional characters.

## The Brighton Earthship

It's August 2009 in Stanmer Park on the outskirts of Brighton. I meet Mischa Hewitt and we walk past allotments and permaculture gardens to the Brighton Earthship. I can't think of anyone better in Brighton to talk to about sustainable housing than Mischa. He is project director for the Earthship and a director of the Low Carbon Trust, he helped to run Brighton's hugely successful Eco Open Houses event in 2008, and he has now set up his own sustainable building company, Earthwise Construction.

We enter through the south-facing glazed wall and Mischa opens roof windows to cool the building and to allow air to circulate. The Earthship is a welcoming and open space, full of natural light and giving no sense of being underground, despite the fact that this building is set deep into the south-facing hillside.

Plant-filled troughs across the front window show where greywater is recycled and used for flushing toilets, electricity comes from photovoltaic panels on the roof and the wind turbine humming outside, and hot water is from a solar thermal system. Earthships (see http://earthship.com) are designed to maximise passive solar gain for space heating and to use thermal mass to absorb this heat and release it when the sun sets and air temperatures fall. Additional heating comes from a wood-burning stove in one corner. Much of the building is constructed from recycled materials – cans, bottles, old car tyres, and reclaimed stone and timber (see www.lowcarbon.co.uk).

## The first of many?

The Brighton Earthship is not a home but a community centre designed and built as a model passive-solar, low-carbon building. Though not a home, it feels like a superb place to live in, and I can understand why there were plans for a development of earthships, some of them affordable, overlooking the Brighton Marina.

Mischa, along with Kevin Telfer, a freelance journalist who regularly works with Kevin McCloud and *Grand Designs*, has written *Earthships: Building a zero carbon*

The Brighton Earthship functions as a resource centre and venue for events as varied as permaculture and weddings.
Photograph: Mischa Hewitt

*future for homes*. The opening paragraph gives an enthusiastic outline of what earthships are about:

> "Earthships are not whacky, 'way-out' or extremist buildings from the lunatic fringe. They should not be regarded as the domain of hippies, sock-and-sandal-wearing folk, assorted eco-nuts and survivalists . . . earthships are a serious, rational and well-designed architectural response to some of the challenges that face humankind in the 21st century. They are also visually arresting, charismatic and extremely comfortable for those who live in them; indeed, they are often described as low-carbon living in luxury. Not only do earthships address the fundamental question of how to provide safe shelter for their inhabitants, they have a thorough and holistic engagement with vital issues of sustainability, notably zero-carbon and zero-waste living, through recycling and reusing waste, energy saving and generation, water harvesting and recycling, and even food production."[1]

Reclaimed granite flooring in the Brighton Earthship.
Photograph: Mischa Hewitt

OK Mischa, I'm convinced! I promise never to wear socks with sandals again as long as we can all live in earthships. Unfortunately this possibility is virtually excluded by the conclusion to Mischa and Kevin's book. Earthships as a mass zero-carbon housing solution are practically a non-starter, for a number of reasons. Low housing density, the need for south-sloping sites and high labour input – possible for exemplar builds with volunteers but expensive for commercial building – stack the odds heavily against earthships. But there is another problem. More than three years of thermographic studies of the completed building by Mischa and the University of Brighton suggest that this building might not be as suited to the UK climate as hoped.

"I have a huge investment in this building," says Mischa. "It took four years of my life but if I had to start over again I don't think an earthship would be my choice of building for the UK climate." Mischa

gathered huge amounts of data on the performance of the building for his MSc thesis and concluded that earthships are probably not the best design for British patterns of temperature, sunlight, wind and rain. But surely all the money, not to mention blood, sweat and tears, haven't been wasted? No. Many of the lessons learned from this project can be employed elsewhere. Another scenario outlined in Mischa and Kevin's book is as follows.

"To employ all the sustainability measures used in earthships but modify the design to increase density, drive down construction costs and facilitate lower labour requirements. Mike Reynolds has had the idea to stack earthships and it could be argued that a development like BedZED is not dissimilar in concept from the idea of stacked and terraced earthships, with south-facing passive solar glazing, thermal mass, passive ventilation, greenhouses and other sustainability measures including water harvesting and photovoltaic arrays. The Hockerton Housing Project also has generic similarities, particularly due to the fact that it is earth sheltered, while achieving a slightly higher density through a terracing approach . . . earthships surely have to continue to evolve to suit the specific requirements demanded by the UK housing environment".[2]

## Eco Open Houses

The discussion moves on to 'Eco Open Houses', which took place in Brighton over two weekends in June and July 2008. "Brighton has a long history of holding Artists' Open Houses," explains Mischa. "People were already looking at the art on the walls but we wanted them to look at the walls."

eco
open
houses

See how you can
save money on utility
bills while saving
the environment

# Eco open houses
# in Brighton and Hove
## 28–29 June and 5–6 July 2008

**14 HOUSES RENOVATIONS & NEW-BUILD FREE ENTRY**

**Visit a house for a chance to win an energy smart meter! See p24**

The first Eco Open House event in Brighton attracted hundreds of visitors.

In early January 2008, Brighton Permaculture Trust, representatives from Brighton & Hove Council, the Low Carbon Trust and a few others agreed to organise an Open House event focused on sustainable buildings. By the end of January an amazing £20,000 was promised to organise the event, produce printed and online guides, gather feedback from visitors and evaluate the whole project. Support came from Legal & General Plc, South East England Regional Assembly and the South East England Regional Development Association, which donated 20 smart meters for participating households.

Less than six months later, more than 2,500 visits to 14 houses marked the event as a resounding success. "We did include new eco-builds but renovations are far more important," says Mischa. "Most of us live in older properties. Sixty-nine per cent of homes in Brighton & Hove were built before 1939 and these buildings have the highest energy use, hence improving their energy performance must be a priority."

The householders themselves led the tours, supported by knowledgeable volunteers from the Brighton Permaculture Trust, the Sustainable Building Association (AECB) and students from the Centre for Alternative Technology MSc course in Architecture. Some houses also had tours arranged by industry professionals involved in the buildings, including Duncan Baker Brown of BBM Sustainable Building and Pooran Desai of BioRegional.

Perhaps the most important feature of the Brighton event was the thorough evaluation of the whole project. Visitors were asked to complete feedback forms and pledge to reduce their personal energy consumption. A Southampton University student analysed the pledges and concluded that, if all the promises were kept, 4,000 tonnes of $CO_2$ would be saved over three years. In financial terms that's £475,000 in heating costs and £31,000 in electricity – a handsome return on the £20,000 invested in the event, and savings continue year after year.

## What did the visitors think?

Feedback from visitors, householders, volunteers and the organizers was overwhelmingly positive, with most visitors saying they were inspired to make changes in their own homes. Questionnaires showed that a large majority of people visiting the houses were over 40, women slightly outnumbered men, the self-employed outnumbered those in full-time employment, and most were homeowners.

Media coverage of the event was excellent, with numerous television, radio and newspaper articles including the *New York Times*. The dedicated website (www.ecoopenhouses.org) has thousands of unique visitors and remains available as an excellent resource with detailed information on each house.

There are many lessons from this event for would-be Open House organizers, such as how to get the message across to potential visitors. Word of mouth was found to be most effective, followed by the 28-page brochure and email contact. But it is difficult to extrapolate from the well-funded Brighton event – 20,000 brochures were printed at a cost of £7,000 and nearly £3,000 was spent on the website – to events with fewer resources.

## Eco house pledge

If you have been inspired by a house you have visited, you might like to consider an eco house pledge. Keep this to remind you of your pledge.

| I pledge to... | Approximate cost of change | DO NOW | DO IN A YEAR | DO BY 3 YEARS |
|---|---|---|---|---|
| **Reduce my gas use for water and space heating** | | | | |
| Turn my central heating down by a couple of degrees | | | | |
| Put on an extra jumper instead of turning heating up! | | | | |
| Turn radiators off in rooms I don't use | No cost and saves money! | | | |
| Use heavy curtains to keep heat in | | | | |
| Make sure my heating is not on when I'm out | | | | |
| Take quick showers instead of deep baths | | | | |
| **Start monitoring my gas use and notice how much I'm saving** | | | | |
| Check my boiler is running efficiently | £65 | | | |
| Insulate my loft | £100* | | | |
| Replace my boiler with a very efficient one | £800* | | | |
| Insulate external walls if possible, or fill cavity wall | £450–£1,500* | | | |
| Insulate the ground floor | £500–£2,500* | | | |
| Install under floor heating (it works with warm water not hot water, therefore saving lots of energy. Runs off normal boiler; works well with solar thermal) | £2,500 to install | | | |
| Invest in solar thermal energy to preheat water for central or space heating | £3,000–£4,500* | | | |
| **Reduce my electricity use** | | | | |
| Always turn off unnecessary lighting | No cost and saves money! | | | |

*continued over...*

| ...continued from back page | Approximate cost of change | DO NOW | DO IN A YEAR | DO BY 3 YEARS |
|---|---|---|---|---|
| **Reduce my electricity use** | | | | |
| Always turn plugs and electrical items and technology off | No cost and saves money! | | | |
| Start monitoring my electricity use and note how much I'm saving | | | | |
| Switch to a green energy supplier that invests in renewables (wind/ solar/tidal/biomass) | An extra £10 per quarter | | | |
| Get intelligent energy saving plugs for 'white goods'. (Try centre for alternative energy online shop www2.cat.org.uk/shopping) | £25–75 | | | |
| Replace all my lights bulbs with energy efficient versions | £100 | | | |
| Install photovoltaic (solar)panels or tiles – depending on situation but could supply all electricity needs for low energy light bulbs and more | £5,000–£7,500* | | | |
| **Save water** | | | | |
| Installing a water meter (free from my water company) and start monitoring how much water I can save by simple measures see www.southernwater.co.uk | No cost and saves money! | | | |
| When buying new, buy low water use shower heads, washing machines and dual flush toilets | | | | |
| Get a water butt for watering my garden | £25 | | | |
| Invest in a rainwater harvesting system – to flush toilets, and to use with my washing machine | £5,500 | | | |
| **Use natural materials** | | | | |
| Use non-toxic, local and even recycled materials for insulation, plastering, decorating, floorboards etc. where possible. (To reduce the likelihood of 'sick building syndrome' which plagues well-sealed, well-insulated buildings AND to promote local green industries of which there are many in Brighton and SE England) | Costs of green materials: about twice the norm | | | |

* see council grants page for possible grant funding or try www.lowcarbonbuildings.org.uk

Eco Open House visitors were asked to pledge themselves to energy-efficiency measures.

By 2009, without the funding available in 2008, the Brighton event was reduced to just six venues as part of a wider Heritage Open Door programme.

While the aim may have been to promote eco-renovation, the breakdown of visits by house type showed that people were far more interested in 'sexy' new-build eco-houses than in worthy-but-less-exciting refurbishments. Seventy-two per cent of visits were to the seven new builds, while only 28 per cent of visitors saw the seven retrofits. Other Eco Open House events have altered this balance by the simple expedient of excluding new builds, but the real challenge is to make refurbishment 'sexy'.

## Eco Open House in Lewes

Julia Waterlow from Transition Town Lewes (TTL) visited the Brighton event. When we met she said: "I thought it was so good to see practical things that ordinary people are doing that I decided we should do the same thing in Lewes." So she did. "I spoke to Mischa, got support from the TTL Energy Group and went to the Head of Environmental Services at Lewes District Council. They realised an Eco Open House event would tick lots of their sustainability boxes and agreed to fund the publicity."

In June 2009, ten houses in Lewes welcomed more than 600 visitors, an energy fair showcased the work of local insulation and renewable energy companies, and the BBC broadcast *The Politics Show* from one of the homes and discussed sustainable housing. Of course it chose the only new-build house in the event as its location!

Does Julia have any advice on organising Open House events? "Speak to people who have done it before. Read the 'Step by Step Guide' from Ecovation in Oxfordshire and don't make it too big!"

Transition Town Lewes *presents* Open Eco-House Weekend Sat 20 – Sun 21 June 2009

*Visit houses in and around Lewes to find out what others are doing and what you can do to make your house more ecofriendly and cheaper to run.*

Inspired by the Brighton event, members of Transition Town Lewes organised their own Open Eco-House Weekend. © Julia Waterlow

## Dryad Housing Cooperative

In 1990 Brighton & Hove Council helped 16 young homeless men build their own homes. The idea was for the young men to end up with a home they could rent from the council, but also to learn some building skills along the way. The houses were Walter Segal designs, which can be built with relatively few skills, and the project went well until the homes were finished, the tenants moved in and the council left them to get on with it. Unfortunately the all-male tenants, many of them still in their teens, lacked the social skills and cohesion to form a successful community. Houses were damaged and eventually seven were left empty and derelict.

After a few years, a group of 'caretakers' – so much more accurate than 'squatters' – moved in, repaired the seven properties and another four that subsequently became empty, and eventually secured a 10-year occupancy agreement with the council through Southern Horizon Housing Association. Dryad Housing Cooperative now had a home, but also responsibility for rent collection and arrears management, maintenance and repairs, allocations and lettings and good governance.

Rachel Laidlaw currently chairs Dryad and Flo Scott helped write 'Save Cash and Save the Planet', Dryad's Green Policy. We meet in Flo's pleasant timber-frame house and share a delicious cake made with fruit from her small garden and the surrounding woodland. It's easy to distinguish Dryad properties from those still directly rented from the council. The former have rainwater butts beside drainpipes, chimneys for wood stoves and something else – something less tangible that hints at a sense of community. But this is gradually changing as some of the council tenants also start collecting rainwater and growing vegetables.

"It was really good to be part of the 2008 Eco Open House event," says Rachel, "but what people really see here is an example of a community moving towards more sustainable living rather than just houses that have been renovated to make them more energy-efficient."

Dryad Housing Cooperative took part in the Eco Open House event in Brighton.

## Chicken or egg?

We have a 'chicken and egg' discussion about Dryad's Green Policy and the community that has developed. Did people come together as a community because of shared environmental goals, or were they able to develop a green policy because they already had a strong sense of community? As with all chicken-and-egg debates, there's no clear answer, but that doesn't really matter.

Dryad's Green Policy is firmly rooted in the realities of their lives. "We all have low incomes but that doesn't mean we can't do things to make a difference," says Flo. So they started with simple changes in behaviour, such as encouraging members to walk or cycle rather than use cars, and to use on-site composting and improved recycling. Rents are spent on maintaining the buildings and on improvements such as installing wood-burning stoves and rainwater harvesting. Regular workdays are used to improve the shared environment, and the area is now a haven for wildlife thanks to tree planting, nesting and bat boxes and the provision of habitats for solitary bees. Not content with improving its own environment, Dryad influences the wider community by being a good example of how people can work together to create a greener lifestyle.

'Save Cash and Save the Planet' covers the usual issues such as composting and recycling but goes a few steps further in recommending that residents use a green energy supplier and eco-friendly paints and buy locally grown foods. Plans for the future include loans to enable residents to buy AAA-rated appliances, and installing solar water heating and maybe even a community wind turbine. A nearby piece of woodland could house a low-impact yurt or straw-bale building for communal activities, and there are also plans to improve the biodiversity of the area.

We walk around the site and Flo points out the shared wood store built on a community workday and the Magpie recycling area, which residents pay for because it enables them to recycle tetra paks and plastics that the council won't collect. Trees planted in the early 'caretaking' days have matured, and fruit-laden branches sway in the breeze. Butterflies and bees flutter and buzz in the busy gardens. It's already clear that the sustainability of these homes cannot be separated from the community now established here, and this is confirmed when I ask Flo's children what they like best about living here. "The people," they answer without hesitation. "Definitely the people."

## OneBrighton

The New England Quarter in Brighton, just a few minutes' walk from Brighton's Central Station, is an 8.7-hectare development on land once occupied by a railway locomotive works. In 1997 the site was sold to the New England Consortium, which included Quintain Estates and Development, Network Rail and J. Sainsbury Developments Ltd. Their initial 'master plan' included, in the words of the local Indymedia, "a car park, two hotels, yuppie flats, inadequate key-worker bedsit-style accommodation and, of course, a Sainsbury Megastore."[3]

### Community objections

A campaign group, Brighton Urban Design and Development (BUDD), was established to fight the proposal and "stimulate, encourage and initiate sustainable urban design and development through an inclusive participatory process, to combat social exclusion and to generate schemes that integrate social, cultural and environmental benefits to Brighton". One of BUDD's early activities was a protest meeting attended by 300 people who overwhelmingly rejected the proposed development. Petitions, marches and rallies followed, and the Consortium's planning application was rejected. BUDD was even awarded a council grant in recognition of its work in "providing a process for disparate communities of interest to develop their views and become involved in the planning and decision-making process."

The Consortium went back to the drawing board and employed URBED (Urbanism Environment Design), a non-profit-making urban regeneration consultancy.

"We got involved in 1999 and started working on an alternative masterplan which eventually evolved into the scheme that was built. This

OneBrighton may not be everyone's idea of eco-housing but it's certainly a striking part of the Brighton landscape. Photograph: BioRegional Quintain

OneBrighton residents are encouraged to recycle using convenient storage bins. Photograph: BioRegional Quintain

A resident at OneBrighton tends a plant in a communal terrace garden. Photograph: BioRegional Quintain

was subject to a huge amount of debate and objection from various quarters but it was never rejected. In terms of community consultation we participated in a community workshop for the site in about 1999. This was organised by the council to write a brief for the scheme and as part of it we prepared a sketch scheme. Most of the discussion and the subsequent brief reflected just the sort of scheme that we were preparing; a mixed-use high-density neighbourhood. The overwhelming point of contention was the inclusion of the Sainsbury's store. After that we organised consultations including meetings with individual groups, BUDD, The North Laine Traders etc. . . . as well as an exhibition and drop-in and a very stormy public meeting that I spoke at. As part of this a number of the scheme's opponents came around, although BUDD remained implacable."[4]

David Rudlin, a director of URBED

In 2002 a modified planning application was approved by the council. Opposition continued, with protests focusing around an occupied shop that served as a cafe and centre for activists, particularly those involved in the campaign against the new Sainsbury's store.

The development attracted further controversy in 2004, when the Beetham Organization Ltd bought part of the site and submitted a revised planning application which included a 42-storey building. The application was firmly rejected.

## So what happened?
When I visited the New England site in August 2009 most of the building work was finished. Sainsbury's had their new store, and two 'posh' hotels stand beside the railway line. A 600-place car park for people using the station has been built, but apart from the 190 parking places below Sainsbury's there is little other parking in the area for the 1,000 or so people expected to occupy new homes or to work in the hotels and commercial buildings. But this is a city-centre location next to a mainline station and, even ignoring environmental considerations, a car is more liability than asset.

So what did all the protests, marches and petitions achieve? Part of the answer is in the new development I am here to see. BioRegional is well known as the developer of the groundbreaking BedZED eco-housing in London. Following controversy over plans for the New England Quarter it was invited to submit proposals for a 'green' development on part of the site. The result is OneBrighton.

I met Daniel Viliesid, Sustainability Integrator for BioRegional Quintain Ltd (BQL), as building work drew to a close. Residents would start to occupy the 172 homes in just a few weeks, but the site was still busy with construction workers. We changed into hard hats, protective boots and high-visibility jackets and Daniel gave me a tour and brief history of the site.

"BioRegional always made it clear that we wanted to work with the big developers and construction companies," said Daniel, "So when the opportunity to develop this site came up we approached Quintain, eventually created BQL, and agreed to use Crest Nicholson as the builders. This gives us the opportunity to really influence the mainstream in construction."

In 2008/9 Quintain gross profits were £36 million, and it has high-profile projects in Wembley and Greenwich. In 2008 Crest Nicholson had assets of nearly £1 billion. They are certainly mainstream. Since it was formed in 1992, BioRegional has established itself as a leading entrepreneurial charity with high-profile sustainable enterprises around the world. As well as being the developer of BedZED it is well known in the UK for its collaboration with the Worldwide Fund for Nature (WWF) in developing the concept of 'One Planet Living' (see box, page 97).

'One Planet Living' follows ten basic principles, and Daniel showed me how the OneBrighton development adheres to these principles. A host of features contribute to the 'zero carbon' tenet. Wood-fibre insulation, triple glazing, airtight construction, energy-efficient appliances, woodchip-fired heating and roof-mounted photovoltaic panels all play a part in making these flats 'Ecohomes Excellent' under the old Building Research Establishment's Environmental Assessment Method (BREEAM) or Code for Sustainable Homes 4 under the new system (see pages 161-2), with SAP ratings in the mid-80s (see page 49). Many of the building materials were sourced locally, and recycled materials were used where possible. Cement use, for example, was cut substantially by using an industrial waste product. Rainwater harvesting for the terrace gardens, water-efficient appliances, on-site composting and easy-to-use recycling facilities – the list of environmentally friendly features goes on and on.

## No parking

A couple of things struck me as particularly beneficial. Parking is limited to spaces for people with disabilities and five places for City Car Club, to which all residents receive an initial free membership. If you have a bike it's a different story, with secure cycle storage at several sites in the two blocks. Then there are the conscious attempts to foster community among the residents – one of the most successful features of BedZED, where residents claim to know, on average, 20 of their neighbours. OneBrighton features communal terrace gardens where residents can meet, as well as a community 'extranet' to facilitate community interac-

tion and to give access to information such as local bus timetables.

"Some features come from the consultation we ran with the local community," says Daniel. "For example, delivering organic vegetable boxes is difficult in blocks of flats so, following suggestions made during the consultation process, we installed storage boxes on the ground floor. The terrace gardens also came from the consultation."

OneBrighton meets all the criteria for 'One Planet Living', but in some cases it seems little more than ticking the box. The principle of local and sustainable food has resulted in herb planters on balconies and rooftop allotments, but these are just 1m$^2$ and there are just 28 between the 172 homes in the two buildings. Daniel argues that these are "an important resource for people living in the inner city even if they can only make a minimal contribution to food production."

Although the rooftop solar panels generate only around 2 per cent of electricity consumption, the use of a green energy supplier is far from token. A high-voltage supply from Green Energy UK is sold on to residents through a local energy supply company, set up and managed by BQL. So the supply is less expensive and is green. Residents can opt out but are unlikely to do so because any alternative would almost certainly cost more.

## Conclusions

- Natural building techniques should be appropriate to the climate, so we should keep an open mind about what works in the UK and what doesn't.

- We can learn from mainstream developers as well as from 'natural' builders.

## One Planet Living

Ecological footprinting shows that, if everyone in the world consumed as many natural resources as the average person in the UK, we'd need more than three planets to support us. If everyone consumed as much as the average North American, we would need five planets. The concept of 'One Planet Living', developed by BioRegional and WWF, uses ten principles of sustainability as a framework to help us enjoy a high quality of life within a fair share of the Earth's resources.

The ten principles of One Planet Living are:

- Zero carbon. Making buildings more energy-efficient and delivering all energy with renewable technologies.

- Zero waste. Reducing waste production, reusing where possible, and ultimately sending zero waste to landfill.

- Sustainable transport. Encouraging low-carbon modes of transport to reduce emissions, reducing the need to travel.

- Sustainable materials. Using sustainable products that have a low embodied energy.

- Local and sustainable food. Choosing low-impact, local, seasonal and organic diets and reducing food waste.

- Sustainable water. Using water more efficiently in buildings and in the products we buy; tackling local flooding and watercourse pollution.

- Natural habitats and wildlife. Protecting and expanding old habitats and creating new space for wildlife.

- Culture and heritage. Reviving local identity and wisdom; support for, and participation in, the arts.

- Equity, fair trade and local economy. Inclusive, empowering workplaces with equitable pay; support for local communities and fair trade.

- Health and happiness. Encouraging active, sociable, meaningful lives to promote good health and well-being.

See www.oneplanetliving.org

- Community protests and direct action can make a difference.

- The history of Dryad shows how important people and community cohesion are to sustainability.

- With the right people and support, Eco Open House events can be organised quickly and effectively. But make sure you run an event that encourages behaviour change rather than just eco-house voyeurism.

- Beware of the 'tick-box' approach to sustainability.

# CHAPTER 7
# NEW BUILD

*"Go, friendly bombs, don't fall on Slough*
*It isn't fit for humans now*
*But we can make it right again*
*With hemp and lime and new straw bale"*

**With profuse apologies to John Betjeman**

Although making existing homes sustainable is the priority, not all buildings can, or should, be retrofitted. But where do you draw the line? Paul Morrell, the government's Chief Construction Advisor, believes we should demolish many houses built in the 1960s and 1970s because it is impossible to refurbish them. Problem areas include Newcastle city centre, Slough and Aylesbury.

> "In the sixties, everything was built cheaper, faster and nastier. If you are going to try to fix buildings, then really you won't have too many problems with anything built earlier than the fifties or after the eighties. Although you can do some things . . . like replacing the roofs, there are probably some places that need to come down entirely."[1]

> Paul Morell, the government's Chief Construction Advisor

Demolish large numbers of buildings and you need to replace them. George Monbiot, well aware of the environmental costs of building new homes, wrote a column in 2007 headed: "Three million homes – yes, I am sorry to say, we need them."[2] If he is right, then how can we do this in a sustainable way?

Mainstream builders offer two approaches. On one hand there are high-tech, expensive eco-homes with all the latest gadgets but little regard for sustainability in materials. The other approach is the step-by-step modification of conventional designs. Neither route offers the "revolution in the way we build, design and power our homes" that even the government says is needed.[3]

So what's happening in new build and what can we learn from it?

A development of earth-sheltered social housing at Long Sutton in Lincolnshire shares energy from the Skyrota wind turbine.
© Jerry Harrall, SEArch Architects

## Autonomous homes

www.cropthornehouse.co.uk

Nearly 20 years ago Brenda and Robert Vale demonstrated the possibilities for sustainable housing when they built the 'Autonomous House' as a showcase for self-sufficiency through energy conservation and generation, water harvesting and sewage treatment. The Vales went on to design Hockerton Housing Project before moving to New Zealand, but the autonomous house concept is still popular with one-off self-builders – at the time of writing there's an ongoing blog for the Cropthorne Autonomous House near Birmingham – and the Vales have developed the idea further. Autonomous houses, they claim, cost no more than conventional builds. You just make them 25 per cent smaller.

The Long Sutton development also has areas for growing food, rainwater harvesting and a sewage system integrated into the development. © Jerry Harrall, SEArch Architects

## The Wintles – sustainable community or green ghetto?

'The Wintles', a development of 40 homes at Bishop's Castle in South Shropshire, won awards for 'green' and sustainable housing and featured on the BBC's *Newsnight* as a twenty-first century exemplar home. It also won the *Daily Telegraph* 2008 'House-builder of the year award' – a slap in the face for the Wimpeys of this world and possibly indicating an 'establishment' open to new approaches. The houses meet numerous sustainability criteria – effective insulation, airtight doors and triple glazing, solar water heating, heat recovery and ventilation and the use of natural and recycled materials. Two thousand trees were planted even before planning consent was granted; 3 hectares are set aside for communal use, including an orchard and allotments; cars are restricted to the edges of the development and, to quote from Rob Hopkins' blog, this "pioneering green housing development . . . has

A path winds between houses at The Wintles.
Photograph: Bob Tomlinson

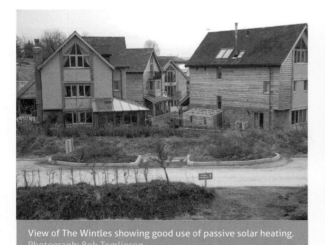

View of The Wintles showing good use of passive solar heating.
Photograph: Bob Tomlinson

Houses around the village green at The Wintles. Notice the absence of cars parked in front of homes.
Photograph: Bob Tomlinson

a strong sense of community."[4] It has also, with some justification, been called 'a ghetto for the very rich', although 'middle class' is probably more accurate

Bob Tomlinson and Carole Salmon are the driving force behind the Living Village Trust, which developed The Wintles, and, when we met in November 2009, Bob outlined the story behind the development.

## Permaculture inspired

The journey began in the early 1990s, when Bob met Bill Mollison, an Australian considered by many to be the father of permaculture, in Bristol. Bob and Carole were inspired by Mollison and developed plans for a sustainable community incorporating many of the design principles of permaculture. Their ideas attracted attention, including form a wealthy patron; the Living Village Trust was formed, and they approached planners in South Shropshire. The response was along the lines of 'you will need an act of Parliament to build anything like that!'.

So the Trust modified its plans and purchased the Six Bells pub in Bishop's Castle. The pub had been empty for four years but came with a plot of land and consent for five homes. Within a few years the Six Bells, reopened with its own CAMRA-rated micro-brewery, was thriving, new businesses were established in adjacent workshops, and five eco-homes were built. But this was just a stepping stone. When a site on the edge of Bishop's Castle won consent to build 40 homes, the Trust saw an opportunity to really show what the Living Village ethos could achieve.

The site, owned by a former mayor of the town who was keen to see a development that would really benefit the community, had planning conditions that put off many conventional developers. But these restrictions were not an obstacle to the Trust. So, in

1999, after selling the Six Bells development and borrowing money from Triodos Bank, the site was purchased and plans developed for what Bob calls "a neighbourhood rather than a housing estate". Among those involved were Christopher Alexander, author of *A Pattern Language*, the classic book on designing sustainable homes and communities; Keith Kritchlow, an expert in sacred geometry, who designed the labyrinth orchard; and Leon Krier, an urban planner best known for his work on Poundbury Village near Dorchester.

Of course there were problems: the initial design group was too large and diverse, and the resulting conflicts hampered progress; planning officers didn't take the proposals seriously, and banks, always wary of unconventional projects, placed unreasonable conditions on loans. But by 2003 obstacles were overcome, the council agreed on detailed planning consent, and most homes in the first phase had been sold off-plan.

## High prices

Around half the initial homes were sold to Shropshire people, and the rest to incomers to the county. Later phases, built after the development attracted media interest, were bought almost exclusively by people outside the county. Apart from some homes developed with a housing association, prices range from £300,000 to £475,000 – hence the 'ghetto for the rich' jibe.

Why so expensive? "Build costs were 20-25 per cent higher per square metre than for bog-standard homes," says Bob, "but since this only applies to the build and not land or other development costs it doesn't mean that eco-homes are automatically that much more expensive." The main reason for the high price is simply that that was the market rate. Initial sale prices were around 35 per cent higher than those for equivalent houses elsewhere, but people preferred a three-bedroom house at The Wintles to a five-bedroom conventional house on a soulless estate elsewhere. Even at these higher prices there was a certain amount of speculation, with some buyers selling early and profiting by up to £100,000.

And it's not just the eco-design or the built-in community that makes The Wintles so popular. The houses are beautiful. A creative mix of stone, brick, timber, plaster, tiles and the intelligent use of colour is striking.

Is it replicable on a wider scale? As Rob Hopkins says:

"In terms of design as if beauty mattered and energy efficiency yes, but in terms of that resulting in houses unaffordable to most, perhaps not. However, as a mainstream development that embodies the spirit of *A Pattern Language* and which places a far higher priority on the need for beauty than most conventional development, this is an important place. It was a brave development by a visionary developer, one who took risks and who put their money where their mouths were, at a time when many others talked about the need for sustainable building but did nothing."[5]

## Credit crunch victims

Unfortunately the final phase of building at The Wintles was a casualty of the credit crunch. The Royal Bank of Scotland suspended its agreement to fund construction costs and, despite sale of the homes already being agreed, the Bishop's Castle company created to run the development was forced into bankruptcy. But that isn't the end of the story. There are plans to relaunch the Living Village concept and a number of projects are in the pipeline. The most advanced of these is in the former mining village of Winchburgh in Scotland, where LXB Properties took advantage of falling land prices to purchase 400 hectares. LXB has applied to build 3,500 homes, schools and a retail scheme and the Living Village Trust is responsible for a pilot of 29 homes as the first phase of a 300-house eco-neighbourhood. How close this is to the Living Village ethos remains to be seen.

## The Living Village ethos

- Houses should be in car-free clusters of around 10-12 households that have their own identity and 'gateways'. These then make up wider eco-communities of 40 to 70 households. (A small child must be able to give you directions to his or her house by identifying 'landmarks', and 10-12 representatives from households can get together informally around a table to discuss common concerns without the need for formal meetings.)

- Homes must be designed to accommodate a full range of households and types of people.

- Cars may need to get close to houses for deliveries and other vehicles need to get to the houses to comply with regulations, but the key thing is that the motor vehicle does not dominate and is 'put away' out of site rather than parked in front of the houses. Through-traffic, preferably pedestrians and cycles, add life to neighbourhoods, but 'dead ends' are not a good idea.

- Developments should have land set aside for woodland, orchards and allotments.

- The houses should be ultra-energy-efficient, include passive solar design and wood-burners for heating.

- Designs should reflect the local vernacular and be made as much as possible from local materials.

## How group dynamics can make or break a project: The Wintles experience

**Bob Tomlinson, founder of Living Villages**

Getting any form of cohousing project from idea to finished building will take years, quite often decades.

The biggest problem is that it takes a very determined person to stay the course, and usually people's circumstances change during the process and they leave the group. This means that the interest group is continually changing and new members have to be brought up to speed and brought down to accept the dreary realities of a construction project.

Running a democratic decision-making process when the group is continually changing is a challenge.

Ideally, a core team accepts responsibility for carrying the project through, and new members accept that it takes time to get fully integrated with the decision-making process.

My advice would be to have the core team work on the visualisation of the place that is to be created; this visualisation 'document' is the key element that serves as the bedrock of the project.

The core team must also protect the vision from the construction industry 'professionals'. Group dynamics often sap energy and enthusiasm from the process and inordinate amounts of time gets spent on personal issues. This leaves the core team exhausted, and when it comes to translating the vision into drawings and proposals the easiest option is to let the architect or project manager get on with it. Sadly, this often results in the original vision being distorted to accommodate the new designer's ideas, or a reduction to the lowest common denominator occurs to cope with cost constraints.

So:

- Create the vision.

- Identify the core team to carry that vision.

- Put an appropriate and robust structure in place, to cope with the group dynamics.

- Expect to get old during the process!

---

- Designs should encourage residents to stay for their lifetime and also to work for the next generation of their family.

## Low-carbon miners?

www.sev.org.uk

There's a wonderful irony in the fact that one of the UK's most successful low-carbon developments is run by former miners. In 1994 Ollerton Colliery in Nottinghamshire closed, 600 miners lost their jobs and an entire community faced a bleak future. Then something remarkable happened.

Stan Crawford, former National Union of Mineworkers branch secretary, tells the story. "We had to do something to stop the local community from dying. We held a public meeting in the village and decided we had had enough of decisions being made about our future by someone else. We wanted to be in charge of our own futures."

So redundant miners and people from the council estates of Ollerton did something extraordinary. They formed a non-profit-making Industrial and Provident Society, a fully trading company where profits are reinvested rather than being used for shareholder benefit. Crawford negotiated with British Coal and, after two years of haggling, they bought the 36-hectare site for £50,000. Crawford, who already had valuable experience as a former Labour leader of the local council and of the board of directors, wisely rejected an offer from British Coal to sell the site for £1 plus a hefty slice of the profits. It's now valued at around £70m!

## Muck and brass

"We used to say 'where there's muck there's brass', but we'd had enough muck when mining came to an end," says Crawford. So Sherwood Energy Village Ltd (SEV) was established, to create clean jobs in a low-carbon community. The first step was raising £4.5m to clear the site. Geological experience from mining veterans was immediately useful, first in shifting thousands of tonnes of polluted soil, and then in creating Britain's largest sustainable urban drainage system.

Next came jobs. Business units were established with an impressive portfolio of green technologies, including rainwater harvesting, green roofs, ground source heat pumps, solar water heating, wind turbines, photovoltaics, passive solar gain and passive ventilation. The introduction of sustainable urban drainage systems (SUDS) ensured that a 1-in-150-year storm in 2007 passed without any flooding of the site. Circular dykes carry heavy rainfall for long enough for the water to drain into the sandy aquifer below without any run-off into the Trent and other local rivers. There

is already more work than there was at Ollerton Colliery when it closed and the site will eventually provide 2,500 jobs.

The latest phase of regeneration is housing, with 196 properties being built on the same commercial and unsubsidised basis as the office and industrial units. Plantings on two former slag heaps have matured to give the new houses a pleasant view, with mixed young trees merging neatly into a large copse of ancient woodland. The houses are sold freehold, from £94,000 for a one-bedroom home to a minimum £200,000 for four bedrooms, and SEV retains control over sustainability standards by acting as its own developer.

The achievements of SEV were recognised in 2005, when it was judged "the most enterprising place in Britain" by the government's Enterprising Britain Competition, and in 2008 SEV took the Royal Town Planning Institute's Silver Jubilee Cup, the top prize in planning, as "an outstanding example of citizens taking their community and environment seriously". But I'm sure the real prize is the pride the members of this community can take in the future they have built for themselves.

## Self-build

Around 20,000 new homes a year are classified as self-build, so self-builders are just behind Taylor Wimpey in terms of house completions. The popularity of self-build has grown significantly in the last 30 years, but still accounts for only 12 per cent of all homes built. Figure 8 shows comparable figures for other developed countries.

Self-build ranges from doing little more than finding a plot of land and paying professionals to do the rest, to

Crawford was on strike during the 1984 miners' strike and says:

"I honestly don't believe I am doing anything different now than I was then. You are fighting for your community, for the place you live and work. It is just using different tools to do it."

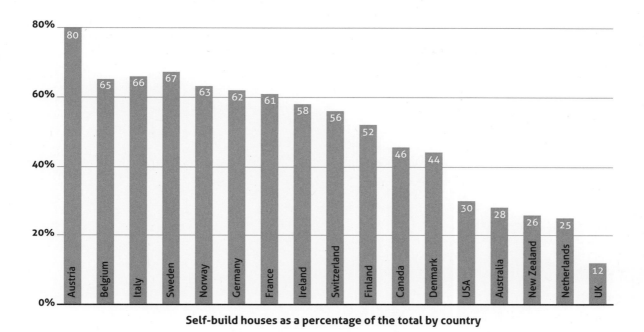

Figure 8. Percentage of housing built by self-build in 'developed' countries. © National Self Build Association

really getting your hands dirty and taking on most tasks. Over 100 self-build community projects have been set up in the last 20 years. The norm is for 10-20 people to work collectively on all the houses.

Self-build is intrinsically more sustainable as the builder/occupant has a vested interest in a home that is energy-efficient. The National Self Build Association (NaSBA) estimates that an extra 25,000 self-build homes would save around 100,000 tonnes of $CO_2$ per year. The opportunity, particularly in community self-build schemes, to exchange time and labour for a less expensive home helps the supply of affordable housing.

## Segal homes

Self-build and Walter Segal are almost synonymous, and the Walter Segal Self Build Trust is still a valuable source of information and inspiration for self-builders. The Segal method simplifies the building process, enabling people with only elementary skills to build their own homes, and recent modifications mean that the buildings can be extremely energy-efficient. For hundreds of self-builders in the UK, using Segal designs and methods of construction is uniquely empowering. Ken Atkins of the Lewisham Self Build Housing Association talks of the "indescribable feeling that you finally have control over what you are doing".[6]

Hedgehog Self Build Housing Cooperative in Brighton uses a
Segal design modified by Architype architects.
Photograph: Architype

## Hedgehog houses

Architype, which specialises in self-build and community housing, designed Hedgehog Housing, a cooperative of self-built timber-frame homes in Brighton. The
houses have grass roofs, extensive south-facing
balconies and windows and 'Warmcell' insulation, and
are built from British-grown larch and Douglas fir.
Even though this Segal development was completed
in 1996, the houses achieve very high levels of energy
efficiency, and the timber construction locks up carbon
for at least the lifetime of the building.

## The Yards – self-build in Bristol

Passing the organic supermarket, the 'Artrageous'
scrap store and the City Farm should have prepared
me to expect something special when I visited 'The
Yards' in Bristol. But rows of drab terraced houses and
small industrial units surround this self-build project,
and I was surprised by the sudden riot of colour, the

varied design and the people-friendly community that
self-builders have established here. Jackson and Anna
Moulding welcomed me to their home and we drank
tea as they outlined the roots of the project.

In 2000 the site, a former scaffolding yard squeezed
between railway lines but very green for an inner-city
area, attracted the attention of McAlpine, which put in
an application to build 35 houses on less than one
hectare. Local people, fresh from success in establishing a community nature centre on land surrounding
the railway lines, formed the Ashley Vale Action
Group (AVAG) and opposed the application.

"We hoped to get the application deferred to give us
time to talk to the land owner," explains Jackson, "but
to our surprise their plans were rejected, enabling us
to buy the site and gain planning consent for a
mixed-use development."

There was already an example of self-build in the
adjacent road, a quirky house with a sculpted tower
and hobbit-house door, so AVAG formed a non-profit-
making company and raised the purchase price by
sub-selling plots to self-builders and to a housing
association that built homes for the elderly. Most of the
original directors of that company already had homes,
and their aims were to develop imaginative and
environmentally friendly housing and give local
people a step on to the property ladder. The 20
self-build homes cost between £60,000 and £160,000
including site costs – far less than other local houses.
"We were renting some rooms nearby," says Jackson,
"and building this house, which cost us about £70,000,
was the only way we could afford a home of our own
in this area."

I looked around the spacious open-plan kitchen and
living area with light flooding in past balconies at
front and back, three bedrooms, an office area and a

mezzanine giving extra space above the living room. This was a welcoming and distinctive home, an amazing place to live and work in, and a stark contrast to the standard boxes churned out by the large-volume house builders.

We walked around the small community and passed children playing on the road and in green areas at the centre of the site. Self-builders were encouraged to use a shared palette of materials and to have a commitment to sustainability, so, although the Mouldings' house is unique, it shares many characteristics with neighbouring

## Quoin Building wins award

The renovated 1960s office building won the Regen South West Green Energy Award for 'Best Housing Scheme' for 2009.

Jackson Moulding and Paul Brana-Martin received the award on behalf of Quoin Common Hold and Ashley Vale Action Group from David Wheeler of the Homes and Communities Agency, and Jonathan Dimbleby hosted the prestigious awards ceremony.

Jackson Moulding in front of some of the self-build homes at The Yards in Bristol. Photograph: Chris Bird

buildings. High levels of insulation and natural materials are the norm and most houses have photovoltaic panels funded by the Department of Trade and Industry's domestic photovoltaic field trial.

Few restrictions were placed on self-builders. Jackson described the approach as being 'here's the plot – get on with it'. People built to different designs, budgets and timescales, and that may have contributed to the success of the project and to the cohesiveness of the community that now exists. Neighbours help with strenuous tasks and know the favour will be repaid if the need arises.

The development was in three phases, and the second phase, an arc of six self-finish homes, with solar thermal panels and green roofs, occupies the centre of the site. The third phase of the development was refurbishment of the Quoin Building, a "horrendous 1960s concrete office block with metal-framed Crittall windows". This is now an attractive externally clad building with biomass heating, solar thermal and photovoltaic panels and double glazing throughout. "It's probably the most sustainable building on the site," said Jackson as he showed me the office units, community room and six flats.

The site provides 42 homes, offices and work units and a shared social space. Children have safe play areas and a real community has developed. The benefits over McAlpine's original plan for 35 off-the-shelf boxes are clear, so why is it so difficult to make projects like The Yards happen?

The Ashley Vale residents had a number of advantages. Previous experience in opposing inappropriate development and in establishing a community nature reserve gave them confidence in objecting to the planning application from McAlpine, and there was already a

## Taking the self-build message to Glastonbury

In 2009 and 2010 Ecomotive, a self-build group that grew out of the Ashley Vale development, had a stand at Glastonbury Festival. Networking was the main aim and the space allowed those interested in self-build to exchange ideas and advice and work out problems. The group also had an interactive map of the UK, for people to identify the areas where they would like to build and contact others in the same locality.

positive example of self-build in the area. Sympathetic councillors were another important factor, and the initial group had the skills to take the project forward.

"The group that formed had all the right elements," said Anna, "a couple of people worked for the council, others knew about roads and highways and planning issues, someone else was an architect and we brought a strong green agenda. Perhaps more important was that there were a lot of 'doers'. We made things happen."

### Land is the problem

If there is one critical factor that made The Yards possible it was the availability of affordable land. NaSBA, which Jackson Moulding helped to launch in 2008, sees the difficulty in acquiring land as the key obstacle to self-build housing solutions. NaSBA is urging the government to bring about the following changes.

- Identify 50 sizeable plots of public land that could quickly be made available to self-builders. These sites should provide more than 2,000 plots.

- Each of the proposed new eco-towns (see pages 114-5) should be required to provide sites for at least 500 eco-self-builders.

- Every local authority should be tasked with providing sites for at least 30 self-builders a year.

- A new organisation should be set up to facilitate the process of servicing, splitting up and selling sites to self-builders.

- Developers could be required to make a certain number of plots available as part of Section 106 planning agreements.

- Private-sector landowners should be encouraged to look at the economic benefits of selling off some of their current land holdings to self-builders.[7]

## New-build medley

New build does have the advantage of giving more scope for innovative designs, and there are plenty of projects where people grab the opportunity with both hands. The following is a somewhat breathtaking race around a few of the most interesting new-build projects in the UK. It starts with the smallest and works up to some substantial plans for eco-towns.

## A studio for £3,300

The West Country artist's studio designed by David Lea is not strictly a house – but it could be. The building mixes bent saplings, cement reinforced with cow hair, chicken wire and straw for insulation to create an 'Arts and Crafty' version of an African mud hut. A simple but beautiful structure built by the artist herself, with occasional support from the architect.

## Will Anderson's Tree House

www.treehouseclapham.org.uk

Will Anderson's house in Clapham, the subject of his book *Diary of an Eco-Builder* and of a TV programme, shows what can be achieved on a small urban site.

Tree House is extremely well insulated for warmth in winter, uses passive cooling to keep temperatures

Will Anderson's Tree House shows what can be achieved on a small urban site. Photograph: Will Anderson

down in summer . . . and it's beautiful. Why is beauty important?

"Very occasionally, when the accumulating evidence of global climate breakdown saps my optimism, I wonder what difference our radical eco-specification will actually make. But I have no such doubts about acts and works of beauty. After all, if we cannot sustain a delight in life itself, whatever future we face, what is it that we are fighting to preserve?"[8]

Will Anderson

## Gap House

This house in Bayswater sits between two listed buildings and is just 2.5m wide at the front but opens up to a large L-shaped living area at the rear. Making use of the 'dead' space between two buildings means that all three homes become more energy-efficient.

## Denby Dale Passivhaus

This house in West Yorkshire is conventional in appearance and construction, but is one of the first homes accredited to Passivhaus standards in the UK. The total build cost for the detached three-bedroom property was £140,000 and the project was managed by the Green Building Company, construction division of the Green Building Store. During construction the project supervisor, Bill Butcher, wrote a regular diary on the construction for *Building* magazine and the entries are still accessible online – see www.building.co.uk.

## Hockerton Housing Project

www.hockertonhousingproject.org.uk

We'll slow down a bit for this housing project in Nottingham, because "the world's first earth-sheltered, self-sufficient, ecological housing development" is the perfect place for a short rest.

Nick Martin, project founder, became interested in sustainable development in the early 1990s, acquired the site and, with family and friends, formed the nucleus of the group. They recruited others by advertising and set about the lengthy task of developing their ideas and getting planning consent. A few people were lost on the way, but the group held together through developing the organic gardening area and through regular meetings 'spiced with a little wine', and founded Hockerton Housing Project Ltd as a cooperative responsible for the project. All adult occupants are on the management team.

Hockerton had to overcome a series of hurdles, but in 1996 made UK post-war planning history by obtaining special permission to build a sustainable housing development on 10 hectares of agricultural land. The key to victory was building a sustainable community that included businesses and housing. Most lenders wouldn't consider the project, but the Co-operative Bank provided loans that were later converted to mortgages with the Ecology Building Society.

The architects were Brenda and Robert Vale, and Hockerton is still a ground-breaking development and a great place for information and training on all aspects of sustainable housing.

Off we go again.

Designed by Stride Treglown, Great Bow Yard was described by Kevin McCloud as "excellent examples of just how environmentally well-thought-out a house can be."
Photograph: Robert Delius, Stride Treglown Limited

## Great Bow Yard

Great Bow Yard in Langport, Somerset, was built by the Ecos Trust, a registered charity that aims to give examples of sustainable design and construction and to persuade planners, builders, developers and estate agents that this is a practical way to build and meets a real and unsatisfied demand from house buyers.

Langport is a mix of 12 houses and flats in two terraces, constructed of reclaimed brick with lime mortar, timber frames and structural insulated panels (SIPs). Timber is FSC- and PEFC-certified with the cedar cladding sourced from South Wales. Half the insulation is cellulose sandwiched within the SIPs, plywood is used instead of MDF, and natural paints are used throughout. Energy costs are kept low by passive solar heating and ventilation, solar thermal heating and PV panels.

## BedZED

www.zedfactory.com

Beddington Zero Energy Development, BedZED for short, a collaboration between Peabody Trust, BioRegional and Bill Dunster's ZEDfactory, is located in South London and comprises 100 homes, community facilities and enough workspace for 100 people. Iconic rooftop ventilation 'funnels' make the development instantly recognisable.

These characteristic roof cowls above the sedum roof make BedZED instantly recognisable. Photograph: Zedfactory

Residents moved into BedZED in 2002 and in 2009 BioRegional published *BedZED Seven Years On*, which assesses how 'green' the development and residents actually are.[9] The outcome is disappointing. BedZED may be a great place to live in, but the ecological and carbon footprints for residents are only slightly below the UK average, mainly because, although residents use less energy at home, they lead relatively affluent lifestyles. The real value here is in the lessons the project holds for future initiatives.

## RuralZED

RuralZED may have learned some of these lessons. Zedfactory claims that these kit homes are made from sustainable materials, last for a minimum of five generations and are available to meet various specifications up to Code for Sustainable Homes Level 6 (see pages 161-2) and beyond. A terrace of six RuralZED houses in Upton, Northamptonshire, built for the Metropolitan Housing Trust, became the first Code 6 homes available on the open market. Two are for rent, two for shared ownership and two for sale. As Code 6 homes they are exempt from stamp duty.

## Coin Street Community Builders (CSCB)

www.coinstreet.org

This company, limited by guarantee, was established by local residents in 1984, following a campaign against office development on London's South Bank. CSCB's aims and objectives include opposing "developments which are likely to have an adverse effect on the environment of the South Bank" and recognise the "need to sustain the Earth's resources". The company transformed a largely derelict 5-hectare site into a thriving mixed-use neighbourhood with cooperative housing, shops, galleries, restaurants, sports facilities and open spaces. These developments, now over 25 years old, may not be particularly eco-friendly, but they met a real need for good-quality affordable housing and community.

In September 2009, CSCB overcame objections from English Heritage and Westminster Council to proceed with the 20-hectare Doon Street Development. Over 300 homes in a controversial futuristic tower will subsidise swimming and leisure facilities for local people. It is unlikely that the tower will be built from sustainable local materials or be environmentally friendly in any meaningful way, but Coin Street shows just how much can be achieved from what started as a community campaign against office buildings.

## Hanham Hall

www.hanhamhall.co.uk

Barratt Homes isn't the first construction company that comes to mind when you think about sustainable

Cutaway showing the environmental features of new homes at Hanham Hall near Bristol. © Barratt Homes

housing but, at Hanham Hall near Bristol, is it rising to the Carbon Challenge set by English Partnerships (now part of the Homes and Communities Agency). Around 180 Code for Sustainable Homes Level 6 homes are under construction, and the original Hanham Hall, a Grade II* listed building, will be refurbished as the centrepiece of the development. Community facilities, green spaces, cycle routes, allotments, an orchard, greenhouses and a 'sustainable living centre' complement the buildings. It looks good on paper but I'm not sure Barratt really understands the concept of sustainable building. Why do I say that? Because its video of the project consists of nothing but a massive digger destroying a building. Surely it could have thought of something more appropriate?

## Design for Manufacture

Nonetheless, Barratt and its like are not going to disappear overnight, so sustainable building has to spread to the mainstream. On the surface, Hanham Hall looks like a good start. The Code 6 homes should achieve the costs set by the Design for Manufacture Competition,[10] where two-bedroom homes with a floor area of 76m² were built for just £60,000. This competition brought entries from six developers over numerous sites. Costs were kept low by using factory-built homes rapidly assembled on site.

Perhaps the most striking of the winning designs were the 'eco-hats', a little different from the standard Wimpey homes, designed by Rogers Stirk Harbour and Partners and built by Wimpey at Oxley Woods in Milton Keynes. Richard Rogers is behind such environmentally friendly buildings as the Millennium Dome, the Pompidou Centre and Terminal 5 at Heathrow, and some reviews suggest that living in an eco-hat might be a little like living in one of these public spaces.

These striking homes were built as part of the Design for Manufacture competition. Photograph: Design for Manufacture, Department for Communities and Local Government

## Graylingwell

www.graylingwellchichester.com

This development of a hospital site in Chichester, West Sussex, includes 750 new homes and refurbishment of the existing buildings for homes, commercial and community use. Before obtaining planning consent, the developers arranged lengthy consultations with local people and organisations, and the submitted proposals include many suggestions from the community. The consultation began with a well-advertised weekend workshop in Chichester, followed by an open Graylingwell forum, which held three further evening meetings. More than 200 people took part. The success of this consultation can be measured by the fact that the Chichester Society, which has over 750 members and frequently argues against planning applications, supported the proposal. There is also a Community Liaison Panel, designed to continue consultation through the development phase.

John Templeton was one of the Chichester Society members who attended the Community Planning Weekend in 2008. He also represents the Society on the District Council's North East Chichester Forum, which keeps a watching brief on Graylingwell and other developments. He said:

> "We were extremely happy with the consultation process and, although not everyone got their own ideas included, or specific concerns addressed, everyone had ample opportunity to put their comments forward . . . overall there is pleasure and growing pride that Graylingwell will be an exemplar of sustainable development".

Graylingwell aspires to be a zero-carbon development, defined as zero carbon dioxide emissions resulting from actually living in the home. This is achieved through high levels of insulation, use of passive solar heating, combined heat and power plants and an average of 23m² of photovoltaic panels per home, bigger than a football pitch in total. There are also impressive – for a mainstream development – plans to reduce the ecological footprint of the site by encouraging walking and cycling, by using local and recycled building materials and by incorporating orchards and allotments.

## Eco-towns

Graylingwell is a big development, but it is dwarfed by the eco-towns proposed by the Department of Communities and Local Government in 2007. The first four of ten eco-towns are planned for Whitehill-Bordon in Hampshire, St Austell in Cornwall, Rackheath in Norfolk and Bicester in Oxfordshire. The criteria for eco-towns include at least 30 per cent affordable housing, zero carbon (excluding transport), a minimum of 40 per cent green space, higher recycling rates and making use of waste in new ways.

# Tesco secretly backs an eco-town

By Jane Merrick, Political Editor, The Independent, Sunday 6 April 2008

One of the Government's new eco-towns is being secretly backed by Tesco, it emerged last night. The supermarket giant plans to build a sprawling 'environmentally friendly' store at the heart of the proposed town in Hanley Grange, Cambridgeshire.

A shortlist of 15 eco-town sites featuring zero-carbon buildings was unveiled last week, but not Tesco's involvement. The Sunday Telegraph reported that development company Jarrow Investments, which is behind the Hanley Grange plans, owns much of the land on behalf of Tesco.

The move will be seen as an attempt by Britain's biggest supermarket to further extend its influence in retail by environmentally friendly gloss.

Not surprisingly, the plans are controversial and it's unclear if the new government elected in May 2010 will proceed with the same plans. There are claims that eco-towns are just a way for the government to sidestep local planning controls and doubts about the sustainability of these developments. Jonathan Manns, Lecturer at University of Cambridge and Property Consultant with Knight Frank LLP, argues that eco-towns could be a diversion from the more productive task of retrofitting existing housing – a task that would also result in wider and fairer availability of good-quality affordable homes.[11]

## Conclusions

- Good examples can come from unlikely quarters – as can be seen from Sherwood Energy Village.

- It's important to see through the 'greenwash' that puts 'eco' in front of an old policy, product or service to disguise it as a real step towards sustainability. We have to distinguish between rhetoric and reality.

- Profits drive poor practice.

- Access to land is the biggest obstacle to self-builders, who almost always build to higher standards than conventional ones.

# CHAPTER 8
# SOCIAL HOUSING

*"Ask me my three main priorities for government and I tell you insulation, insulation and insulation."*  With begrudged apologies to Tony Blair

## Social housing in the UK

Social housing in England is managed by local authorities and housing associations, cooperatives and trusts. About 2.1 million dwellings are managed by local authorities, directly or through ALMOs (arm's-length management organisations), and another 2 million by non-profit-making organisations.

This is a big fall from the early 1980s, when almost a third of the housing stock in England was in the social sector. A quarter century of less building and council house sales have substantially reduced the role of social housing. Over 1,648,000 local authority dwellings in England alone were sold at a discount through the Right to Buy scheme between 1979 and 2006. However, the growth of housing associations, partly through transfers of council stock, means that social housing overall still accounts for 21 per cent of all housing, one of the highest percentages in Europe – a valuable opportunity for government, local authorities and housing associations directly to influence a big chunk of existing housing through the Tenant Services Authority (although this is likely to be axed by the new coalition government) and by other means.

There are some excellent examples of both new-build and retrofitted sustainable housing. At present these are the exception, often enabled by additional funding, rather than the rule. Even the Beacon Councils, which are held up as shining examples of good practice, are still way behind what we need to achieve to stand any chance of zero-carbon housing by 2050. The challenge is to build from these exceptions.

## A fourth option

Government policy on financing improvements to social housing is based on moving responsibility away from the direct control of local authorities through stock transfer (so-called large-scale voluntary transfers), ALMOs and the use of private finance initiatives. Where councils or tenants refuse these options they are starved of funds for maintenance and improvements.

Many argue for a fourth option, where an investment allowance from government would allow councils to use their borrowing powers to raise funds for a massive programme of improvements to bring social housing up to the highest standards of energy efficiency. And because millions of homes would be involved, the economies of scale could be enormous.

This type of direct investment is a quicker way of improving homes and, as the Audit Commission has demonstrated, it is cheaper for the taxpayer by an average of £1,300 per home.[1]

## Local authorities

Local councils are directly or indirectly responsible for over two million social houses and, in theory at least, are responsible to us. So what are the good examples and how can we encourage other councils to follow?

### Housing crisis

The average house price is now eleven times the average income in England, rising 156 per cent between 1997 and 2005, while earnings rose just 35 per cent over the same period. But high demand has still not resulted in any major sustained increase in supply. The lack of housing supply contributes to price increases and puts enormous additional strain on social housing, as an increasingly large proportion of the population can meet their housing needs only with some form of financial subsidy. Waiting lists for social housing in England grew dramatically from 1,040,000 households in 2001 to 1,635,000 in 2006. England needs to build 70,000 new social homes a year, but in 2005/6 managed less than 40,000, and this number fell sharply with the credit crunch in 2008. The situation is similar in Scotland, Wales and Northern Ireland, where the shortage of affordable housing increased waiting lists and the number of people in housing stress or homeless.[2]

And remember that behind every statistic and name on a housing waiting list is a crowded family where children struggle with their schoolwork, parents are crushed by depression and stress and families live in conditions that were familiar to Dickens and Engels.

This photograph of a woman reading a letter has added resonance when we learn that she is reading an eviction notice. The composition reproduces Vermeer's 'Woman reading at the window'. Photograph: Tom Hunter, 1997

### Kirklees Warm Zones

The mark of a good idea is that everybody claims it! This is certainly true of the Kirklees District Council (KDC) Warm Zones scheme. In 2007 Kirklees decided to provide insulation free of charge to everybody.

Insulating lofts, cavity walls and hot-water tanks is the most cost-effective energy-saving measure you can take. The payback time can be as little as a year or two, and carbon savings are early and significant. It's a no-brainer.

Most Warm Zones schemes limit free insulation to people aged over 70 or on benefits. This creates problems. For a start, not all households in fuel poverty receive benefits and installations are scattered, making it difficult for contractors to reduce travel and costs by insulating large numbers of houses in a given area.

There are good arguments against even modest charges for insulation. When Kirklees was considering its scheme, a proposed charge of £65 was rejected because the cost of administration, chasing payments and pursuing defaulters would be uneconomic for such a small sum. Even £65 would be unaffordable for some households on low incomes but not qualifying for benefits, while, at the other end of the spectrum,

Installing loft insulation.

there are plenty of wealthy people who don't know or care how much energy they use, so a small charge would still be a barrier. In the end all parties agreed that money was just another layer of hassle that would limit take-up and reduce the efficiency of the scheme.

So how did Kirklees, a district with a population of 375,000, which includes the town of Huddersfield, come to take this approach? Andrew Cooper, a Green Party councillor, makes a reasonable claim that the free insulation scheme resulted from a Green Party amendment to the 2007 budget. The Liberal Democrats were in minority control of the council at that time, and they claim to have initiated the Warm Zones scheme, without mentioning that it was subsequently amended by the Green Party. And the Conservatives, now council leaders, take credit for actually implementing the scheme. Even Labour claims credit, because £10 million out of the £21 million costs come from Scottish Power as part of the Carbon Emissions Reductions Targets (CERT) set by the then government.

The wonderful thing about this all-party consensus is that we can all campaign to get our local councils to copy it. Just stress the role played by whichever particular party happens to be in control in your area! So far only a few councils have introduced similar schemes, the largest being Sheffield (see page 179).

## Power to the people

Having taken the first step with free insulation, Kirklees followed with a scheme enabling homeowners to install renewable energy. RE-Charge offers interest-free loans secured by a legal charge on the property that is repayable only when the house is sold – effectively an interest-free mortgage. The only up-front cost to homeowners is a £100 contribution to the cost of setting up the second charge on the property.

## Five reasons for free insulation?

- Insulation is the most cost-effective energy-saving measure you can carry out. In Kirklees, after CERT money is taken into account, it costs just £7 per year on the average council tax bill over 25 years. Energy savings per household average around £200 every year.

- The Local Government Performance Framework includes National Indicators that strongly support action on energy efficiency. NI 186 looks at per capita reductions in $CO_2$ emissions in the local authority, and NI 187 looks for reductions in fuel poverty.

- The government is legally obliged to meet the EU 2020 Renewable Energy Target of producing 15 per cent of total energy from renewable sources by 2020. Reducing energy consumption plays a substantial role in meeting this target.

- Ask councillors to imagine how popular they would be if they reduced council tax by £200 without cutting jobs or services. That's effectively what Kirklees has achieved.

- Savings on fuel bills are likely to be spent locally, hence boosting the local economy, and these savings increase with rising energy costs. Installing insulation also creates local jobs and training opportunities.

RE-Charge covers biomass boilers, solar water heating, air and ground source heat pumps, hydroelectric and solar photovoltaic systems. Micro systems for combined heat and power are also covered if such systems become available, but wind turbines are not part of the scheme. The loan is in addition to any available grants.

Not surprisingly, this is an extremely popular offer, and Yorkshire Energy Services, the energy advice centre that administers the scheme, gives technical advice and arranges installations, is very busy. Three million pounds is allocated to the three-year programme, of which 10 per cent is ringfenced for houses in fuel poverty. This is expected to support installations in around 330 houses, but year one alone saw 257 applications. This may tail off in years two and three, but demand is likely to exceed the funds available. A breakdown of the first 115 installations shows 29 solar water heaters, 75 photovoltaic systems, five ground source heat pumps and six biomass boilers.

RE-Charge didn't appear from nowhere. Kirklees has a long history of supporting renewable energy, including SunCities, one of the largest domestic photovoltaic energy projects in the UK. This scheme alone was responsible for 5 per cent of the total UK photovoltaic energy output in 2005. Not bad, considering that the population of Kirklees is just 0.6 per cent of the total for England and Wales.

SunCities was a European-Commission-funded project that began in 2000 and aimed to install 3.05 megawatts of solar electricity on 2,000 homes in Germany, the Netherlands and Kirklees. In Kirklees this included a total of 351kWp solar electricity systems and 63 solar thermal systems. Around 518 households were involved, including elderly tenants and families with young children, who benefit from free power.

The project attracted funding of up to £1.8 million to Kirklees and gained nationwide attention through winning an Ashden Award for Sustainable Energy, a British Renewable Energy Association Award and a Green Apple Award.

Kirklees District Council also backed the installation of around 100 solar water heating units in social housing, as well as wind power, photovoltaic systems and solar water heating for schools and a new civic centre. Use the search engine on the Kirklees website (www.kirklees.gov.uk) to find detailed case studies.

## Straw-bale council houses

It's not every day that building four council homes in a Lincolnshire village makes the national news, but that's exactly what happened for North Kesteven District Council (NKDC) in March 2009. Why the interest? This was the first local authority in the UK to approve straw bale as a construction method for council housing.

In September 2009 I arrived on site in the small village of Waddington, four miles south of Lincoln, to spend a day with Amazonails (if you don't get it try saying it again) a non-profit-making social enterprise building company. Barbara Jones, one of the company's founders, was running a two-day course on the basics of straw-bale building and I went along to see what all the fuss was about.

I soon discovered that this isn't just any straw-bale building. When NKDC decided to build with straw, it went the whole hog and approved a design using load-bearing straw-bale walls. Let me explain: many straw buildings use a load-bearing timber frame to support the roof and, in two-storey buildings, the upper floor. Straw bales are packed in after the frame is in place, to provide excellent insulation. Single-storey buildings often use straw-bale walls to carry the weight of the roof. This saves material costs, but one disadvantage is that you don't have a roof in place to keep the bales dry while building. There are also

hybrid buildings, which use a lightweight frame. All this is explained in Barbara's excellent *Building with Straw Bales*.[3]

But this building is special. The roof, temporarily covered in plastic sheets, rests on scaffolding and will be lowered by a crane only when the last bale is firmly in place . . . and there are two floors. "We've actually built two-and-a-half-storey buildings with load-bearing walls without any problems," says Barbara, "and we would like the opportunity to build up to four storeys high, because I'm confident such buildings are possible."

Bruce King, a leading campaigner for sustainable building in the US, argues that load-bearing straw-bale buildings shouldn't go beyond a single storey. "But that's based on someone testing one bale in a laboratory," says Barbara. "Our experience is based on real buildings." The evidence must be strong, because the local planners gave their seal of approval.

Tidying up inside the Kesteven straw-bale council houses.
Photograph: Steven Hills, North Kesteven District Council

## Laying foundations

And straw isn't the only sustainable feature of this building. The foundations, deeper than originally intended because of infill discovered when the build started, are limecrete over shingle. "It took a lot of persuading to convince the planning department that this was OK," explains Barbara. Amazonails then had to repeat the arguments to Taylor Pearson, the main building contractor, who wanted to lay a standard concrete slab. But these debates are worthwhile because they usually end with converts. "That's why we prefer to work with local building officers rather than use a private company we know will be more sympathetic. As a social enterprise, part of our job is spreading the word to sceptical council officers." Taylor Pearson is now convinced of the value of limecrete and enthusiastic about the merits of straw.

Finished straw-bale council houses. Photograph: Steven Hills, North Kesteven District Council

As well as being less expensive – around £110,000 per home, but that will decrease as local builders become familiar with the techniques – these homes are extremely well insulated. Barbara expects them to achieve Code for Sustainable Homes Level 4 or 5 (see pages 161-2), and no heating is installed apart from a wood-burning stove for very cold weather.

Other innovations on this site hold lessons about sustainability, but before I tell you about that a little background about Amazonails is in order.

## Amazonails

Barbara Jones worked as a carpenter on building sites during the 1980s but soon realised she would not survive in the 'macho' culture of the construction industry. She took time out to visit the US, fell in love with straw-bale construction and made a second visit, on a Churchill travel fellowship, to gain more experience of straw technology. Amazonails was established by Barbara and Bee Rowan in the 1990s, pioneered straw-bale technology in the UK and adapted North American techniques for use in the wetter UK climate. But Barbara and Bee also think it's important to change the culture of building sites:

> "The atmosphere on our building sites is qualitatively different to that found on the majority of other building sites elsewhere. This is not by chance. We deliberately encourage a feeling of being part of a group, of all working together to achieve a common aim. Each person's past experience and level of skill is valued and appreciated . . . Our building sites are happy places. People are well motivated, look out for each other, share experience and have fun. Inevitably this means that we achieve a lot, health and safety is excellent, and the quality of our work is high."[4]

On the Lincolnshire site this difference in culture – and I'm not just talking about the vegetarian lunch, fruit in the tearoom or the absence of sexist pin-ups – is apparent when we gather in a circle before we start work and hold hands. Barbara leads us in focusing energy on 'Angel Cards' spread across the floor, then Pete, an architectural technician, picks a card. He reveals 'Clarity', which becomes our theme for the day. Now, I am just about the least spiritual person you can imagine, but I do appreciate the importance of ritual. Most building sites are full of unacknowledged rituals that lead to competition rather than collaboration, poor craftsmanship and a high accident rate. In 2008/9 there were 53 fatal accidents in the UK construction industry, the highest total for any industry and second only to agriculture in terms of risk per number of employees.[5] So what could be better than a simple ritual to reinforce our unity of purpose and interdependence?

## Why Kesteven?

So why is this groundbreaking build happening in a small village few people have ever heard of? "North Kesteven has a reputation for innovation. We are open to new ideas," answers Stan Ogden, one of the councillors behind the build. "We may not have the land to build as many affordable homes like these as we would like, but we can provide models for other people to follow." Marion Brighton, leader of the council, reinforces this view. "The district council not only hopes to share its expertise and knowledge with other organisations but also with residents, by inviting them to come and watch the whole process of the houses being built."

North Kesteven District Council even has its own straw logo.
© NKDC

Local people have signed up to work on the build, and there's been local and national television and press coverage as well as a lot of interest from building and environmental publications. Kesteven has put straw-bale affordable housing on the agenda.

## Rolling out the idea

But could major construction firms build thousands of straw buildings every year? The raw material is certainly available – the UK's annual surplus of straw could build over 250,000 super-insulated, three-bedroom homes a year – but are there other obstacles? As Barbara shows us how to 'dress' each bale to ensure it fits tightly, sometimes rejects bales altogether, and stresses the importance of design detail and building technique to ensure that bales remain dry during and after construction, the answer becomes clear. Natural materials like straw vary in ways that concrete blocks and bricks don't. Builders on piecework and subcontractors working to a fixed price may be loath to spend time assessing the quality of their materials. Construction companies interested in short-term profit rather than long-term quality would not produce good straw-bale homes.

I have no doubt that construction workers could acquire the necessary skills, but could the industry develop the culture in which those skills could be effectively used? The problem is similar to that seen with Passivhaus building (see pages 163-4), where a new mindset is needed to ensure the attention to detail necessary to construct an airtight building. It can and must be done, but the more focus there is on speed and profit, the harder it becomes.

There are certainly farmers in the UK who would like to see straw-bale construction take off. Among the many people visiting the Lincolnshire site are representatives from the National Non-Food Crops

Centre, which is already backing the use of hemp as a sustainable building material (see page 193) and would love a new market for thousands of tonnes of straw.

I left the Amazonails course with new confidence in load-bearing straw-bale construction and with great respect for this pioneering company. In 14 years it has built well over 100 straw-bale buildings; won numerous awards, including the Grand Designs Eco Home award in 2008; and, most important of all, made building accessible to people excluded by the prevalent culture of the construction industry.

## Housing associations

Making all new homes 'zero carbon' and meeting Code for Sustainable Homes Level 6 by 2016 looks increasingly unlikely, but some builders already build to, and beyond, this standard. The big construction companies littering our countryside with boring and energy-inefficient boxes are put to shame by builders and developers demonstrating that we need not wait until 2016.

Just a few months before this book was published, the first development of homes in the UK built to the demanding Passivhaus standard was completed. Are they exclusive homes built by a cutting-edge developer? No, these are modest homes for the elderly, built by a housing association.

### Passivhausing Association?

This 28-unit bungalow scheme, built by Gentoo and completed in summer 2010, is part of the Racecourse Estate in Houghton-le-Spring, Tyne and Wear, and is the first certified Passivhaus scheme on this scale in the UK. Passivhaus homes rely on passive solar gain and airtightness, super-high standards of insulation and triple-glazed windows. The buildings have a mechanical ventilation system that provides excellent air quality and efficient heat recovery, so only a small heater, integrated into the ventilation system, is required. Annual heating costs will be around £40. Ironically, many of the residents are retired miners, still entitled to a coal allowance. Coal fires in a Passivhaus? No way!

Gentoo argues that it is "relatively straightforward" to build to all levels of the Code for Sustainable Homes using designs familiar to the UK and without recourse to renewable energy sources beyond solar hot water and photovoltaics. A Gentoo report looks at a range of house types and concludes that "PassivHaus is ideally suited for zero-carbon housing." The limiting factor is cost. The Passivhaus- based design in this report costs around £21,000 more than an equivalent house built to 2006 Building Regulations.[6]

However, this cost must be seen in context. Code 6 housing has almost zero energy costs and, from April 2010, is actually an income generator because of

A section through the Passivhaus social housing development built by Gentoo. © Gentoo Sunderland

## Biased building codes

"Building codes are inherently biased against green materials," says Barbara Jones. The big building companies do a lot of lobbying when new building codes are being developed, so it's no surprise that building codes are biased in favour of hi-tech and conventional building materials. The Code for Sustainable Homes does give some points for green materials but fails to acknowledge the real value of sustainable materials with low embodied energy.

Furthermore, National Home Energy Ratings, which are a theoretical assessment of energy efficiency, usually underrate homes built with unconventional materials.

"Eighty-five per cent of the Kesteven build is natural materials with low embodied energy," says Barbara. [See Table 2.] "The reverse is true for most conventional builds, but that fact won't be acknowledged in any official assessment of energy efficiency."

| Embodied energy of materials used in a typical straw-bale building | | |
|---|---|---|
| **Embodied energy** | **Materials** | **Percentage volume of all materials** |
| Extremely high | Plastic straps, lead flashing, hinges, locks, handles, nails and screws, galvanised downpipe | 0.14% |
| Very high | Double glazing | 0.09% |
| High | OSB, external plywood, Tyvek membrane | 2.19% |
| Medium | Baler twine, floorboards, wooden gutters, cork underlay, celenit fibreboard, door/window frames, lime plaster, hessian | 7.34% |
| Low | Local timber | 5.28% |
| Very low | Straw bales, sheepswool insulation, hazel, clay plaster, cedar shingles | 84.95% |

Table 2. Percentage volume and embodied energy for materials in a typical straw-bale house. Around 90% of materials have low or very low embodied energy and also act as a carbon store. From 'Energy assessment of a straw-bale building', Carol Atkinson, MSc Architecture thesis (2008). Available at www.homegrownhome.co.uk

feed-in tariffs for electricity from renewable sources. Furthermore, Gentoo believes that as it develops experience, particularly with renewables, costs will come down. The fitted cost of photovoltaics, for example, could fall by at least a third.

Ian Porter, Managing Director of Gentoo Sunderland, says: "Passivhaus provides the perfect solution for our customers, our organisation and the planet." Other housing associations obviously agree, and in 2010 Hastoe Housing Association built 14 rural homes to Passivhaus standards in Wimbush, Essex.

## Peterborough Carbon Challenge

Gentoo is also part of the English Partnerships Carbon Challenge scheme and is involved in building 450 homes on a 7-hectare site in Peterborough. All the homes must be built to Code 6. Six groups were invited to submit bids, but several builders, developers and housing associations withdrew after claiming the project was too expensive. pPod, a consortium of Gentoo, Morris Homes and the architects Brown Smith Baker, is the preferred developer for phase one of the scheme, which also includes shops, community facilities, orchards and allotments.

Building the UK's first PassivHaus development in Sunderland and zero-carbon homes in Peterborough is pretty good evidence of green credentials, but Gentoo also has a refurbishment project to justify its collection of sustainability awards. Three reports outline Gentoo's Retrofit Reality project, covering 139 of the properties Gentoo owns and manages.[7] A variety of energy-efficient products, solar thermal panels, A-rated condensing boilers, energy-efficient showers, external insulation and double glazing were fitted. The effectiveness of these measures is assessed using a

## Gentoo Green

Why has Gentoo pursued an ambitious green agenda while others find reasons to do nothing? One answer may be the decision of Gentoo Group, which oversees the development, construction and housing association arms, to create Gentoo Green. This section, complete with its 'Green Teams' and 'Environmental Champions', exists to inspire the rest of the group to behave in a sustainable way, with the aspiration to "give the planet a little something back".

Gentoo Green is tasked with creating a culture where the environmental impact of actions and decisions is considered, and the company goes beyond mere compliance with legislation. Ecological and carbon footprints have been measured and environmental impact assessments undertaken, a mobile exhibition unit takes the energy-efficiency message to customers in their own communities, £6 million has been spent on energy efficiency to save residents an estimated £4.2 million each year and to reduce $CO_2$ emissions by 7,524 tonnes, and Gentoo has switched most of the group's electricity demands to a 'greener' supplier.

Perhaps this extract from the Gentoo website sums up its ethos:

> "Experience tells us that people are very quick to assess the commercial cost of doing something but very rarely the commercial and indeed wider aspects of not doing something."[8]

Gentoo has chosen to do something, and when a company with a turnover of more than £140 million and assets in excess of £1 billion starts moving in the right direction that sends a powerful message.

control group of 40 homes. Gentoo is also doing extensive educational work with tenants to ensure that products are used to the greatest benefit.

Retrofit Reality tackles questions such as how difficult products are to install and use, what the benefits are to people living in the homes, and what maintenance they require. The research has financial support from the Tenant Services Authority and Low Carbon Buildings Programme. Gentoo is also working in partnership with Northumbria University and is funding two PhD students to assist with the technical and behavioural aspects of the project. Lessons will be applied to the 30,000 homes managed by Gentoo.

## Hemp housing

As we have seen from the rise in interest in straw-bale building, construction materials are a vital factor in sustainable housing. In 1999 Suffolk Housing Society acknowledged this by building the first homes in the UK using hemp.

The project built two pairs of homes of exactly the same design, one using traditional block and render, the other using hemp and lime around a timber frame. The two hemp houses now stand on a small social housing development in Haverhill, Suffolk. Every step of their construction and occupation has been closely monitored to compare their performance with the otherwise identical 'traditional' houses.

Suffolk Housing Society, which manages nearly 2,000 homes in the East of England, had support from the Housing Corporation and St Edmundsbury Borough Council, but the project really happened because of the enthusiasm for using hemp from local architect Ralph Carpenter. Carpenter had seen the method in France, where the hemp-processing system was developed.

The Building Research Establishment (BRE) carried out extensive research during the project, to demonstrate that hemp and lime construction is a viable low-energy alternative to brick and concrete blocks. It looked at relative structural, thermal, acoustic, permeability and durability qualities; reduction in waste generated on site, and environmental impact and construction costs for the two systems.

Its report concluded that the hemp buildings, although costing more, performed as well or better than the 'brick and block' homes and, as concern over the environmental impact of construction increases, so very low-impact materials such as hemp, lime and local timber will come into their own.[9]

Clay Field Sustainable Housing, also in Suffolk, was constructed with a sprayed hemp/lime mix, and the development has a biomass community heating system (fuelled by locally sourced wood chips) that heats all the homes from a single boiler.

Hempcrete social housing in Suffolk. The building with the green roof houses the biomass community heating system (fuelled by locally sourced wood chips) that heats all the homes from a single boiler. Photograph: CFA Marketing Communications and Suffolk Housing Association

## Hemp twinning

During the Haverhill project links were established with a housing association in Northern France, Hennebont Blavet Habitat, which has a larger-scale development using the same methods of construction. Suffolk Housing Society and Hennebont now have wide ranging ties to see what they can learn from one another about providing and managing social housing in the two countries.

## Moving the earth

Peddars Way Housing Association won first place at the Campaign to Protect Rural England awards ceremony in 2004 for its Earth Sheltered homes at Honingham in Suffolk. Completed in 2003, the dwellings were designed by the well-known eco-architect Jerry Harrall and were the first earth-sheltered social homes in the UK.

The single-storey homes, all facing south, use passive solar gain as the main heat source and passive ventilation techniques for cooling. Earth sheltering, where earth is banked around the walls and roof, maintains an internal temperature of around 20°C without the need for any additional heating or cooling systems, although a back-up heating system is installed to cope with extremely low temperatures.

The floors and walls are designed to make major excavation unnecessary, the foundation is made of a reinforced concrete slab and the walls are of cavity construction, comprising two leaves of concrete blocks. A tanking membrane is applied to the outer surface of the roof, walls and floors, and polystyrene boards on top of the tanking add extra insulation. Earth laid over the roof and walls to a minimum depth of 750mm is covered with a woven nylon membrane, through which evergreen herbaceous shrubs grow.

Jerry Harrall, Managing Director at SEArch Architects Ltd, said:

"The bungalows are very simple to build. The quantity of materials required for their construction is significantly reduced in comparison with the construction of conventional homes. Fewer tradesmen are required due to the absence of plastering, skirting boards, stud work, lintels, foundations or embedded services. The design of the buildings is commercially viable and could therefore be used by other forward-looking housing associations across the UK."[10]

Earth-sheltered housing designed by Jerry Harrall at SEArch Architects and managed by Peddars Way Housing Association. Photograph: Jerry Harrall, SEArch Architects

## Greening the Box

www.greeningthebox.co.uk

Jerry Harrall and SEArch Architects are also behind a low-tech retrofit experiment designed to transform social housing. The Greening the Box (GTB) initiative, adopted by Wherry Housing Association, demonstrates that retrofitting can transform 'hard-to-heat and hard-to-treat' properties into models of sustainability – a greener alternative to knocking down old stock and building new.

21 The Street, in the Norfolk village of Ringland, is solid-walled, off the gas network and typical of the rural houses managed by Wherry. After a 16-week retrofit, the property is now home to a family of four who agreed to take part in a three-year monitoring programme covering life-cycle analysis, thermal performance and energy consumption.

The complete refurbishment of the property cost nearly £100,000, but only an estimated £36,000 of this was spent on the eco-retrofit. Windows have been double-glazed as a matter of course, but those on the north elevation have been made smaller, while on the south side more and bigger windows increase natural light and passive solar gain.

Apart from a wood fire – "an open fire warms the human spirit", says Harrall – the only heating is a low-grade electric underfloor system. Solid 9-inch external walls are clad with an extra 100mm of polystyrene insulation. Factor in the heat contribution from appliances and humans – the average person emits 90W of heat – a ground floor of dense concrete, and the superstructure of the building acts like a storage radiator, holding on to its summer heat for the winter months. By upgrading the volume of active thermal mass Harrall estimates that the last net contribution of solar heat from September won't leak out until three months later.

Other features include 600mm of insulation in the roof, a rotating cowl to draw air through the house, breathable walls to reduce condensation, a 1,000-litre

Greening the Box. Rear view before refurbishment . . .                . . . and after. Photographs: Jerry Harrall

rainwater tank and solar water heating. Estimated annual $CO_2$ emissions are now just half a tonne, compared with nearly eight tonnes for the control house next door. Energy bills are likely to be less than 25 per cent of the control house.

Learning how to get the best out of the new home will be the major challenge for its new residents. Harrall says: "we've given them a green Porsche, or a Tesla, where they've been used to a Ford Anglia. We've got to get them driving it to its optimum performance."

This is being achieved through education about how the house works, as well as through a few rules. Rugs are allowed but no carpets, which might hamper the movement of heat to or from the thermal mass in the floor, and residents are encouraged to leave doors open to allow the free movement of air around the building.

The Circle Anglia Group, which includes Wherry, is looking closely at the experiment before it decides whether to roll out the project to other houses.

## Exemplar refurbishments

There are numerous examples of 'exemplar refurbishments' and environmentally friendly innovations by housing associations. In 2007 **Hyde Housing Association** and ECD Architects established an effective package of retrofit measures to achieve an 80-per-cent reduction in $CO_2$ emissions for a typical three-bedroom mid-terrace house in London. Figures 9 and 10 on the following pages show how the reduction was achieved.

**Parkway Housing Association**, part of Great Places Housing Group, has four bungalows with green roofs and solar panels in Wybourn, Sheffield. The roofs,

planted with low-growing, low-maintenance sedum, help to insulate the properties and slow rain water run-off, putting less strain on the drains.

The **Bourneville Village Trust** claims that its refurbished eco-home in Selly Oak, Birmingham, is the "Greenest Home in the UK". It has every eco-feature you can think of, and the Trust is monitoring to see what works and what doesn't by comparison with a similar but unmodified house.

Way back in 1995, **St Pancras Housing Association** decided to meet the objectives set down in its environmental policy and to reduce tenants' energy costs by installing a combined heat and power plant for tenants in 95 flats, a community centre, ten commercial units (which helps make the scheme viable) and the housing association head office. Electricity rates for the scheme were set at a level that repaid the capital investment in less than ten years, with tenants' costs reduced by 25 per cent.

### Greening Birmingham

After residents expressed concerns about energy efficiency and rising fuel bills, the Family Housing Association (FHA) in Birmingham worked with Birmingham City Council and Urban Living to install new technologies in a Victorian semi being de-converted from a house in multiple occupation into a large family home. The eco-house opened in June 2006 and is currently occupied by FHA tenants and used to promote and demonstrate energy-saving systems.

But this was not just another one-off exemplar. Following the success of the eco-house, the FHA decided to make Summerfield, where the eco-house is, an 'Eco Neighbourhood'. By April 2008, 329 homes had solar thermal panels installed completely free of charge for owner–occupiers, depending on certain eligibility criteria, with the aim of reducing fuel poverty.

FHA also teamed up with Digital Birmingham and Be Birmingham for the 'Living Labs' project to develop a system to measure, display and influence domestic energy consumption. The project is called DEHEMS

(Digital Environment Home Energy Management System) and funded as part of a European Union initiative. Fifty households in the Summerfield and Lozells area, comprising a range of property types and sizes, some with good energy-efficiency products already in place and others without, are taking part. The home energy systems in each property provide data on household heat loss and appliance performance, to enable improvements in energy use. FHA is

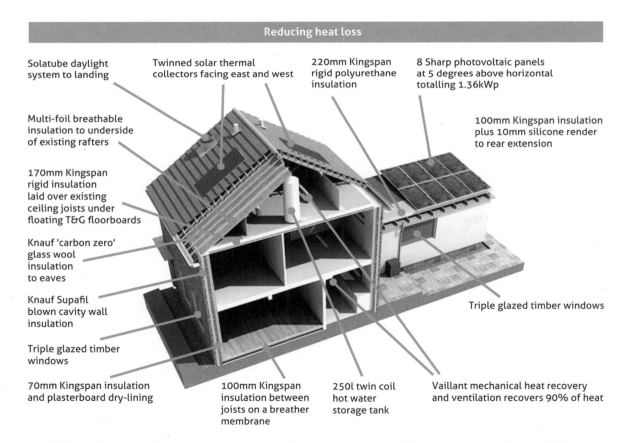

**Reducing heat loss**

Solatube daylight system to landing

Twinned solar thermal collectors facing east and west

220mm Kingspan rigid polyurethane insulation

8 Sharp photovoltaic panels at 5 degrees above horizontal totalling 1.36kWp

Multi-foil breathable insulation to underside of existing rafters

100mm Kingspan insulation plus 10mm silicone render to rear extension

170mm Kingspan rigid insulation laid over existing ceiling joists under floating T&G floorboards

Knauf 'carbon zero' glass wool insulation to eaves

Knauf Supafil blown cavity wall insulation

Triple glazed timber windows

Triple glazed timber windows

70mm Kingspan insulation and plasterboard dry-lining

100mm Kingspan insulation between joists on a breather membrane

250l twin coil hot water storage tank

Vaillant mechanical heat recovery and ventilation recovers 90% of heat

Figure 9. This model shows how Hyde Housing Association and ECD Architects achieved an 80% reduction in $CO_2$ emissions. © ECD Architects

also working with the Green Doctor Service (see pages 26-28) in neighbourhoods throughout Birmingham to provide free home energy advice.

And there are new jobs as well. The Lozells Eco project has created employment opportunities for women, with five trainees having the opportunity to become qualified solar panel installers.

## Involvement of local schools

The eco-house gave FHA the opportunity to work with primary school children on promoting energy efficiency, and it invested £20,000 in helping more than 500 children in local schools to develop an Eco website, radio station and energy advice DVD. The aim is to create a new generation of energy-wise consumers and use 'pester power' to influence adult behaviour.

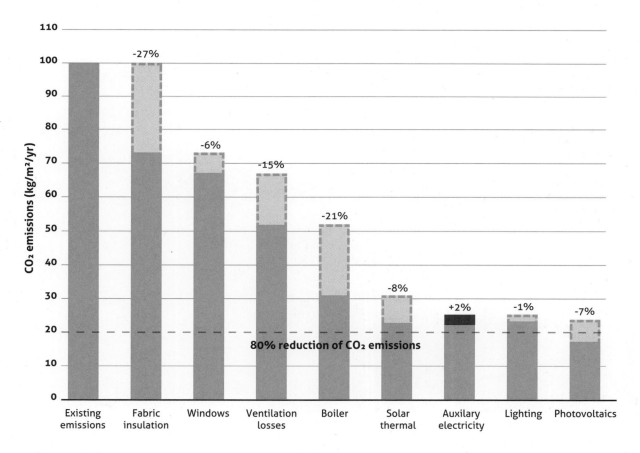

Figure 10. This chart shows the percentage contribution to the 80% cut in $CO_2$ emissions made by each improvement. © ECD Architects

## Green future for the Black Country

www.bcha.co.uk

Black Country Housing Group (BCH) is really pushing the boundaries. As well as initiating new and refurbished 'eco-home' developments, it has its own environmental consulting arm and is testing the world's first hydrogen-fuel-cell system for electrical power and hot water in the home. BCH is concerned about the security of gas and oil supplies as well as about global warming, and a key aim of the trial is to find out how fuel cell technology can replace fossil fuels. e²S, its environmental consultancy, offers specialist environmental, economic and social consultancy services for clients including local authorities, housing associations, architects and manufacturers.

Its Bryce Road development used 'green tendering' to get best value by fixing a price and asking: "Who can deliver the most features for this budget?" Phase 1 achieved homes with a SAP rating of 100. Phase 2 is more experimental and uses pre-assembled timber and steel frames, concrete-panel systems and factory-assembled kitchen and bathroom pods. The homes are

New technologies on trial at Black Country Housing Association's Eco-Pod test centre. Photograph: Black Country Housing Association

super-insulated and airtight with managed ventilation, and water is pre-heated with solar panels. There are also sun tubes (a reflective tube that delivers light even around corners) and provision for a waste segregation system.

On-trial technologies are monitored and demonstrated from a subterranean 'Eco Pod' centre. The Eco Pod is also testing ground source heat pumps, solar water heating, photovoltaics, wind generators, grey water recycling, rainwater harvesting, composting toilets and a storm-water management system.

## Changing behaviour – the Oak Meadow experience

In 2005 Devon & Cornwall Housing Association (DCHA) completed Oak Meadow, with homes built to high environmental and 'healthy living' standards. Before moving in, residents had several meetings with DCHA and were encouraged to adopt measures such as energy and water conservation, reducing car use, growing vegetables, recycling and reducing waste sent to landfill. The experience, claims DCHA, "highlighted for us that it wasn't just the residents that needed to change their behaviour to become 'green' – it was the organisation too!"[11]

So DCHA, which manages over 10,000 homes, applied to the Environmental Action Fund for a three-year grant to develop a partnership approach to promoting and monitoring sustainable consumption and reduction of waste in the social housing sector. The Sustainable Living Project, which involved over 500 residents and numerous partners, looked at two themes:

- how to manage the housing stock sustainably and offer environmentally responsible housing services

# Heat pumps in Cornwall

### Denys Stephens, Penwith Housing Association

Penwith Housing Association (PHA), a member of Devon & Cornwall Housing Group, manages 6,000 homes throughout Cornwall. When we began using ground source heat pumps (GSHPs) for heating, PHA already had a strong reputation for excellence in energy-efficiency work. The in-house technical team had developed the expertise, and the board and senior management team wanted to bring its benefits both to its customers and the condition of the stock. The use of GSHPs became possible because of the presence in Cornwall of GeoScience Ltd (whose heat-pump business now trades as EarthEnergy Ltd), one of the first companies in the UK to promote the technology. A visit of the Association's Environmental Working Party to GeoScience's offices led to a meeting with representatives of South Western Electricity, who wanted to pilot GSHPs in housing. This resulted in PHA building the UK's first social housing with GSHP, at Marazion in 1998.

This helped to establish the viability of the technology in well-insulated new homes. But in Cornwall, particularly in rural areas without mains gas, there is a real need for affordable heating that is not easily met with traditional systems. In 2003 the Association began working with GeoScience on retrofitting GSHP to existing homes – this became part of the Powergen (now E.ON) 'HeatPlant' scheme. The aim was to produce a replicable and affordable method of installing the technology in existing homes. The new Clear Skies funding programme provided the opportunity to take the idea further, and the Chy An Gweal site near Penzance was chosen as a deserving location. Residents struggled to cope with solid-fuel heating and, while the homes were well insulated, running costs were high and SAP ratings low.

At a meeting held in April 2003, residents of Chy An Gweal became the first social housing tenants in the UK to be offered GSHP systems alongside conventional alternatives for heating. Their enthusiasm to take advantage of the potentially clean, low-cost, low-carbon

Fitting the pipes for a retrofitted ground source heat pump in social housing. Photograph: Denys Stephens, Penwith Housing Association

and effective heating offered by GSHP systems confirmed that the project should go ahead.

Details of the multi-award-winning project are recorded in several online case studies (see www.managenergy. net/download/nr269.pdf, for example), but one of the most important outcomes was that it encouraged other social housing landlords to install GSHP. In the 'Completing the Loop' project funded by the Energy Saving Trust, partners worked with ESDConsultancy (now Camco) to promote the use of GSHP in social housing, which resulted in numerous projects around the UK. It is now regarded as a standard retrofit technology.

- how to inspire and enable residents to adopt a sustainable lifestyle in their own homes.

One outcome was the Residents Environmental Green Guide, which gives advice on issues such as energy, water, recycling and transport and includes case studies. The final project report suggests that encouraging residents to adopt sustainable lifestyles can only be achieved through:

- provision of tailored advice to households on the basis of their homes' environmental potential

- taking advantage of procuring low-cost services and goods, for example, energy tariffs, water butts and compost bins

- signposting and referrals to local services including financial advice, energy efficiency and healthy living

- community development opportunities promoting green and healthy behaviour

- residents being consulted and involved in procurement and service design decisions

- promoting an honest message to residents that their homes are not going to become super-green overnight, and that this can be achieved only through working together and making lifestyle choices.[12]

## Conclusions

- There are good models of sustainable social housing, but they have yet to become the norm. Local authorities and housing associations should be responsible to their local populations and

### National Housing Federation

The National Housing Federation (NHF), 'the voice of affordable housing', represents 1,200 independent housing associations in England. NHF members provide two-and-a-half million homes for more than five million people.

The NHF is a delivery partner in a €1.5 million Intelligent Energy Europe (IEE) project called 'Powerhouse' to share knowledge and promote expertise around building and retrofitting to greener standards. The project provides accessible information and tools to assist retrofitting for 39,000 non-profit-making organisations managing over 22 million homes in 19 EU states. IEE already publishes reports on over 450 European energy-efficiency projects, including many that are directly relevant to homes and communities.

See ec.europa.eu/energy/intelligent

residents. The Sustainable Communities Act enables local organisations to propose legislative changes to their local authority for onward transmission to the Local Government Association and Parliament. Bringing about legislative changes in this way is a long shot, but a proposal on self-build affordable housing from Totnes was shortlisted.

- The Tenant Empowerment Programme[13] enables social housing tenants to gain independent advice, training and information to challenge, influence or control how housing services are delivered, and can be used to promote sustainable housing.

- Local authorities and housing associations should be working for us and not the other way round. There are a number of ways in which we can influence their practice both as individuals and collectively, as follows.

> Make sure local councillors, planning officers and housing associations are aware of examples of sustainable housing.

> Write letters, send web links, inform the local media about what's happening elsewhere and ask why your council / local housing associations aren't following best practice.

> Invite councillors and local officers to a 'Global Cafe' event to discuss and learn about sustainable housing.

> Make sure you invite people with responsibility for social housing in relevant activities, e.g. in Totnes we included them in a trip to Oak Meadow.

> Establish or work with residents' associations on sustainable housing issues.

> Get involved in local consultations on planning and sustainability issues.

# CHAPTER 9
# SUSTAINABLE HOUSING IN STROUD

## Hill Paul

Step off the train in Stroud and the first thing you see is Hill Paul, a magnificent restored red brick mill. The mill was built in 1898 as a clothing factory and was open until 1989. The distinctive red bricks were made from local clay and sand in the nearby village of Stonehouse. One of those red bricks, 'C. Jefferies Stonehouse' stamped in the frog, is in Stroud museum, but it's a long time since the Jefferies fired bricks in Stonehouse or anywhere else in Gloucestershire.

The doors and windows of the mill are framed in local Cotswold limestone. Within a few miles there were quarries and lime kilns, and all the building materials were probably transported to the site by rail or on the adjacent canal. Only the modern roof extension is constructed from materials that aren't local.

Hill Paul is a striking building, but in 2000 a wrecking crane almost destroyed this piece of history to make way for new housing. The mill had stood empty for nearly ten years and, although Hill Paul stands in a conservation area, Stroud District Council did not use its powers to ensure the structure was maintained. Attempts to get the building listed also failed. A developer applied for permission to demolish, and Stroud District Council agreed. Hill Paul was for the wrecking ball.

But local people, fresh from successful rooftop protests against the destruction of other heritage buildings,

Hill Paul. This striking building was saved from demolition by direct action from the Stroud community.

had other ideas. Hill Paul Regeneration Group was formed, the building was occupied to prevent demolition, and a company was established to buy the building. Shares were sold at £500 each and raised over £85,000 in two weeks, with no guarantee that investors would ever get their money back. Eventually the developers conceded defeat, Stroud District Council backed down and Cherbury Homes turned the building into an attractive apartment block.

Hill Paul is not an energy-efficient building – energy and environmental impact ratings for a typical apartment are in the E to F range. But if Hill Paul had been destroyed and replaced, the embodied energy in any new structure would have taken decades to recoup. When campaigners saved Hill Paul they also saved thousands of tonnes of carbon embodied in high-energy materials, demolition and construction, and the transport of waste and building materials around Britain and probably from all over the world.

So I've barely stepped off the train and I'm already impressed by what people in Stroud have achieved. They may have failed to stop Tesco, McDonald's and an ugly new cinema, but they saved Hill Paul. Well done Stroud!

## A meeting in Woodruff's

It's a short walk from the station to Woodruff's, which claims to be the oldest organic vegetarian cafe in the UK, where I'd arranged to meet Philip Booth, a district councillor for the Greens and a Transition Stroud founder. On the way I passed shop window displays advertising 'Transition Stroud Eco-Renovation Open Homes', and posters about the launch of the 'Stroud Pound', a new local currency. A farmers' market, voted best in the country, is planned for the next day, as is the launch of a Fair Trade campaign. Stroud is a busy town.

I hadn't met Philip before but I'd read his blog, www. ruscombegreen.blogspot.com: "the ninth most popular green blog in the country", he tells me. He has lots of energy. (Like Tigger, but with focus and direction.) In the same sentence Philip complains that he needs to cut back on the issues he campaigns around and then outlines some new project. Philip Booth is an activist.

I'd come to Stroud to see the town's 'Eco-Renovation Open Homes' event, so who better to talk to than Philip, who ran the first 'Stroud Open Homes' event in

2008. But first I needed to understand the context. What sort of town is Stroud?

"We were just 20 minutes too late to elect the first Green Councillor in the country," says Philip, and you can hear the competitive edge in his voice despite the fact that this was back in 1985. The Greens have run Stroud Town Council for many years, have half a dozen councillors on Stroud District Council (SDC), and won their first Gloucestershire County Council seat in 2009, when they took an impressive 19 per cent of the county vote. The Conservatives dominate both the district and the county councils, but until May 2010 the local MP was David Drew from Labour. Stroud has a relatively good record on sustainability and was one of the first councils to sign up to the 10:10 pledge to cut carbon emissions by 10 per cent by 2010.

Councillor Philip Booth holding programmes for the Stroud Eco-Renovation Open Homes event. In the background is the retrofitted Randwick Village Hall. Photograph: Philip Booth

SDC has a Climate Change Panel that makes annual recommendations, and in 2009 invited Richard Heinberg, a forceful exponent of the need to prepare for peak oil, to give a presentation. After this event Transition Stroud initiated a council sub-group on peak oil and climate change.

"But we should be doing much more on housing," complains Philip. "We've only just realised how much power town and parish councils have to make things happen around energy efficiency and renewables." This power stems from the Sustainable Energy and Climate Change Act, which empowers councils to do more on these issues.

Philip explains how they tried to use Kirklees District Council's Warm Zones scheme (see pages 117-18) as a model. Unfortunately SDC was unwilling to borrow the money to finance a similar scheme, even though it is eventually self-financing. It has also rejected plans for a £7 million 'revolving energy fund' to give householders loans for solar thermal energy. "But we are still working on them," says Philip hopefully.

## Stroud Eco-Renovation Open Homes

www.stroudopenhomes.org.uk

Stroud District Council has funded 'Target 2050', a £300,000 project to create a range of exemplar retrofitted homes, put extra money into renewables and, in 2009, agreed to back a second Stroud Open Homes event. The idea is simple. People who reduce the carbon footprint of their homes by improving energy efficiency or installing renewable energy open their homes to visitors who learn directly from the experience of real people in real homes. There are no entry charges.

In 2008 Stroud Open Homes had 11 properties open over the weekend. "It was a great success,' said Philip,

"but after all the work that went into that weekend I swore I'd never do it again without some funding. So in 2009 we managed to get £1,500 from SDC, £500 from the Town Council, and Ecotricity paid for the leaflets, which is probably another £1,000."

In 2009, with a "fantastic effort" from Helen Royall, who coordinates the event, over 20 homes were involved. In 2010 the event focuses on eco-renovations and is designed to give visitors the clear message that this is something they can and should be doing.

Leaflet for the Stroud Eco-Renovation Open Homes event in 2009.

Homes that took part in 2008 are joined by many of the 'exemplar' homes from the Target 2050 project. "The real challenge is how to move on from a weekend where people look at things to actually getting them to do stuff," says Philip. Motivating factors include follow-up support and solar clubs, where people get together and buy discounted solar panels – a practice common elsewhere in Europe but unusual in the UK. In 2009 visitors were asked to make pledges on everything from installing insulation or swapping to a green electricity supplier, to installing solar technologies. "How to make it everyday normal? That's the problem," says Philip as we leave the cafe.

## Tranquility House

www.tranquilityhouses.com

One home not in the Stroud Open Homes programme was the Tranquility House. It was included in 2008 but not in 2009. Why?

"Tranquility is a really important building," says Philip. "It raises all sorts of important issues that need to be discussed, like the solar room on the south of the house and computerised air flow. But our event wasn't the right forum and in 2008 some visitors felt disempowered by the cost and complexity of the building rather than inspired. It's also a new and very expensive building, so far less relevant to most people's concerns than the retrofits we want people to emulate." His concerns are understandable, as other reports mention visitors being given hour-long lectures. My initial request to visit Tranquility was met by an offer to discuss the matter 'on neutral territory', and my subsequent email agreeing to this went unanswered. In contrast to the friendly welcome and collaborative spirit that marks Open House events around the country, Tranquility seems characterised by secrecy and the desire to plough a lone furrow. But it is a

fascinating building and I was sorry not to see it during my time in Stroud.

## Springhill Cohousing

www.therightplace.net/coco/public

"We have a quota of fourteen cats. That's seven per acre," explains Max Comfort. "Dogs have to be interviewed with their owners to make sure they won't be a danger, particularly to the children who live here, or bark too much. Dogs have to be interviewed but the humans are self-selecting," he adds with a wry grin.

This is Springhill, the first new-build cohousing development in the UK and a model that many groups have tried to repeat, though so far without success. Max, one of the founding residents, shows me round and explains their policy on pets. All the main problems with cohousing seem to begin with a 'P'. Parking, parenting and painting are the other three, but monthly meetings for residents, training in conflict resolution and general goodwill solve most disputes.

As we saw in Chapter 5, cohousing is intrinsically more sustainable because residents share facilities. At Springhill residents have the choice to eat communally three evenings a week, so one large kitchen is used rather than 15 to 20 small ones. While many of the 50 or so adult residents do own a car, there is ready access to a car club and a lot of informal car sharing. Built in 2004, the timber-frame houses are well insulated and had photovoltaic panels installed as part of the build. Many residents have since added solar thermal water heating.

But at Springhill sustainability is about community as much as about energy. Communal areas host a variety of activities: here residents socialise, and verandas overlook walkways, so people interact as they walk past each other's houses and everyone looks out for each other. "It's like Neighbourhood Watch but nicer," said Max. It's certainly a safe environment for the 25 children who live here, but there's something more. Another resident, Lee James, has three children. He told me: "My children have good relationships with people of all ages and from all sorts of backgrounds. They regularly have conversations and interact with neighbours they've grown up with and are more confident people because of that. It's a great environment for kids."

## Not affordable

Springhill residents own their own homes or rent from one of the owners. The freehold is held by a jointly owned company and residents have 999-year leases. Initial build costs were much higher than anticipated and this is not 'affordable' housing. Furthermore, so many people want to live here that there's an estimated 15-20 per cent premium over local property values. Not surprisingly, the community, well mixed in other respects, is overwhelmingly white and middle class.

"That's a challenge for cohousing,", admits Max. "How can we build genuinely mixed communities and integrate affordable housing?" The answer may be in plans by Gloucestershire Land for People to develop the nearby Cashes Green Hospital site, where half the development will be cohousing and half of that will be affordable. Land for People is currently negotiating with English Partnerships to develop the site.

Another challenge is the age mix. "Thundercliff Grange, a cohousing project in Rotherham, is so popular that nobody leaves. Consequently the residents have all got old together and it's becoming an elderly population. How can that be addressed other than when residents start to die off?"

Max believes there's a real place for cohousing in communities built to Code for Sustainable Homes Level 6 (see pages 161-2). "Managing the infrastructure associated with that level of renewable energy works best in the cohesive communities you get with cohousing." He's probably right, but establishing communities like Springhill is not easy. Max and others regularly host visits, speak at meetings around the country and support dozens of cohousing groups around the UK. But in the five years since Springhill was completed only one other group, Halton near Lancaster (see pages 78-80), is set to develop new-build cohousing.

Part of the problem is money. The Springhill site was purchased by one resident who had the funds to act quickly, buy the land and transfer ownership to the cohousing group that formed later. Max believes the best option is a small core group to drive projects forward, but says there needs to be new funding routes available. He discusses some of the possibilities on page 174.

Another problem is suspicion about what is still an unusual form of housing development. The initial planning application for Springhill was rejected because one councillor argued they were "dead weird . . . were going to eat together, would be bulk-purchasing and dragging furniture across the park at night"! It was also difficult to find a contractor and other professionals who understood and were sympathetic to cohousing.

## How was Springhill financed?

Springhill was originally the brainchild of one man, David Michael, whose deposit of £150,000 for the one-hectare site was enough to persuade the vendors to accept his £500,000 offer in the summer of 2000. David skilfully negotiated a contract where full payment and exchange of contract would wait until completion. He quickly gathered a group around him who became directors and shareholders in a limited company that was to own the site. By September some 15 households had signed up, each buying £5,000 in company shares. By March 2001 21 households were involved, with plot fees ranging from £36,000 for a five-bedroom house to £18,000 for one-bed flats. This repaid David's deposit, covered the balance required to purchase the site and established a fund to cover professional fees and administration costs. Unfortunately, at the eleventh hour, the vendors claimed other purchasers were interested and proposed a 'sealed bids' sale. This was avoided by agreeing to pay an additional £50,000.

A year later, after a few problems, planning consent was granted. Traditional 'self-build' mortgages were not possible because the houses would be leasehold, so negotiations began with Triodos Bank for a commercial loan to cover the build cost. Eventually the necessary money came from the Co-operative Bank, which was far more helpful. As soon as funds started to be drawn, the householders began sharing interest payments, with amounts varying with plot size. It soon became clear that the estimate of £70 per square foot for build costs was very optimistic: the final cost was £4.2 million – £120 per square foot.

While recognising the importance of David Michaels' "drive and determination, financial savvy and imagination" Max Comfort is keen to emphasise that Springhill did not happen because of a fairy godparent with deep pockets. "This is inaccurate and could deter other projects," says Max. "Lancaster cohousing group have just exchanged contracts and they had no benefactor."

## The Open Homes weekend

The best thing about Eco Open Homes events is the range of buildings to choose from and the easy access to homeowners who have become experts in the eco-renovation of that type of house and are keen to share their experience. As Philip Booth put it: "This is all about giving people the chance to see, touch and hear at first hand from homeowners about their eco-renovations: the highs and the lows, what worked and what didn't." But until I set off to visit a selection of these homes on my bike I had no idea about the major drawback to the 2009 Stroud event. All the open homes seem to be at the top of mountains!

## A farm far away!

Jane and David Godsell at Far Westrip Farm are in the programme because they've installed a wood-pellet boiler. I can see their farm in the distance when a helpful local man points it out, but somehow I have cycled to the top of the wrong mountain and must descend past clusters of beautiful Cotswold stone cottages and fields with grazing sheep before struggling up another steep lane.

Far Westrip certainly has a wood-pellet boiler, and David Godsell explains how it is far more efficient than his old oil-fired boiler – and we agree there's something obscene about the fact that it would actually be cheaper to burn grain than wood pellets. But there's a momentum about lowering carbon footprints, and the Godsells have also fitted solar thermal and photovoltaic panels as part of the Target 2050 project. David shows the meter running backwards as the PV produces more electricity than they are using.

Like many householders in the project, the Godsells believe they could have got better deals from suppliers not on the approved list of installers, but Severn Wye Energy Agency is addressing that problem by adding more installers to the list.

Adjacent to the wood-pellet boiler is the kit David uses to make biodiesel from used rapeseed oil. It costs him about half as much as white diesel and he has no problem with the supply of raw materials or their quality. A hundred metres from their farmhouse a pole supports a wind monitoring device and, if average wind speeds are high enough, they hope to install a wind turbine. See what I mean about momentum!

## A stone house in Stonehouse

Simon Pickering owns a listed building in nearby Stonehouse, downhill all the way from Far Westrip! Many of the visitors have similar listed houses and want to learn about internal wall insulation and secondary double glazing. Some discover that what Simon says won't work for them, while others leave satisfied that his solutions are appropriate for their own situation.

That afternoon, at the energy fair where local installers display and explain their products, I meet Simon again and ask why he opened his house to visitors. "Because we were asked and because it's a good idea," he answers. "People see the difficulties but also the ease with which some of the problems of dealing with listed buildings can be overcome." He explains that conservation officers are twitchy about changes to listed buildings, so you have to give them confidence that you are not going to do anything outrageous. "Then they are fine; mildly ineffectual, but fine."

Simon is another Target 2050 householder, and now uses far less energy than predicted for the changes they made. "It's probably the way we live," he suggests. "We set the thermostat to 18 rather than 21 and that makes a big difference." I later discover that Simon worked for several years on Bird Island in

Antarctica, where he studied declining populations of Wandering Albatrosses. It helps to explain why 18 degrees is perfectly acceptable to Simon, whereas my own partner, who was born and grew up in Bangladesh, regularly threatens to leave me whenever I turn the thermostat below 21!

## New house retrofit

Paul and Clare Sheridan live in a new development, grace the front cover of the event brochure, took part in the Stroud Open Homes weekend in 2008, are both active in Transition Stroud and, to cap it all, Paul works for Severn Wye Energy Agency (SWEA). They live in a modern detached house on which they have mounted solar thermal and photovoltaic panels. "You'll find us easily," Paul told me. "Just look for the house with all the panels on the roof."

Visitors examine solar thermal and solar PV panels on a retrofitted house in Stonefield. Photograph: Philip Booth

Why are they taking part again? "It was great fun last year," replies Clare. "We got a lot of feedback suggesting that people would make similar changes themselves and we also made a few new friends!" In 2008 the couple opened their home for the whole weekend, but in 2009 they wanted to visit a few homes themselves so were opening only for the Saturday morning.

Paul's experience of working for SWEA on the Target 2050 project confirms many of the lessons from Eco Open House events. Out of 190 applicants for Target 2050, 20 were selected with the aim of reducing their carbon emissions by 60 per cent. Up to £6,000 was available to each home as match funding, plus other grants. The 20 participating households have already spent an additional £50,000 on improvements and this will rise as more installations are completed. The project is on target to achieve the 60-per-cent reductions and establish a range of exemplar homes.

"The crucial lesson, and this crops up time and time again," says Paul, "is that people are looking for lessons from a home just like their own. That's why we ensured there was a range of solid-walled houses in Target 2050 and Eco-Renovation Open Homes. There are just so many houses like that in this area."

### Internal or external cladding?

At the top of Bisley Road (Bisley Mountain!) are two open homes that really demonstrate the value of this event. Both are Edwardian solid-walled houses in the 'hard to treat' category and both have loft insulation and double glazing. Neither is a listed building, so they had a choice of internal or external insulation. Nick and Carol at number 44 chose external insulation, while Dave and Fiona at number 18 opted for internal insulation. Both had good reasons for their choice, on the basis of the detail of their homes, and it is precisely this detail and experience that is so valuable to other householders.

## More than just books from the library

One of the spin-offs from Stroud Open Homes is the availability of home energy monitors from local libraries. Gloucestershire County Council funded the trial scheme, administered by SWEA, and it now operates in nine libraries across the county.

Lewisham was probably the first council to make energy monitors available through libraries, where they can be borrowed just like a book. Three weeks is long enough for householders to monitor energy use, discover just which items gobble up the power, and remind themselves about appliances left on standby. In Lewisham an average 70 per cent of monitors were on loan at any one time, and the council increased the number available to 40.

## Conclusions

- Change gathers momentum. A farmer installs a wood-pellet boiler and gets interested in other renewable energies, local people rescue part of their architectural heritage and then have the confidence to challenge the wrecking balls in defence of other buildings. The Open Homes weekend goes from strength to strength, a few Green councillors exert influence way beyond their numbers and one cohousing development inspires others.

- Perhaps Philip Booth's question about how to make sustainable housing the norm is already being answered by the actions of people in Stroud. After all, as Plato said: "The beginning is the most important part of the work."

# CHAPTER 10

# NEW TRICKS WITH OLD BRICKS

*"There is no question that there is some unsettling times in the housing market."* With no apologies to George W. Bush

The Empty Homes Agency, a campaigning charity that highlights the waste of empty property and works to bring it back into use in a sustainable way, estimates there are 650,000 empty homes in England. Around 300,000 of these are empty for more than six months, and 150,000 could easily be returned to use.[1] English Partnerships, now part of the Homes and Communities Agency, estimates that 400,000 residential units could be created in empty commercial and industrial units. Together these provide a huge supply of potential new housing.

But do we want to use inefficient old buildings rather than build new homes? There's a lot of information available about the carbon emissions of housing, but relatively little about emissions from building a house in the first place. It's often assumed that replacing old homes with new eco-homes is the way to save energy. This view is encouraged by the media, which sees new build as 'sexy' and newsworthy; and by developers, who profit more from demolition and rebuild than from refurbishment. Even bodies such as Oxford University's Environmental Change Institute, in its report on the '40% House', makes a case for over three million house demolitions by 2050.[2] It's easy to think that new is good and old is bad, but research by the Empty Homes Agency suggests otherwise.

## Smaller footprint for refurbished houses

The research, published in 'New Tricks with Old Bricks',[3] compares three new builds with three comparable refurbished houses. Bath University produces data on the embodied energy of building materials, and a quantity surveyor was used to calculate the amounts of materials needed for each build. This showed that the average new build resulted in 50 tonnes of $CO_2$ emissions, compared with just 15 tonnes for the refurbished homes. Most of this difference came from the retention of existing foundations, brickwork and masonry – all energy-hungry materials.

National Home Energy Reports were compiled for each home to assess ongoing energy use. While the new-build houses were slightly more efficient, the difference was so small that it takes decades – usually more than 50 years – for the new homes to make up for their higher embodied energy costs. All the evidence suggests that the earlier we reduce carbon emissions the more impact it will have on global warming. This weighs the scales heavily towards refurbishment, since the initial benefit is a saving of 35 tonnes of $CO_2$ over new build. And the research did not take account of demolition, the disposal of building waste, the environmental impacts of mining and quarrying, water use, habitat loss or the pollution associated with many building processes. Around 24 per cent of all waste is generated by construction and demolition, so these are not inconsiderable impacts.[4]

The government stresses the importance of refurbishment. Planning Policy Statement 3 says: "Conversions of existing housing can provide an important source of new housing. Local Planning Authorities should develop positive policies to identify and bring into residential use empty homes and buildings." And 'Homes for the Future', a report from the Department for Communities and Local Government, states that "We . . . need to make the most of existing homes and buildings."[5]

## VAT discrimination

Yet VAT regulations in the UK discriminate against refurbishment. New build homes are zero-rated, while refurbishments are charged at 17.5 per cent. The 'New Tricks' research showed the average refurbishment cost to be 39 per cent less than the average new build – a saving that would be greater if differences in VAT were eliminated.

Homes empty for more than two years incur a 5-per-cent rate of VAT for refurbishment. This did not apply to any of the case studies in 'New Tricks'; had it done so, it would have reduced the average cost of the refurbishments by approximately £10,000. Refurbishment costs on some homes empty for more than ten years can be zero-rated, but this applies only to material costs for DIY projects, or possibly where the resulting home is purchased by a social housing provider.

## Spot the empty home

There are nearly a million properties empty in the UK, a problem highlighted by BBC television in January 2010. *Britain's Empty Homes* followed Empty Property Officers, whose job is to get empty buildings into use. The programmes ranged from neglected historic buildings and mansions in Belgravia to derelict inner-city terraced homes.

The Empty Homes Agency website offers excellent advice on how to find empty properties and report them to local authorities. It even gives advice on how you can purchase and develop these properties yourself. Many empty homes are in relatively good condition. A study commissioned by Kent County Council in 2005 showed that the average cost of returning empty homes to a habitable state was about £6,000.[6] A similar study, commissioned by the Greater London Authority, found the cost to be just over £12,000.[7]

There are many good examples of housing refurbishment. Hill Paul in Stroud (see pages 136-7) is an example of an industrial building refurbished as housing, while many of the flats in Sheffield's Park Hill Estate (see page 177) were empty when refurbishment began. Other examples of unused buildings are not so obvious.

## LOTS more potential homes

Living Over The Shop (LOTS) is an idea for identifying unused property above shops and bringing it back into use. It has the advantages of reviving town centres and reducing crime, because new residents overlook streets. The idea first became popular in the 1990s, but projects frequently foundered because of a perceived incompatibility between residential and commercial activity. In England a 2001 survey of 370 buildings by

Chichester District Council found that 21 per cent had empty spaces. Of these, about two-thirds were suitable for refurbishment, with the potential to create accommodation for 275 people.[7] The scheme was relaunched by the Northern Ireland Housing Executive in 2007, when grants of up to £30,000 were made available towards conversion costs. There was so much interest that funding soon disappeared.

## Hidden homes

Southwark Council in South London has a 'Hidden Homes Initiative' to identify wasted property on its council estates. Unused laundries, garages, storage areas and rent offices, identified with help from residents' groups, are converted into homes at roughly half the cost, and considerably less carbon, of new build. Twenty-five new homes have been created.

One problem is the lack of designers with experience of this type of conversion. On the plus side is the fact that many sites are at ground level and are therefore particularly suitable for people with disabilities, who need level access. Another 300 potential sites have been found, but the council lacks money to develop them. Its solution is to develop some, including those with river views, for sale, and use the profits for more social housing. In 2009 Southwark had a housing waiting list of 15,000.

## Squatting – an environmental duty?

Bringing unused property back into use is inherently sustainable, as it prevents the decay of buildings and reduces the need to build new houses. But mechanisms for local authorities to identify and reclaim unused homes are far from effective. Squatting can fill the gap.

Squatting consists of occupying an abandoned or unoccupied space or building, usually residential, that the squatter does not own, rent or otherwise have permission to use. Robert Neuwirth, an author who lived with squatters in Africa, South America and Asia, claims there are one billion squatters globally.[9]

In many countries squatting is a civil rather than a criminal offence, and squatters often have a positive effect on the properties they occupy. In Berlin it is called *instandbesetzen*, a combination of words for renovating and occupying.

In the Netherlands, an empty building unused for 12 months, where the owner has no pressing need to use it, can be legally squatted. The only illegal aspect would be forced entry. There are squatters 'conversation hours', with advice from experienced squatters, and 'unofficial' squatting is discouraged. Some residential squats eventually achieve a legal status. Poortgebouw in Rotterdam was squatted in 1980 and two years later the residents agreed to pay rent to the city council. They are still there today. In Denmark the 'free' community of Christiania still exists, nearly 40 years after local residents first occupied the abandoned military barracks.

In Britain squatting has been a form of radical direct action since the Levellers and Diggers of the seventeenth century. There was a huge squatting movement involving homeless ex-servicemen and their families after the Second World War, when thousands of people occupied sites as diverse as former military bases and luxury apartments.

Squatting was popular in the 1970s, particularly in London, and often led to squatters being rehoused or reaching agreements with local authorities. The Advisory Service for Squatters maintains an active

Black Thursday is a small organisation but is able to capture media attention through actions like this high-profile squat in a luxury Paris mansion. website: http://squattercity.blogspot.com

website, advertises fortnightly advice sessions, and regularly updates the *Squatters Handbook*. It even has archive pictures of the London Squatters Union banner, held up by Jeremy Corbyn, a Labour MP and one of the few who increased his majority in the 2010 election, and by his brother Piers, now better known for his arguments against anthropogenic climate change.

## Building conversions

We've all seen those episodes of *Grand Designs* where a couple turn an old factory or water tower into a stylish home. A cohousing group has done it with a hospital in Sussex (see page 77) and Land for People hopes to do the same with Cashes Green Hospital in Stroud (see page 140). Converting buildings is much better than knocking them down, and the bigger the building the more energy and materials are saved by avoiding demolition.

## Squatting with class

In October 2009 a £13 million mansion in one of Paris's most exclusive areas was squatted to highlight the lack of affordable housing in the city. The seventeenth-century mansion, once the home of Isadora Duncan, was occupied by the French squatters' group Jeudi Noir (Black Thursday – Thursday is when newspapers print ads for places to rent), until a court ordered their eviction in January 2010.

The squatters, including students, a lawyer, architects and a pianist, pointed out that the mansion had been unoccupied for more than 40 years and the owner has a string of sumptuous properties, including an estate on the Riviera, hunting grounds in Sologne, and land in the Arcachon basin in the south. She also has another luxury town house behind the Musée d'Orsay in Paris. Meanwhile over 1.2 million people are on waiting lists for social housing.

Interestingly, the 87-year-old owner had tea with the squatters and went away satisfied with their treatment of her property. It was her family who persisted with court proceedings.

## Greenhouse in Leeds

www.greenhouseleeds.co.uk

The Shaftsbury Hostel in the Beeston Hill area is a former workers' hostel built in the 1930s. Until 1998 it was used to house single homeless people. It's a large and monolithic building that once accommodated over 500 people. It's also listed.

The building lay empty and derelict from 1998 until 2004, when the Leeds-based developer Citu identified it as a potential site and worked with Leeds City

Council to develop Greenhouse: "a scheme aimed at championing the regeneration of the Beeston Hill and Holbeck area as well as setting a benchmark for sustainable development".

The aim was to achieve BREEAM (Building Research Establishment's Environmental Assessment Method) 'Excellent' (see page 164) and, if possible, a carbon-neutral building achieved through using ground source heat pumps fed from an 80-metre borehole, solar thermal water heating and wind turbines. There are also plans for an off-site wind turbine nearly 100m high (a feature that makes it one of the tallest structures in the city), an electric car-share scheme and electric shuttle.

Chris Thompson, director of Citu, said: "What makes Greenhouse unique is that not only is it a 'green' development by building standards but the groundbreaking technologies it uses are aimed at ensuring sustainable living by changing residents' behaviour patterns."

Each resident can view utility and media bills from their TV, so they see their energy use translated into carbon emissions and – crucially – pounds. This helps people to focus on reducing their carbon footprint and ultimately changes behaviour.

Apartments are fitted with A$^+$ appliances and water-efficient taps and showers. There's access to allotments, secure cycle storage, and during the build 90 per cent of waste materials were recycled. As well as homes, the development has offices, a cafe and leisure facilities. The £27 million scheme, creating 172 homes, is expected to save 169 tonnes of carbon and 3.8 million litres of water a year compared with a conventional development. Citu claims this makes it around 60 per cent more efficient than an average new build . . . but do the sums and you'll find the saving is only around 1 tonne per home per year.

To be fair, Citu doesn't claim this development is going to save the planet. Its sales material reads: "Greenhouse may not save the world, but from small seeds great ideas can grow."

The Greenhouse is certainly popular. Phases 1 and 2 were sold off-plan and, with prices starting at £59,000 for a studio flat, it is relatively affordable.

## Roscoe Towers

I know it's exciting to watch concrete tower blocks being demolished. A few carefully placed explosives . . . BANG . . . a massive collapse and then just a cloud of dust and a pile of rubble. But what a waste of embodied energy! Two 1950s tower blocks on the Roscoe Street Estate in Islington demonstrate a clear alternative. The towers were refurbished by the Peabody Trust and ECD Architects with high-performance double glazing and external insulation giving a 60-per-cent reduction in $CO_2$ emissions and an enormous saving in the energy that would have been required to build replacement homes.

The UK and Europe abound with derelict factories, unused military barracks and empty hospitals. Two initiatives, Cabernet and Rescue Europe, look at good examples of reusing these buildings and developing brownfield sites (see www.cabernet.org.uk and www.rescue-europe.com).

## Urban regeneration

There are hundreds of neighbourhoods, particularly in inner cities, that have been neglected for generations. Can these communities be regenerated rather than demolished?

## Pathfinder – a missed opportunity?

The government's Housing Market Renewal 'Path-finder' programme to 'revitalise communities' where declining population, derelict and abandoned homes and poor services are leading to deteriorating social conditions was launched in 2001. Nine communities in the North and Midlands were identified and a total of £2.2 billion allocated for a mix of refurbishment, demolition and new build. Unfortunately, as the example of the Toxteth Street Neighbourhood in Manchester shows, real opportunities have been squandered.

Plans to redevelop the area, often used as a background for dramas such as *East is East, Life on Mars* and *Coronation Street*, were first unveiled in 2001. In 2005 Manchester City Council approved outline plans by New East Manchester and Lovells Partnerships for demolition and redevelopment, and the resulting shadow of compulsory purchase and demolition took its toll. By March 2007 over 70 per cent of homes were empty and sealed. Over 500 Victorian terraced houses were due to be demolished, but the remaining community fought back and, in collaboration with the campaigning organisation SAVE Britain's Heritage, won a public inquiry into the compulsory purchase order (CPO). SAVE commissioned Brian Morton MBE, a leading structural engineer, to challenge claims that the houses were unsound. Morton said:

> "The existing houses are built to a surprisingly high standard . . . most are in good condition, and all are easily capable of refurbishment . . . I simply do not accept that surveys carried out in 2000 and 2005 indicated that 77 per cent of dwellings surveyed were assessed as unfit or defective."[10]

Morton believed the cost of refurbishment would be less than half the cost of demolition and rebuilding.

SAVE and Mark Hines Architects developed rival proposals with the support of local residents. These offered "a viable alternative to demolition and a fresh approach to rehabilitating terraced housing". The plans included prefabricated hemp 'overcoats' for the rear of the basic two-up/two-down properties. These provide space for a bathroom, a larger second room on the first floor, and vastly improved insulation. The rear yards were transformed into private and communal gardens, and landscaping on the street side provides a pedestrian-friendly environment without banishing cars. Family houses are created by converting two houses and gardens into one, and energy efficiency is improved by communal heat and power networks supplied by green energy.

> "Judged on community benefits, environmental impact and cost, rehabilitation and refurbishment are clearly the way forward. It is less

These prefabricated Modcell panels can be used for retrofit extensions to terraced housing as well as in new buildings. Photograph: Mark Hines Architects

Rockfield Road before refurbishment . . .                    . . . and after. Photographs: Affordable Homes Development Company

destructive, helps preserve the existing community, saves money and offers revitalisation without losing the enduring qualities of these characterful and much-loved terraced streets."[11]

William Palin, secretary of SAVE

The collaboration spawned a study looking at how existing terraced housing can be upgraded, which is being published as *Streets of the Future: Unlocking the benefits of terraced housing.*[12] Palin believes these ideas offer a model for how similar properties could be transformed across the country.

But Toxteth was not to be the crucible to test these ideas. Manchester City Council and the New East Manchester 'regeneration' agency identified the Toxteth Inquiry as a 'must win' case and invested heavily in making sure they won. The council admitted it had failed to take into account the environmental impact of demolition and refused to disclose figures for the cost of the redevelopment. Despite this, in February 2009, local residents and SAVE lost their bid to overturn the Compulsory Purchase Order and to save a community from the bulldozers.

Most residents have now moved but, ironically, the downturn in the housing market makes early redevelopment of the site unlikely. It's little consolation that SAVE's position is vindicated in a report on Pathfinder by the Commons Committee of Public Accounts, which warns of "a risk that demolition sites, rather than newly built houses, will be the Programme's legacy" and concludes that "the needs of those who wish to remain in an area should not be overlooked in developing more mixed and sustainable communities".[13]

## The Chimney Pot Park story

Communities that take decades to build can be destroyed by bulldozers in a few weeks, but communities are about a lot more than houses and, as Chimney Pot Park demonstrates, saving homes from demolition doesn't always save the community.

The *Salford Star* is an independent online magazine with 'attitude', written and produced by people in Salford and relying heavily on input from locals. It gives the community a voice; makes public bodies a bit more accountable; informs, campaigns and entertains . . . and it has its own brand of investigative reporting, which came close to winning the prestigious Paul Foot Award for Campaigning Journalism in 2007.

In August 2006 the *Star* published an 8,000-word account of the redevelopment of the Langworthy and Seedley area of Salford, an area close to Salford Quays and on the Metro route into Manchester City Centre.[14] The question it sought to answer was simple. Were houses being refurbished for the current community or were they future commuter homes for young professionals working on the Quays?

The developer, Urban Splash, had over 200 awards for its innovative urban regeneration projects. A *Guardian* supplement on 'Greener Housing' featured the eco-friendly remodelled terraced houses at Chimney Pot

Park,[15] and many types of council and housing associations place the 'Splash' high on the list when choosing a development partner. But is this reputation justified?

Nearly two thousand homes were remodelled by Urban Splash in Salford. The design literally turned the houses upside down, with living areas and kitchen upstairs and bedrooms below; a new balcony and terrace were added and energy efficiency greatly improved . . . and they were supposed to be affordable.

Hazel Blears posed for the cameras in Chimney Pot Park alongside Deputy Prime Minister John Prescott and Urban Splash chief Tom Bloxham. "These plans", announced Blears, "will create exciting, affordable homes and help boost the regeneration of Seedley and Langworthy". Bloxham himself mentioned a sales

Cutaway model showing the 'upside-down' designs used to retrofit homes in Chimney Pot Park in Salford. © Urban Splash

Chimney Pot Park terrace before refurbishment . . .                    . . . and after. Photographs: Urban Splash

figure of around £50,000 per house. Over £15 million of public money was spent, but what did Salford get for its money?

## Unaffordable homes

When the homes came on to the market, the average price was £120,000 plus another £5,000 or £10,000 to park – way above Salford City Council's own financial definition for affordable housing (£57,600, i.e. 3 x £19,200, the 'lower quartile household income' for the city). In fact the 'lower quartile' income of the area around the Urban Splash development was then £13,933, putting an affordable house for this community in the £42,000 realm. The average price of the Urban Splash houses was almost three times this figure. Despite all the hype, only a dozen houses were bought by local people. Even if local residents could stretch themselves financially, only seven out of the 108 houses that went on sale were priced at £99,950. The rest cost up to £146,000. The promises of politicians, spin doctors, developers and community workers were empty: houses were not affordable for people living in Seedley and Langworthy.

Yet large amounts of public money were poured into the scheme. Around £12 million came from English Partnerships and Pathfinder, with more from Salford City Council. A conservative estimate for the total amount of public money invested in the Urban Splash development would be around £15 million, but nothing in the agreement between the company and its public sector partners set aside properties for local people. In short, house owners were told that their houses were being demolished, only to see them done up by Urban Splash a few years later and put on the market for up to ten times what the council paid in compensation.

According to the *Star*, Urban Splash didn't pay anything for the land, relocating and compensating the existing residents, or getting the site ready for development. That's been done through a battery of public funding under titles such as 'Strategic Site Assembly', 'Strategic Investment' and 'Developer Support'.

During its investigation the *Star* found that much of the information around the project was 'commercially sensitive' and therefore confidential. Minutes were missing or marked 'not for publication', and even concerns by local councillors "relating to the increased purchase price of the houses being sold by Urban Splash, which Members felt are too costly for some local people" were omitted from minutes. The true nature of the financial arrangements between Urban Splash and Salford City Council is masked in secrecy. What is clear is that local people are angry at being moved out of their homes and community with little compensation and no chance to move back into the remodelled houses. Salford's affordable housing policy requires that 20-25 per cent of all new housing developments should be affordable, but even if some do become available they are likely to cost around £300,000 each in subsidy!

## VAT (again!) versus sustainability

New build is zero-rated for VAT, while refurbishment is rated at 17.5 per cent. The negative impact of this policy is clear from the changes it caused to the Salford redevelopment. The scheme was originally designed to use as much of the existing structure as possible, but was altered to ensure that the development qualified as new build. Rather than the existing party walls and first-floor structure being retained, they were demolished. VAT rules contradict the sustainability agenda and effectively create a subsidy for new build.

Demolition is also VAT-free and, since councils usually fund demolition at an overall cost of nearly £20,000 per home, this is another strong financial incentive for developers to favour new build.

The Sustainable Development Commission proposes equalising VAT rates for new build and refurbishment and imposing VAT on all demolition, to be paid by the organisation producing the replacement housing. Councils should no longer directly fund demolition.[16]

When pushed by the *Star*, Bob Osborne, Salford's Head of Housing, admitted: "It's never been about affordable housing *per se*. It's been about rebuilding the community . . ." This is reminiscent of comments made by the US during the Vietnam War: "Sometimes it's necessary to destroy a village in order to save it."

The *Star* quotes around a dozen residents, and the recurring theme is that local people are being forced out to make room for "yuppies who want to live in a chic and shallow version of Coronation Street". The following comment is typical.

> "I was ousted out of the Urban Splash houses because I lived on Reservoir Street. I got a Homeswap and was moved out of mine into another one. I'm not happy when I look at what they are selling them for and how much they gave me. I got £9,000 for my house, I got a valuation on my new one of £27,000, and I've got a balancing charge against the house of £18,000. If I sell my new one I have to pay that back . . . where's the swap? There is no swap."
>
> Susan Copeland, former resident of
> Reservoir Street, Salford

People complain about the profits made at their expense and about the injustice of being excluded from their former homes, but mostly they are concerned about their loss of community.

Since 2006 the *Salford Star* has been hit by loss of council grants and a decline in advertising revenue. The unpaid editor, Stephen Kingston, continues to investigate irregularities in the Chimney Pot Park development, Urban Splash is still getting large amounts of public money, and Salford Council and the Homes and Communities Agency are still making it difficult for people to find out what's really going on.

## Top-down versus bottom-up

William Palin, Secretary of SAVE Britain's Heritage, believes the key problem with Chimney Pot Park, Toxteth Street and many other Pathfinder developments "is that part of the stated aim is to get rid of the community . . . to rejuvenate the area by bringing in more 'economically active' people".[17] Palin also points to good examples of refurbishment carried out using Pathfinder money within existing communities. Just a stone's throw from Toxteth – so close you can almost hear the bulldozers – Manchester City Council is refurbishing the Ashton Road area, and in the Bensham and Saltwell area of Newcastle and Gateshead 1,200 homes are getting facelifts.

"The most successful schemes", says Palin, "are always driven from the bottom up, from the community, rather than top-down like Pathfinder, and often depend on simple things such as regular maintenance and unfussy upgrading and extending of properties." An evaluation of Pathfinder in October 2009 does show that refurbishments (37,571) outnumbered demolitions (10,133) across the nine areas.[18] Interestingly, there were only 1,200 new builds, suggesting that this process has stalled or that there are long delays between demolition and replacement. The ratio between demolitions and refurbishments is similar in information provided by Liverpool City Council in response to a Freedom of Information request, but this response also stated that there were over 1,000 new builds in the Liverpool area alone.

It's difficult to obtain overall data on how communities are affected by the refurbishments, but one criterion used to judge the success of the programme is a rise in house prices. These increased in Pathfinder areas by 70 per cent between 2003 and 2007, which may be good for owner–occupiers who remain in their homes but not for displaced residents priced out of their own community.

It's also difficult to establish what is meant by refurbishment. Pathfinder works with different partners in each of the nine areas, each of which is broken up into many different projects. Refurbishments are often 'facelifts' to front elevations, which improve appearance but have little impact on energy performance. Refurbishment to the government's Decent Homes Standard (see pages 164) does not even require a basic measure such as cavity-wall insulation.

## Conclusions

- We must defend the history and the embodied energy in our built environment.

- Local authorities can use compulsory purchase orders if they can demonstrate a 'compelling case in the public interest'. They have the power to purchase and refurbish unused buildings and derelict sites and we should encourage them to use these powers.

- We should draw attention to unused and under-utilised buildings and, if necessary, use direct action to bring buildings back into use.

- The key to using existing buildings in the most sustainable way is a well-organised community.

- VAT regulations undermine sustainability and we should campaign to change them.

# CHAPTER 11

# LAND, PLANNING PERMISSION AND FINANCE

*"Men and women lead, money follows."* With apologies to Anon.

On the A5 near Capel Curig in North Wales is Ty Hyll, the 'Ugly House', built under ancient law, when anyone who built a house between sunset and sunrise, with walls, roof and smoking chimney, could claim the freehold. It's no longer that simple, but there are ways through the legal, financial and organisational minefields.

The three main obstacles to developing sustainable housing are finding the land, meeting the requirements of planning consent and building regulations and, of course, raising the money. This chapter also looks in some detail at community land trusts and mutual home ownership, because these structures can provide a route through these obstacles.

## Land

A survey by Norwich and Peterborough Building Society found that 70 per cent of homeowners in the UK have considered building their own home but, despite this apparent enthusiasm, only 10 per cent of houses in the UK are self-build.[1] This contrasts with 48 per cent in France and 55 per cent in Germany. Why the difference? The answer is access to land. *Homebuilding in the UK*, a report by the Office of Fair Trading (OFT),[2] found that most large building firms own a strategic reserve of potential building land, equivalent to between three and seven times their annual output, which is drip-fed into the market. This may be partly for reasons of planning difficulties but there is a strong suspicion that it is also to keep land prices high.

Despite this, the OFT is not particularly concerned that 90 per cent of building land in the UK is swallowed up by firms building identical boxes. Meanwhile, self-builders who, according to the OFT's report, "adopt new technology earlier than speculative house builders . . . and tend to pay particular attention to the sustainability of their homes", are denied the land on which to build superior homes.

The result is starkly visible in Lloyd Kahn's book *Home Work: Handbuilt Shelter*.[3] This stunning sequel to the classic 1973 book *Shelter*, also by Kahn, show-cases the ultimate in human ingenuity, building construction and independent lifestyles. Over 1,000 photographs show homes from around the globe "built with soul, creativity, and designed with a solid understanding of natural materials, structure, and aesthetics". And there are scarcely any from the UK! So, where can you find land?

## Surplus public land

At any one time the government is sitting on around 3,000 hectares of land suitable for building – enough to build a town the size of Slough and have Betjeman turning in his grave. The military has another 1,600 hectares. The Homes and Communities Agency publishes a quarterly register of surplus public land and a list of what it confusingly calls 'smaller sites', which are frequently rather large. There are usually around 750 sites, listed by county, totalling around 5,000 hectares.[4]

## Taking the land – Portugal 1975

We are standing in the centre of a shanty town, rough shelters made of scavenged materials – cardboard, bent corrugated iron, torn plastic sheets. Raw sewage runs between crowded shacks and there is no sign of a water or electricity supply. Shanty town is the right term, although this isn't Africa, South America or Asia. This is Lisbon, a few months after the overthrow of the brutal Salazar dictatorship that ruled Portugal for over 40 years.

A man walks into the open space followed by a group of children, stands a rocket upright in a beer bottle, lights the fuse and steps back. After a few seconds the rocket shoots into the sky and explodes with a loud bang: the signal for hundreds of people to emerge from their shacks and gather in the open space. Some are carrying banners or placards, children wave flags, dogs run around barking. A megaphone appears and soon people are chanting. Among the familiar slogans of the revolution there are demands for land and homes.

The crowd becomes a procession and we march away from the shanty town, along a quiet road to a large and overgrown enclosure. Level concrete areas show where buildings once stood. People have occupied the land to build new homes with electricity, water, a sewage system, a place for children to play and space for people to grow a few vegetables and flowers.

A makeshift stage is erected and speakers address the crowd, now nearly a thousand strong. We have no interpreter but the joy and enthusiasm of the people needs no explanation. They cheer and clap and raise clenched fists and we do the same. The end of the dictatorship has released an energy they will use to build a new life for themselves, and they are starting with new homes.

Then the crowd falls silent as a line of army trucks and jeeps approaches from the road and turns into the field. It's not clear from the mood of the people what they are expecting. The vehicles drive over the rough ground and form a half circle around the crowd, soldiers jump from the trucks and mingle with the people. There are smiles, handshakes and embraces, crates of soft drinks are unloaded, children are given rides in the jeeps and the crowd relaxes again. This is the army, radicalised by a long war against liberation movements in Africa, which overthrew the dictatorship. They will not stand in the way of these people. One of the soldiers speaks through the megaphone and there are enthusiastic chants: "The workers and soldiers are united and will never be defeated."

Less than a year later the authority of the State is restored and the occupation of land is halted. But the people we marched with have already built their homes – sturdy structures with electricity and water and no sewage in the streets. They have taken the land and built a new future for their children and it's too late for anybody to take that away from them.

### Section 106 agreements

Section 106 agreements are negotiated by local authorities and can require developers to build a certain proportion of affordable homes as a prerequisite for planning permission. A 2006 report from the Joseph Rowntree Foundation[5] includes estimates that half of affordable housing in England is provided through these agreements. However, while some local authorities achieve as much social and affordable housing as possible, others have a poor record and sometimes homes agreed under Section 106 agreements are not actually delivered.

This arrangement also links affordable housing to the general housing market, so when private housing catches a cold, social housing goes down with pneumonia. Self-build housing, which operates independently of Section 106 agreements, is less likely to fluctuate with the rest of the housing market. It surely makes sense to break this unhealthy link.

### Other sources of land

For those of us without the support of a friendly army (see box, left) there are alternatives. You can still find land, with and without planning consent, advertised in local newspapers and specialist building magazines. There are also subscription websites listing self-build sites. You can find them on Google alongside complaints about the service they provide, so be careful what you sign up to.

For the lucky, or the diligent, there are friends, neighbours, local farmers and landowners who may be willing to sell you, or even give you, a plot. Advertise, knock on doors and get on the phone! Ideally you can shake hands on a deal or sign an option agreement to purchase the land at an agreed price if you obtain planning consent.

## Planning consent and building regulations

The complexity of planning laws and building regulations in the UK seems designed to create lucrative employment for expensive consultants who understand this impenetrable maze. It's hardly surprising that big developers have a head start over people who want to build one-off eco-homes or small

### Housing problems in Cornwall

"In the last 40 years the housing stock in Cornwall has more than doubled – faster than anywhere else in the country. Yet the housing problems of local people have got dramatically worse.

More house building has meant more second homes, more retirement homes, etc. Five times as many homes are sold to second-home owners as to first-time buyers.

. . . the planning system is fuelled more by greed than need. We need to rebalance the system to give the poorest in our communities the chance of finding affordable housing rather than continually feeding the desire of developers or those with large gardens to secure personal lottery wins through the planning system."[6]

Andrew George, MP for St Ives, Cornwall

George says planning permission should be required for change of use to a second home and that stronger controls on housing development are needed to deliver more affordable housing by undermining the 'hope value' for land that is inherent in the current system (i.e. sellers are encouraged to hold out for higher prices in the hope that they will eventually gain planning consent).

developments of sustainable housing. There are ways through the maze, but understanding the basics of the planning system is essential.

Significant details change with bewildering regularity, so a good place to start is the government planning portal, which outlines the system (www.planningportal. gov.uk/england/public/planning). Take a particular look at the guide to Local Development Frameworks (LDFs) and Development Plan Documents (DPDs). These, together with the Regional Spatial Strategy, outline local plans for the next 15-20 years, so it's important to be familiar with the overview for your area. DPDs, which are subject to community involvement and consultation, include a core strategy with a general spatial vision and objectives for local development, including site allocations, and a map showing areas earmarked for development.

## The DPD process

Influencing local policies can be crucial in laying the foundations for later sustainable development as well as in preventing harmful development. The Building and Housing Group within Transition Town Totnes, alongside other community groups, spent hundreds of hours responding to the consultation documents from the district council. Over 600 individual and group responses forced the council to backtrack on many of

Dot Reid, a 58-year-old grandmother, applied for planning permission to demolish the home of Tesco Boss, Terence Leahy, and build a community area with trees, a pond and play areas. Her application was to highlight plans to demolish her home and 70 others in order to build Everton's new football ground – and a new Tesco Superstore![7]

their initial proposals, and the final plans, although far from perfect, are more sustainable. So it's important to watch out for consultations on council policies and try to arrange a unified community response that includes parish and town councils, who are usually more responsive to local needs.

Plans formulated by the council after consultation must be submitted to the government's planning inspector, and representations can also be made at this stage. In 2010 the coalition government scrapped the Regional Spatial Strategy, and it is unclear at the time of writing what, if anything, will replace it.

## Rural exception sites

Development is not limited to sites outlined in the LDF. Local planning authorities can approve 'rural exception sites' for 'affordable' or 'intermediate' housing. These sites are defined in Planning Policy Guidance Note 3 as:

"small, solely for affordable housing and on land within or adjoining existing small rural communities which would not otherwise be released for general market housing. The affordable housing provided on such sites should meet local needs in perpetuity and count towards the overall level of housing provision".[8]

The definition of affordable housing is determined by a formula that takes into account local incomes and house prices. 'Intermediate affordable housing' is for people who can afford prices and rents above those determined for affordable housing but below market levels. This can include shared equity. Local planning authorities are likely to include other eligibility criteria, such as being on the housing needs register, or the length of local residency. There is a good argument for renaming 'exception' sites as 'local housing needs sites', to make clear that this is not a favour or an optional extra.

Several Community Land Trusts (CLTs) have obtained planning consent for developments as rural exception sites, as this model is particularly suited to ensuring that affordability is maintained in perpetuity. The earth-sheltered affordable homes at Honingham in Norfolk (see page 127) is an exception site.

This earth-sheltered housing in Suffolk was given planning consent as a rural exception site. Photograph: Jerry Harrall, SEArch Architects

## Not just apples

'Windfall' sites, usually on previously developed land (brownfield), are those areas not considered by the local planning process and therefore not included (or excluded) by the DPD. A study in Gloucestershire showed that, on average, 31 per cent of house building fell into this category, but that in Cheltenham over 90 per cent of all houses were built on sites not previously considered.[9] Windfall sites include buildings or locations that become available after a local plan is agreed – so expect a glut of car parks, garages and petrol stations that fit this category after we have moved beyond peak oil!

There is also a significant paragraph in Planning Policy Statement 7:

> "Very occasionally the exceptional quality and innovative nature of the design of a proposed, isolated new house may provide this special justification for granting planning permission. Such a design should be truly outstanding and ground-breaking, for example, in its use of materials, methods of construction or its contribution to protecting and enhancing the environment, so helping to raise standards of design more generally in rural areas. The value of such a building will be found in its reflection of the highest standards in contemporary architecture, the significant enhancement of its immediate setting and its sensitivity to the defining characteristics of the local area."[10]

This exception is more likely to justify one-off eco-mansions than significant numbers of sustainable houses, but may be useful in some circumstances.

Of course there is a lot more to making a successful planning application than just following the rules. Bob Tomlinson, who developed The Wintles (see page 100) and other sites, explains some of the subtleties.

## Building regulations

Don't confuse planning consent with building regulations. These set standards for the design and construction of buildings to ensure safety and health

# How to work with planning officers

**Bob Tomlinson, founder of Living Villages**

Remember that planning officers are busy people dealing with increasing amounts of paperwork within fixed budgets. They spend most of their time dealing with 'live' projects that are moving ahead, and therefore have little enthusiasm and energy for 'potential' projects that may never happen.

Planning consent is all about policy, precedence and 'planning law'. Opinion, common good, environmental benefit, social ethics and 'beautiful architecture' very rarely feature in the day-to-day realities of the process.

In order to impress the planning officer and be taken seriously you need to show understanding of the process and prove:

- ownership, or the ability to control the outcome, on the piece of land in question

- a valid case for consent

- that you have the resources, skills and determination to see the project through.

Spend time at the library or planning office looking at what the local policy is and at the maps that cover the areas allocated for development. Get a feel for what types of permissions are granted and where they are. If you decide the site has possibility, speak to a planning consultant. They are usually quite approachable and may give a 'free' initial consultation. This is the most effective way to find out if your plans have a 'hope in Hell'. If there is real potential, the consultant may agree to a deferred fee or find a way in which the project can pay its way.

Professional developers will employ a planning consultant to make the case for development on a given piece of land. This will be through a representation to the planners in some form, normally a letter with illustrative plans. The letter will effectively be a list of why the property in question should get planning consent, will refer to local planning policy and past precedent, and will begin to form a very non-emotional 'legal' case for development on the site.

If you apply for planning and get refused, the local authority must give reasons and cite relevant policy and

Bob Tomlinson at The Wintles in Shropshire.
Photograph: Bob Tomlinson

precedent. If you can show a clear case for permission on the site that they dispute you can appeal and a planning inspector will adjudicate. As with any court case, it will be the 'letter of the planning law' that decides the matter. Of course the law is often an ass. So:

- to get the attention of a planning officer, demonstrate that you have done your research and that you mean business

- make the case for your development, talk it through with the planning officer and rework the proposal if necessary

- go through the formal application and see if you can tick the boxes.

If you get this far the project is starting to get real, but getting permission is a long haul. If there are genuine possibilities, make your ideas visual. Descriptions, sketches and three-dimensional drawings are much better than plans and elevations now. Get to know local councillors and find out who might support your development. Show them the vision and listen hard to their advice. If there is strong support for an application that is borderline, then councillors on the planning committee can reject the planning officer's recommendations.

Remember that at the end of the day the planning officer is a public servant and will be aware of the 'popularity' or otherwise of the applications that cross his or her desk. If you have local support, this will help your case.

for people in or about those buildings. They also include requirements to ensure that fuel and power is conserved and facilities are provided for people, including those with disabilities, to access and move around inside buildings. In short, planning consent grants permission to build, while building regulations stipulate how to build. Separate applications and consent are required for the two processes. For minor building work, planning permission may not be required. Check with your local authority.

Technical requirements to meet the building regulations are covered by 14 'Approved Documents', Part A up to Part P. Part A, for example, covers structure while Part L, updated in 2006, deals with the conservation of fuel and power.

### Code for Sustainable Homes

Since 2008 it has been mandatory for all new homes to be rated against the Code for Sustainable Homes (CSH) – see www.communities.gov.uk/planningandbuilding. The Code, part of the drive to improve sustainability of new homes, targets $CO_2$ emissions and water use and includes mandatory requirements in many areas.

CSH has six levels and in 2006 the government published a ten-year step-by-step timetable. From 2016 all new homes must be built to Code 6 or 'zero carbon' performance. From April 2007 a minimum of Code 3 became mandatory on all English Partnerships and Housing Corporation developments. These two bodies subsequently merged to form the Homes and Communities Agency.

CSH awards points across nine categories, from which the final level is determined. The high weighting attached to energy and $CO_2$ emissions makes it almost impossible to reach levels 5 and 6 without using renewable energy systems. Notice that sustainable materials are covered, although this category has a weighting of only 2.2 per cent.

## Design categories under the Code for Sustainable Homes

1. Energy/$CO_2$. Minimise $CO_2$ emissions arising from the operation of the home. 36.4 per cent

2. Water. Reduce consumption of water in the home. 9 per cent

3. Materials. Encourage using materials that have less impact on the environment. 2.2 per cent

4. Surface water run-off. Ensure that peak run-off rates and annual volumes of run-off are no greater than the previous levels for the site. 7.2 per cent

5. Waste. Encourage the recycling of household waste. 6.4 per cent

6. Pollution. Reduce potential global warming from substances used in the manufacture or composition of building materials and reduce nitrous oxide emissions. 2.8 per cent

7. Health and well-being. Improve the quality of life in houses by including good natural daylight, sound insulation and private space. 14 per cent

8. Management. Covers use of the home, construction and security. 10 per cent

9. Ecology. Encourage development of land that has limited ecological value; minimise building footprint and protect existing ecological features. 12 per cent

Consultation on the Code ended in March 2010 and, at the time of writing, it is unknown whether lobbying by the building industry or the change of government in 2010 will weaken the requirements or delay implementation. Although there are many deficiencies in the Code, it is the first in Europe to acknowledge the importance of materials and biodiversity as well as strict energy criteria.

## Requirements for Code 6

(From 'Code for Sustainable Homes: A step-change in sustainable home building practice'.[11])

Zero net emissions from all energy use in the home. This could be achieved by:

- improving thermal efficiency of walls, windows and roof by using more insulation or better glass

- reducing air permeability to the minimum consistent with good health

- using a high-efficiency condensing boiler, or being on a district heating system

- designing the fabric of the home to reduce thermal bridging

- installing appropriate solar thermal panels, solar PV, biomass boilers, wind turbines and combined heat and power systems

- using no more than about 80 litres of water per person per day, achieved through water-efficient taps and appliances, and sourcing 30 per cent of the water requirements from non-potable sources such as rainwater and grey-water recycling systems.

Other minimum requirements:

- surface water management – including soakaways and porous paving

- a minimum number of materials meeting at least a 'D' grade in the Building Research Establishment's Green Guide (the scale goes from A+ to E)

- a waste management plan during construction and adequate space for waste storage.

In fact, a home must include 90 per cent of everything in the Code to achieve Level 6.

## Other building codes

Although only the government's building regulations have the force of law, there are also some excellent guidelines developed by organisations involved in sustainable building.

### CarbonLite

The Sustainable Building Association (AECB) developed CarbonLite (see www.carbonlite.org.uk), a three-step programme that AECB describes as "a unique combination of research materials, technical data, training programmes, discussion forums and useful links and contacts . . . an essential resource in the building sector's drive towards low-carbon living".

### Step one – Silver Standard

Silver Standard would probably be met or exceeded by the UK's top 20-50 housing projects using the best widely available technology. It does not push the technological boundaries radically forward but is a big advance on normal UK building practice. Good energy and $CO_2$ performance is achieved even without the addition of renewables or other 'bolted-on' equipment. The standard is achievable using products and materials available on the UK market at close to current building costs. AECB estimates a 70-per-cent reduction in $CO_2$ emissions.

The Stawell development in Somerset is built to Silver Standard. The homes use solar panels and wood-pellet stoves to ensure a healthy internal environment with low heating and electricity bills. Specially landscaped gardens support wildlife and provide residents with space to grow their own produce, and allotments are available. The terraced properties are a joint venture between the landowners and Ecos Homes Limited.

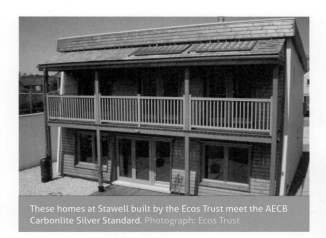

These homes at Stawell built by the Ecos Trust meet the AECB Carbonlite Silver Standard. Photograph: Ecos Trust

### Step two – Passivhaus

This is equivalent to the German Passivhaus Standard (see right), which has not been widely applied in the UK. Passivhaus maximises use of energy-efficiency technologies to achieve an 80-per-cent reduction in $CO_2$ emissions.

Overall, Passivhaus corresponds to best international practice in the design of building envelopes, their services and equipment. All the technology is in use somewhere in Europe or North America. The present leaders are Germany, Austria and Switzerland, where roughly 10,000 buildings meet the standard.

### Step three – Gold Standard

AECB Gold Standard is almost identical to Passivhaus but has stronger requirements for efficient electrical appliances and more electricity-producing capacity. $CO_2$ emissions would be just 5 per cent of those of a normal UK building. Using the Gold Standard should encourage the manufacture of similar technologies in the UK. The Pines Calyx conference centre in Kent (see www.pinescalyx.co.uk) is an example of the Gold Standard.

A big problem with many building standards is the reliance on theoretical rather than actual performance. AECB addresses this through a database of low-energy buildings with monitored energy data. This is a resource for those wanting to understand more about the design and operation of low-energy buildings and to find out what works and what doesn't. Take a look at www.acb.net/cbpd/cbpd_index.php.

> Building standards for domestic refurbishment were launched by the Building Research Establishment (BRE) in summer 2010. The new standards, which identify opportunities to improve the environmental performance of existing homes and set criteria for measuring effectiveness, will be available through the BRE website, www.bre.co.uk.

### Passivhaus

There are nearly 20,000 buildings constructed to the Passivhaus standard worldwide, but only a handful in the UK. A dwelling that achieves the standard typically includes very good levels of insulation with minimal thermal bridges, optimal use of solar and internal heat gains, excellent airtightness and good indoor air quality provided by a mechanical ventilation system with heat recovery (see www.passivhaus. org.uk). A Passivhaus does not need a traditional heating system or active cooling to be comfortable. The small heating demand can be met by a compact unit that integrates heating, hot water and ventilation.

For Northern latitudes, including Europe, a dwelling is deemed to satisfy the Passivhaus criteria if energy demand for space heating and cooling is less than $15 \text{kWh/m}^2/\text{year}$. A typical new-build house in the UK would use around $55 \text{kWh/m}^2/\text{year}$. The total primary energy use for all appliances, domestic hot water, and space heating and cooling must be less than 120kWh/m²/year.

A Passivhaus in Kranichstein, Germany, has been occupied since 1991. In summer the inside temperature on the top floor never exceeds 26°C (79°F), even when outside temperatures are 35°C, while in winter, when the outside temperature is -10°C, the heating system isn't needed.

## Other standards

You may also find reference to some other standards.

All property owned and managed by councils and other social landlords must meet the government's **Decent Homes Standard**, which requires homes to have reasonably modern facilities and to be warm and

This development at Dunnon includes the first Passivhaus project in Scotland. The building on the right has thicker layers of insulation in the roof and reaches the Passivhaus standard.
Photograph: Scottish Passive House Centre

weatherproof. Further details are available from www.homesandcommunities.co.uk/decenthomes.

The Buildings Research Establishment's Environmental Assessment Method (**BREEAM**) is a widely used set of standards for assessing a building's environmental performance. BREEAM Ecohomes was used for residential buildings but has now been replaced by the Code for Sustainable Homes. Other BREAAM categories are still widely used for commercial buildings.

## Raising the funds

Raising money from financial institutions for sustainable housing in the UK almost inevitably means discussing the relative merits of the Co-operative Bank, Triodos Bank and the Ecological Building Society. These names crop up whenever housing projects around the country that are a little bit different – and sustainable housing is still in that category – talk about finance. So what do they offer?

These flats in the eco-community of Vauban, in Freiberg, Germany, reach Passivhaus standard.
Photograph: Tim and Kate Birley

## Co-operative Bank

With 9 million customers, 12,000 employees and assets of £70 billion, Co-operative Financial Services, which includes the Co-op Bank, dwarfs other ethical lenders in the UK. In 2009 it merged with the Britannia Building Society, and "green mortgages that are kind to the planet" are a growing part of its business.

So what are 'green' mortgages? One aspect is the percentage from the Co-op's mortgage business used to fund 'climate care' projects. In 2008, £330,000 was used to fund reforestation in Uganda, fuel-efficient stoves in Cambodia and human-powered water pumps to replace diesel pumps in India. According to the Co-op, these projects offset around 50,000 tonnes of carbon emissions – equivalent to a 20-per-cent reduction in household emissions for each of its mortgage holders.

Another aspect is the availability of 'energy-efficient advances' for existing mortgage holders – effectively a mortgage extension specifically for energy-efficient home technologies. The approved list ranges from insulation up to renewable energy systems such as solar thermal, photovoltaics and even small-scale wind and hydroelectric installations.

## Triodos

Triodos takes pride in lending only to "organisations which create real social, environmental and cultural value, charities, social businesses, community projects and environmental initiatives . . . which benefit the community, care for the environment, respect human freedom and develop individual talents and capacities." Furthermore, as part of its commitment to transparency, it publishes details of all lending, so you can judge its ethical credentials for yourself.

Using the 'Know where your money goes' facility on the Triodos website you can find specific projects it has funded. This means you can search for projects similar to your own as precedents that have won financial backing. You can search by sector – housing brings up over 50 schemes, mainly housing associations and cooperatives – or use a map to find projects in your part of the country.

In 2009 Triodos loaned over £2.3 billion, up from just £386 million in 2004, and there are nearly 14,000 borrowers with average loans of around £130,000.

## Ecology Building Society

Back in 1979 a Yorkshire solicitor was having difficulty getting a mortgage on a property needing renovation. The subject came up at a Green Party meeting and someone suggested starting a building society. In those days it was possible to start with just £5,000. Ten people put in £500 each and the Ecology Building Society (EBS) was registered in December 1980, commencing trading in March 1981 from a tiny upstairs office in West Yorkshire. The initial vision was a building society specialising in properties with an ecological benefit in terms of construction, use of land or lifestyle.

Thirty years later, the EBS has assets of over £80 million and mortgage lending of around £13 million per annum – much smaller than Triodos or the Co-op but vital for projects unable to find money elsewhere. Mortgage applications are judged against EBS criteria, which assess the environmental impact of the project in terms of energy use, pollution and saving resources. Features encouraged by the Society include:

- easily recyclable materials
- use of reclaimed stone, brick, slate or timber
- locally sourced materials
- high levels of insulation
- efficient condensing boilers
- double or triple glazing

- natural paints
- water recycling
- renewable energy systems.

The EBS often lends on properties turned down by other lenders, tries to be flexible and will release funds 'up front' on the unimproved value of a derelict building, releasing further funds as the building work proceeds and property value increases.

Projects often involve support for vernacular building styles, using locally available materials, modern low-impact building technology and the rescue of buildings no longer suitable for their original purpose. So EBS lends on cob and wattle-and-daub as well as on modern timber-frame properties and buildings such as redundant lighthouses, pumping stations and mills. EBS financed Cumbria's first earth-sheltered dwelling and Hockerton Housing Project (see page 110).

## BuildStore

BuildStore, the 'National Self Build and Renovation Centre', has a financial arm that offers an 'Accelerator Mortgage', which, it claims, has enabled over 13,000 people to build their own house. Accelerator is an advance stage mortgage.

## Norwich and Peterborough Building Society

The Norwich and Peterborough Building Society also has a mortgage designed for self-builders and a 'Green' mortgage where it offers £500 cashback for energy-efficiency measures and plants 40 trees when you sign on the dotted line.

## Rootstock

An example of the mutual aid central to housing cooperatives is Rootstock, the ethical investment arm of Radical Routes (see page 85).

## Self-build mortgages

According to the Office of Fair Trading, about one third of all mortgage lenders in the UK provide self-build mortgages.[12] The main difference is that money is released in stages as the project progresses.

With arrears stage payments the money is released once each stage is completed and a valuer has visited the site. This can create cash-flow problems. An arrears stage mortgage can be up to 75 per cent of the total land value and 75 per cent of construction costs, so self-builders need hefty cash reserves available at the beginning of the project, usually raised by selling an existing home and renting or living on site during the build.

With advance stage mortgages, payments are released at the beginning of each stage, which allows for a positive cash flow throughout the build. Up to 95 per cent of total costs can be borrowed, which, combined with the advance payments, makes it possible for self-builders to stay in their current home while building.

One alternative may be a short-term bridging loan, with the level of borrowing based on equity in the existing home and the ability to pay the monthly interest payments. Bridging loans usually last for about three years.

Despite a lower failure rate than that of conventional businesses, housing cooperatives are often discriminated against by banks because of a lack of familiarity with the concept. To counter this, Rootstock has made almost 40 loans to member cooperatives since 1991. Totalling nearly £600,000, these loans have been used to 'top up' bank loans and as 'leverage' for a further £1.5 million from other sources to help finance £2 million-worth of property. During this time only two co-ops have failed while owing money to Radical Routes.

As a lending record this is impressive, and most banks show a higher failure rate. Success is partly because Rootstock lends only to member co-ops and only when other member co-ops agree to the loan. The best people to assess a cooperative project are those from similar projects, rather than bank managers with virtually no experience of co-ops. This type of peer-group lending, also used by some banks, reduces the loan failure rate as well as the costs of assessing loans.

Getting money from Rootstock is not an easy option. Applications take up to nine months and are scrutinised to ensure that loans go only to genuine, fully mutual organisations; every co-op in the network must agree to every loan; and borrowers must participate in the network or risk expulsion and the recall of the loan.

But there are also advantages. Co-ops in crisis may be given loan repayment holidays; and free mediation, help and advice are available if experience is lacking in new co-ops or in established co-ops whose membership has changed.

Money comes from people who purchase shares in Rootstock Ltd. These can normally be withdrawn subject to notice and are repaid at their nominal value, together with accrued interest. Rootstock stresses that

> Of course there's a lot of 'greenwash' from companies eager to cash in on the 'green' pound, so shop around and look beneath the surface of whatever the financial institutions tell you. And remember that keeping debt to a minimum is a key part of your personal sustainability.

investments should be seen as a means of furthering the aims of Rootstock and not primarily as a source of financial gain. Reserves of around £40,000 have been built up to cushion any future losses.

## DIY finance

Many sustainable developments are initially funded through the generosity of supports. Cloughjordan (see pages 209-11), an eco-village in Ireland, raised initial funding in loan stock from the friends and families of members. Loan stock is issued by a company in return for a simple, fixed-interest loan not secured against its assets, so depends on a degree of trust. The land purchased in Cloughjordan increased in value after planning consent was obtained, enabling community members to obtain commercial funds and repay the initial loans.

## Financing refurbishments

In 2008 the Ulster Bank and Solar Century introduced the UK's first solar mortgage. The product, available for existing and new customers in Northern Ireland, offers discounted borrowing for photovoltaic technology as well as full management of supply and installation through an arrangement with Solar Century.

Following the introduction of feed-in-tariffs for photovoltaics from April 2010 and the possibility of a renewable heat incentive for solar thermal, a number of companies are looking at 'pay as you save' schemes to fund renewable energy. In December 2009 the Conservatives announced plans to work with companies such as Tesco and Marks & Spencer to finance domestic renewable energy systems with paybacks from savings on energy bills.

Braintree Council in Essex worked with British Gas to promote energy-efficiency measures through council

Solar panels installed by Solar Century.
Photograph: Solar Century

tax refunds. The scheme was so successful that British Gas rolled it out to over 70 councils as part of its Carbon Emissions Reduction Target obligations.

The Energy Saving Trust is piloting a 'Home Energy Pay-As-You-Save' project to look at paying for retrofits by spreading the cost and offsetting against energy bill savings. The pilot programme tests consumer interest in this style of financial package and involves local authorities, landlords and energy suppliers. Around 400 homes are testing four financial models.

Grant funding is available for communities planning sustainable energy projects, such as biomass-fuelled district heating systems, from the National Energy Foundation's Communities Fund. The charitable fund, launched in 2009, is designed to help communities overcome the financial barriers that stop community-led projects getting off the ground.

Grants for domestic retrofitting and renewables change regularly, but the Energy Saving Trust (see www.energysavingtrust.org.uk) has all the information you need.

## Community Land Trusts

Community Land Trusts offer a structure for providing affordable housing that helps overcome some of the difficulties in finding land, gaining planning permission and raising money. To understand their role it's worth looking at a few examples.

### Stonesfield Community Trust

www.stonesfieldcommunitytrust.org.uk

In recent decades many people have come to see their homes as investments rather than primarily as secure and comfortable places to live. Rising property values; the sales of council housing, which began with the Conservatives under Thatcher; and the perception that it is vital to 'get a foot on the housing ladder' encourage this tendency. Housing becomes a matter of profit rather than of social need, with increasing numbers of people unable to reach that first rung, or to access increasingly scarce social housing.

Rising property prices have a particularly destructive effect on village and market town communities. Stonesfield, a small village in Oxfordshire, saw local people unable to afford houses that were "bought up by middle-aged, middle-class investors who don't need a village shop, don't need a bus service, don't need a primary school, don't need a pub, don't even need a church."[13] So in 1983 Stonesfield became the first place in Britain since Letchworth Garden City in 1903 to establish a Community Land Trust (CLT) to provide permanently affordable housing. Tony Croft, a local activist, donated land on condition that the homes remained affordable in perpetuity, and this principle opened the doors to further community support. A local businessman donated £3,000 to register the Stonesfield Community Trust and to negotiate planning permission. Interest-free loans were obtained from local supporters and the Quaker

Housing Trust. By 1990 the Trust surmounted local objections and built six homes. A few years later it developed a second site with five homes and then a third project with three more homes, workspaces and a post office, which the Trust describes as "the heart of the community". All the properties are well insulated and relatively inexpensive to heat.

By 2005 the first loans were repaid and net income from the Trust's property is now used to fund a local youth service. In a few years' time the Trust will be spending £40,000 per year for community purposes in the village.

## What are CLTs?

A CLT is a mechanism for the democratic ownership of land by the local community, which enables long-term affordable and sustainable development. By separating ownership of the land from its productive use, the value of any public investment, philanthropic gifts, endowments or development gain is captured in perpetuity. In the case of low-cost housing the CLT can either dispose of the freehold but retain its interest as an 'equity mortgage' or grant a long-term, leasehold interest. Both models enable purchasers to obtain a mortgage and give the CLT the right to purchase the property back, at a price defined by a resale formula. This gives the owner a percentage share in equity built through their ownership and improvements, but not the full market value. CLTs are therefore able to re-sell the property at an affordable price or to rent it below the market rate. By taking profit out of the equation affordability is retained and the value of any original bequest is preserved.

## A brief history

The ideas behind CLTs can be traced back to the Chartists and Cooperative movements of the nineteenth century and, even earlier, to the trusts that steward almshouses. Letchworth Garden City, founded in 1903, influenced Gandhi, who promoted a movement that saw over a million acres donated to rural land trusts in India. Next stop for this viral idea was the US Civil Rights movement, where Martin Luther King established CLTs to give poor black people access to land. In the US there are now over 250 such projects.

After Stonesfield showed the relevance of this model for housing in the UK, others followed. Fordhall Farm, where thousands of supporters saved a historic sustainable farm by funding a CLT to purchase the property, is a high-profile example. In Scotland hundreds of the 'community buy-outs', including the Isles of Gigha and Eigg, use a CLT model, and in England there are numerous case studies on the Community Land Trusts website (www.communitylandtrusts.org.uk).

## High Bickington Community Property Trust

www.highbickington.org

Stonesfield may give the false impression that the road for CLTs in rural areas is clear. The experience of High Bickington, however, shows there are plenty of potholes and long diversions.

This small parish in North Devon has a population of around 800 people. In 2000 the Parish Council and High Bickington Community Property Trust began a new form of 'Community Led Planning', which resulted in the High Bickington Parish Plan 2003-2023. The first phase centred on a farm declared surplus to requirements by Devon County Council and included affordable housing, workspaces, a new school, community buildings, recreational facilities and a community woodland of 3,000 broadleaf trees planted by over 100 volunteers and schoolchildren.

High Bickington residents get down to business at their AGM.
Photograph: David Venner, High Bickington Community Property Trust

The plan was as good as it sounds and was approved by Torridge District Council in 2003. Then things started to go wrong. The application was referred to the Government Office for the South West, on the grounds that it was a departure from the Local Development Plan. A Local Public Enquiry was held, after which the planning inspector recommended refusal, a decision endorsed by Ruth Kelly MP, then Secretary of State for Communities and Local Government.

Despite this setback High Bickington, working in partnership with Devon County Council and Torridge District Council, remained determined to meet the community's needs and aspirations. This determination was shared by more than 200 local people who became members of the Trust, and the project received extensive financial support from public and charitable sources.

In 2009 a revised application with less housing was again approved by Torridge District Council and this

time the Secretary of State decided not to intervene. The 'people's plan' for High Bickington won full planning permission for 16 'affordable' homes; 23 homes plus the former farmhouse for market sale; 6 workshops for local businesses; a new 120-place primary school; and community and sporting facilities fit for the twenty-first century.

High Bickington "faced numerous hurdles that have often been placed in our way by the very governmental departments and agencies that say they want local communities to get involved in planning their own future."[14]

After nine years of struggle against bureaucracy the people of High Bickington have started phase one and undoubtedly hope for an easier path with phases two and three!

Tree planting team at work in High Bickington. Photograph: David Venner, High Bickington Community Property Trust

## Birmingham Eco Hub

Don't think that CLTs work only for small villages in the English countryside or remote Scottish Islands. You can't get any closer to the centre of a big city than Digbeth in Birmingham, but that's where a mixed 'demonstration' development is proposing to use the CLT model.

The project, a collaboration between Accord Housing Association, Birmingham Friends of the Earth, Land for People, Birmingham Cooperative Housing Society, Localize West Midlands and Joe Holyoak Architects, involves 18 affordable homes, 6 workspaces and the protection of a wildlife area that has sprung up on the unused land.

The small site is adjacent to *The Warehouse*, FoE's complex of buildings that house a vegetarian cafe, wholefood store and bicycle shop. The two developments will form an 'eco-hub' for Birmingham's Green voluntary sector, so, not surprisingly, the proposals include a high level of energy-efficiency and renewable energy.

The site is owned by Birmingham City Council, which is reluctant to gift or sell to the CLT at a low price until it has seen a full business plan. Jon Morris from Localize, one of the many professionals giving time to the project, explained that the group has been exploring Mutual Home Ownership (see pages 173-4) and has a draft business plan ready to go back to the council.

"I suspect", said Jon, "that the council will want us to go to the Homes and Communities Agency for funding, as this would enable us to pay for the council site. We have a development model they should be interested in but following this route would mean

## Funding for CLTs

In 2008 Community Finance Solutions (CFS), based at Salford University, joined with the Tudor Trust, Esmee Fairbairn Trust and Venturesome to launch a Community Land Trust Fund to which communities in England can apply. The £2 million fund supports fledgling projects and aims to remove obstacles such as difficulty in accessing professional and technical skills to prepare development and business plans, and poor access to risk capital and bank finance.

The fund offers support in four stages. First comes a day of consultancy to assess the feasibility of an idea. Second, once a CLT is established, the fund provides up to £2,500 for professional support to take the project forward. In the third stage up to £4,500 per unit of housing is available to fund the costs of working up a development proposal, submission of a planning application, procuring construction and raising further finance for the project. In the fourth stage, CLTs with a full business plan and planning consent can apply for a loan to supplement private finance to fund the building work.

See www.cltfund.org.uk

more bureaucracy, more hoops for the project to jump through and more delay."

### Legal status

A definition of a CLT was included in the Housing and Regeneration Act 2008, so they are now recognised in law and by government:

> "A Community Land Trust is a corporate body which:
> 1) is established for the express purpose of furthering the social, economic and environmental interests of a local community by

## Reviving community ownership in England: where do Community Land Trusts fit in?

**Bob Paterson, Ashoka Fellow supporting Community Land Trusts**

Community Land Trusts are not a new concept but are enjoying a recent revival. Providing small-scale community-led housing and other community-owned assets, they build on a rich tradition of common ownership.

Inspired by the success of the movement in the United States, Community Finance Solutions at the University of Salford launched a demonstration programme in 2006/7 across England and were able to help CLTs get started, provide them with the tools to succeed and influence national policy. Three years later they are supported by the main political parties and there are 20-30 CLTs and over 150 homes in the pipeline.

If CLTs are to grow in number and reputation, they must show they can achieve national policy objectives and assist in the process of civic renewal in partnership with other organisations they overlap with, including the Transition Towns movement. Here is the case for arguing that the CLT model advances these goals.

### 1. Durably affordable housing for all

CLTs are committed to making housing affordable for income-eligible households, to maintaining the affordability in perpetuity and/or ensuring that capital receipts are recycled within the local community. CLTs can be particularly significant in rural areas in the drive to rescue villages from a 'slow death'[16] and to secure a sense of ownership of the future of a community.

### 2. Fighting asset price inflation

Land and house price inflation are the enemies of sustainable communities and affordable housing. Mechanisms must be found to mitigate the 'boom and bust' model. CLTs help by holding land value out of the market, helping to provide a resilient community-owned social enterprise model.

### 3. Genuine value for money

CLTs are often compared to housing associations, which are the traditional affordable housing providers. Given the likely reduction in public grants and the increasing emphasis on self-provided housing the current mainstream model of producing affordable housing is unsustainable. CLTs are not trying to compete with housing associations but do provide complementary and supplementary provision in areas where there is a need. In addition, they provide the extra security of being backed by the community, which can result in discounted land, labour and other professional costs.

### 4. Place shaping – more than just housing

CLTs also deal with employment, food security, local amenities and renewable energy – community well-being outcomes that local authorities are obliged to deliver.

CLTs can especially contribute to the regeneration of rural areas by re-engineering farm-based businesses and giving new life to redundant buildings and land.

In urban communities residents are demanding a bigger stake in deciding their future. They see themselves as joint leaders, and sometimes joint owners, in local regeneration strategies, and expect to benefit from rising local land values. Tenant-led initiatives are now a standard part of the local authority stock options process, and this can be expanded to include CLTs.

### 5. Empowerment

CLTs enable citizens to work and live together and to meet local needs in a socially active setting, grounded in sound traditional systems of long-term land and property ownership and management. They are not a risky venture or an optional luxury but part of an emerging movement of citizen action.

### What's next?

CLTs have moved from a small group of pioneers to the beginnings of a sector. They punch above their weight in influencing public policy, taking advantage of current political consensus in favour of community-based development. They build on and revive traditional notions of cooperation, community spirit and self-help to improve society and help those in need. Various aspects of CLTs appeal to parties across the political spectrum and politicians, lawyers, architects and many others are eager to associate themselves with this new activity. The story so far shows how much can be achieved. Although there are many barriers and hurdles to overcome, there is great potential for CLTs to continue to flourish and spread in the UK.

acquiring and managing land and other assets in order:

- to provide a benefit to the local community
- to ensure that the assets are not sold or developed except in a manner which the trust's members think benefits the local community.

2) is established under arrangements which are expressly designed to ensure that:
- any profits from its activities will be used to benefit the local community (otherwise than by being paid directly to members)
- individuals who live or work in the specified area have the opportunity to become members of the trust (whether or not others can also become members)
- the members of a trust control it."[15]

A variety of legal structures can be used. In the UK the most common are Companies Limited by Guarantee and Industrial and Provident Societies for Community Benefit. Community Interest Companies and other existing legal entities such as housing associations, development trusts and even parish councils can fulfil the same function as long as the key features of capturing the enduring value of land as an asset for present and future generations and ensuring democratic local accountability are maintained.

## Mutual Home Ownership

Mutual Home Ownership (MHO) is a new form of tenure designed to meet the aspiration of people with moderate incomes, normally excluded from the housing market, to have an equity stake in their home. The model has been successfully used to finance affordable housing developments in the US. This outline is based on a guide from CDS Cooperatives.[17]

The key to a successful and affordable MHO scheme is to make land available at no cost to homeowners. MHO residents pay for building costs but not for the land, which is transferred into the ownership of a CLT, which holds it in perpetuity for the provision of affordable housing in its community.

Residents interested and eligible for the housing, which often falls into an intermediate rather than strictly affordable category, join an MHO Trust (MHOT) registered as an Industrial and Provident Society. This is important for two reasons. First, a mutual housing organisation is excluded from statutory tenancy provision, and therefore is free to use a tenure that gives residents an equity stake through a contractual lease. Second, any payment of equity growth to residents when they leave is tax-free in the same way in which increases in capital value are normally exempt from capital gains tax.

The CLT grants the MHOT a lease of the land at a peppercorn rent. The trust then works with a development partner such as a housing association or private developer, who agrees to build the housing for an agreed price. Finance for this is a standard development period loan. When the housing is complete the trust obtains a long-term corporate mortgage – cheaper for residents because it avoids individual arrangement and transaction fees and evens out interest-rate changes.

The value of the development owned by the MHOT, i.e. the housing but not the land, is divided into units worth, for example, £1,000 each, funded by residents through their monthly mortgage payments. Residents must take up and finance units according to their income and ability to pay, typically around 35 per cent of net income. As their income increases they can take up more units if available.

Members are also expected to make a personal financial commitment of 5 per cent of their equity stake as a cash investment in the trust. This payment, similar to the deposit on a conventional purchase, is security against arrears.

The lease sets out occupancy rights and responsibilities and establishes the right to equity payment when residents leave. This payment is based on a market valuation of the property and on the number of units funded by the member. Ten per cent of this increase is

## New funding models for cohousing

### Max Comfort, architect and Springhill resident

Springhill in Stroud (see pages 139-140), completed in 2004 and much visited by would-be cohousers, is still the only completed new-build cohousing project in Britain.With its social and sustainability benefits – security for families, more affordable lifestyle and community cohesion – there are many people desperate to do cohousing. So why are other projects not being developed?

There are several answers to that question: difficulty in finding sites, backward planning committees, lack of government infrastructural support and, primarily, problems with raising the money.

Springhill happened through the drive and determination of its members, but also because they had money or access to it via a mortgage. It is an undeniably capital project and now, on the rare occasion that one of its properties comes on the market, it sells for a 15-20 per cent premium over 'ordinary' homes in Stroud.

Given that most of us active in cohousing believe that its future should combine mixed tenure, and affordability and ideally be based on a Community Land Trust, how can money be raised for the three big hurdles: purchasing the site, paying the professional fees and funding the build?

One way is a partnership between those genuinely committed to doing cohousing (there are many content merely to talk about it) and more enlightened financial institutions – the Co-op and Triodos, for example. If a group of would-be cohousers put down £10,000 for each household (Springhill members stumped up

Springhill cohousing under construction.

£5,000 ten years ago) and if the bank added to this to create a Cohousing Site Purchase Fund, then the problems of securing sites when they come briefly on the market would be overcome.

The bank would own the site until the cohousers were able to sell their properties and raise the site purchase capital.With the initial facility paid off, another could be established for the build and associated fees, with the site as collateral. This is what happened at Springhill, with excellent support from the Co-op. To guarantee affordability, the site-owning company could rent out some of the properties it had built, paying off the building cost through rental income.

Finally, I encourage those organisations with the means to pilot such new ideas to follow the example of the Springhill pioneers, to abandon 'wait and see', climb down off the fence, take a risk and put their weight behind supporting more cohousing projects.

retained by the MHOT, to strengthen its finances and to create an asset reserve. So if a member is financing 40 units initially worth £1,000 and these increased in value by 50 per cent over the period of occupancy, the member would be paid a tax-free equity payment of £18,000.

Incoming members are accepted on the basis of their inability to buy a home on the open market and of other criteria, for example key worker status. The equity stakes purchased from the member who has just left go to existing members, who can afford to increase their stake because their income has risen, and to the incoming member. So the system gives members an equity stake in their home but, because the land is held outside the market by the CLT, affordability is recycled from one generation of occupants to the next.

## Other legal structures

There isn't room to discuss all the various legal structures here but fortunately the Bodhi Eco-Project, a Scottish group aiming to build a community producing no waste and no carbon emissions, has researched the options – see www.bodhi-eco-project.org.uk/Docs.[18]

## Conclusions

- Access to land, money and planning consent is much easier for the big developers, but that doesn't mean we should give up – there are plenty of success stories to show what's possible.

- People who have already made the journey are generally willing to advise those who follow, so talk to them.

- Working with others is helpful, particularly if you can tap into the support available to CLTs.

- Financial institutions can help, but don't neglect 'self-help' options such as the loanstock used by Cloughjordan or the solution developed by Radical Routes.

- Be aware that the demands posed by regulations and guidelines can push you in the direction of high-tech solutions, and don't forget that low-tech materials can meet these demands in a more sustainable way.

# CHAPTER 12
# SUSTAINABLE HOUSING IN SHEFFIELD

*"In those old days, when weather was fine, it was luxuriously fine; when it was bad – it was often abominably bad, but it had its fit of bad temper and was done with it – it didn't sulk for three months without letting you see the sun, – nor send you one cyclone inside out, every Saturday afternoon, and another, outside in, every Monday morning."[1]*

With no apology required to John Ruskin

## Remade in Sheffield

Both Sheffield and Rome are built on seven hills and, while this industrial town may not be steeped in history to quite the same extent as Rome, Sheffield was once responsible for most of the cutlery on our tables. 'Made in Sheffield' was stamped into millions of knives, forks and spoons, as Sheffield's cutlers supplied a large part of the world. Now, under the slogan 'Remade in Sheffield', this city of over 500,000 people is regenerating its housing.

## John Ruskin in Sheffield

John Ruskin, the collector, art critic and social activist, had a strong connection with Sheffield and in 1871 established a museum here for working people. He also wrote extensively on architecture and made many observations that now seem remarkably prescient. In *The Seven Lamps of Architecture* (1849) he wrote: "When we build let us think that we build forever"; and in *The Stones of Venice* (1851): "We require from buildings two kinds of goodness: first, the doing their practical duty well: then that they be graceful and pleasing in doing it."

Ruskin was quoted by Ebenezer Howard, who wrote *Garden Cities of Tomorrow* – a work that led to the building of 'garden cities' such as Letchworth and Welwyn Garden City, and influenced the design of cities as far away as Canberra in Australia. These promote Ruskin's ideas on town planning, which require "gardens to each home and country air in walking distance".

Perhaps the most prophetic of Ruskin's observations were on climate change. In 1870 he painted a panorama of the Alps along with comments about receding glaciers. In 1884 he published *The Storm Cloud of the Nineteenth Century*, about ominous changes in weather patterns.

Finally, Ruskin was no passive observer. His personal motto was 'Today', and he urged people to act before it's too late.

In 2009 Sheffield City Council was awarded 'Homes for the Future' Beacon Council Status for "their excellent performance in delivering high quality, sustainable new housing."[2] Along with Bolton, Greenwich and St Helens, Sheffield was tasked with providing support and examples of best practice for other councils to learn from. In October 2009 the council held an open day with visits to new-build and refurbished housing in various city locations.

## Regeneration of listed buildings

The most prominent example of Sheffield remade is Park Hill. Built between 1957 and 1961, this was the most ambitious and renowned inner-city housing redevelopment of its time. Residents were moved from slum clearance sites into nearly 1,000 council homes built as a community, with shops, pubs and a school. Viewed from our twenty-first century perspective, this is an unappealing concrete jungle; the only colour provided by coarse graffiti and the endearing 'I luv u will u marry me' spray-painted across a wall. But throughout the 1960s and 1970s the 'streets in the sky' of Park Hill were extremely popular.

Unfortunately the unemployment and lack of invest-ment typical of the Thatcher years sent the estate into decline. Unemployment, crime and social deprivation made Park Hill less attractive, and many properties became empty. These problems did not detract from the architectural importance of the site, and in 1998 it was listed as Grade 2*, which made it one of the most important, and the largest, listed building in England.

In 2002 Sheffield City Council formed a strategic partnership to regenerate the site and create "a sustainable, vibrant, mixed-tenure estate with owner occupation, rented and affordable for-sale properties along with high-quality retail and commercial premises".[3] Existing residents were promised priority to return to the estate and played a role in procuring the Great Places Housing Group as the registered social landlord responsible for affordable housing for rent and sale.

In October 2007 Urban Splash gained detailed planning consent to take the building down to its listed concrete skeleton and refurbish it to create 900 homes, new health and community facilities, shops, bars, an art gallery and other attractions. The aim is to make Park Hill a place to visit as well as to live in.

The first phase will be complete in October 2011, and it remains to be seen if this project avoids the gentrification seen in the Urban Splash redevelopment of Chimney Pot Park (see pages 150-2). However, agreements made with residents and their consistent involvement suggests a better outcome. Around 200 residents have asked to move back when work is complete and, according to the planning application, 200 homes will be available for rent.

One of the original successes of Park Hill was the community achieved by moving neighbours from slums into adjacent properties. One of the key lessons Sheffield City Council claims to have learned in recent years is the importance of involvement from long-standing residents keen to remain in the area. Without this community engagement, attempts to rebuild the 'streets in the sky' could well be just 'pie in the sky'.

## Refurbishing terraced houses

Page Hall is an area of 500 densely packed terraced houses in the Burngreave and Fir Vale Housing

Market Renewal area. Many houses fall way below 'Decent Homes' standard (see page 164) but proposals to demolish the area met with strong opposition from the community, which has a large black and minority ethnic population, who wanted the homes upgraded rather than demolished.

Local people argued for regeneration projects that encouraged individual owners to invest in their own properties. The council responded by launching showcase refurbishments of five empty 'hard to treat' solid-walled properties.

The aim is to demonstrate what can be achieved, transform the run-down image of the area, attract new residents and kick-start regeneration. Architects were invited to submit entries for a competition with four categories, as follows.

- 21st Century Terrace, demonstrating a city living / urban loft concept.

- Eco Terrace, with substantially reduced carbon footprint and installation of solar heating, photo-voltaics and mechanical heat recovery and ventilation in an airtight property.

- Twice the Terrace, with two properties remodelled into one larger home.

- The Healthy Terrace, concentrating on meeting lifetime health needs.

In October 2009 the Eco Terrace and Twice the Terrace were complete and open days and exhibitions planned. Training and information sessions were available to local people to explain insulation grants, the Low Carbon Buildings Programme and aspects of renewable energy. Although the houses will eventually be sold, a DVD of the project is available to provide ongoing education.

These exemplar projects are not without faults. For example, Twice the Terrace was not fitted with solar water heating despite the fact that this would be far more effective in a large house designed for many people than in the small Eco Terrace. Few of the fittings are designed to reduce water use, and kitchen designs do not encourage recycling. However, all the refurbishments make huge improvements in energy efficiency, with the Eco-House moving from an F energy rating to just short of A rating. And it happened because local people said no to demolition.

## Norfolk Park Homes

Many of the buildings in Sheffield's housing stock have been demolished. These include hundreds of flat-roofed houses of an unconventional design not easy to refurbish and, in the Norfolk Park area, 15 tower blocks. But part of this site has been redeveloped with 47 affordable homes that meet Eco-Homes Very Good standard, equivalent to Code for Sustainable Homes level 3 (see pages 161-2). The houses share a system for sustainable urban drainage as well as parking places with power supply for a future electric car-share scheme, and Sheffield's efficient tram system runs nearby.

On 1 November 2008 Councillor Bob McCann, Cabinet Member for Housing, cut the ribbon to open the estate, while Councillor Shaffaq Mohammed, Member for Climate Change and the Environment, planted a tree; the car club was launched and the future looked bright for Norfolk Park. But all was not well. By 28 November *The Guardian* reported that the Environment Trust, which developed the site in partnership with the council, had

These Norfolk Park homes were built by the Environment Trust before it went bust. Photograph: Sheffield City Council

failed to sell any of the Norfolk Park homes and had gone bust. According to *The Guardian*, "The credit crunch has claimed one of the UK's oldest and most innovative community housing and regeneration charities."[4]

The Environment Trust's liquidation also put an end to a novel purchase scheme designed to keep the Norfolk Park homes affordable in perpetuity. Under the scheme purchasers would have paid 70 per cent of market price, with 30 per cent retained by the Environment Trust, effectively as a second mortgage but with no interest payable. When properties were resold they would first be offered to the trust for sale to buyers nominated by the council and the trust. Since the homeowner owned only 70 per cent of the property he or she would be required to sell at this percentage of the market value, so ensuring a measure of affordability.

On completion of the scheme, the Environment Trust intended to hand over the freehold and benefits of any second charges to the Norfolk Park Development Trust, to manage for the benefit of local people. Unfortunately, despite an estimated 15 per cent drop in prices, there were no buyers for the Norfolk Park homes. The credit crunch and problems with Welsh Biofuels, a wholly owned subsidiary of the Trust, ended 30 years of action on environment and renewable energy projects, green homes, education and sustainable enterprises. It also put a stop to ensuring ongoing affordability for the Norfolk Park development.

## Sheffield's Free Insulation Scheme

Sheffield City Council, learning from the success and popularity of Kirklees Warm Zones (see pages 117-18), is offering free loft and cavity-wall insulation to all homeowners and private tenants regardless of age, income or size of property. The six-year scheme prioritises residents aged 70 or over and those on benefits or in fuel poverty, but includes many others.

Council tenants already receive free insulation under the 'Decent Homes' programme managed by Sheffield Homes – an umbrella organisation for tenants' and residents' associations. Housing association tenants are not eligible, but the council scheme places a great deal of pressure on housing associations to follow its lead. Councillor Paul Scriven says: "We don't think that anyone should have to make the choice between heating and eating during cold weather. The scheme will be rolled out to all residents, no matter what age you are or where you live."[5]

Much of the housing in Sheffield consists of solid-walled 'hard to treat' properties, where the choice is between internal and external cladding. In either case this is a far more expensive remedy than cavity-wall insulation. So far no council is supplying the necessary financial support to insulate more than a token number of such properties.

## Not just the council

Look around the 'City of Steel' and you find many examples of people making their homes more sustainable.

### Fireside Housing Cooperative

Fireside Housing Cooperative shares four adjacent houses just a mile from Sheffield City centre. This arrangement came about through a mix of obstacle and opportunity. Fireside began in 1997, with two individuals who wanted to meet their own housing needs. They raised loan stock from friends but failed to find a suitable property. Other people got involved and the group eventually purchased two run-down Victorian houses in a friendly multicultural terrace. Two more houses soon became available, so the cooperative ended up with four houses for a total purchase price of £89,000. Housing improvement grants of £90,000 enabled the homes to be insulated, and new double-glazed windows and boilers were fitted.

In energy terms these homes are far from exemplary. Terry Scully, one of the co-op's founders, explains that they are looking at solar water heating for one of the houses when money is available, and that a shared heating system was rejected because the expertise was not available locally. Lottery money was used for a wind turbine that was demonstrated at various festivals. Food is grown in the shared garden and recycling is well organised. Terry concedes that the six adults who share the houses with three children lack the commitment to spend more on insulation or renewable energy, because this would involve increasing the rent above the current £38 per week.

But in terms of meeting the social needs of residents Fireside is a success. Although the houses are run as separate units, there are doors through adjoining walls. Terry and his former partner, Helen, live in adjacent properties and share the care of their two children. If they had been living in conventional housing there would have been the usual difficulties of finding alternative housing and making arrangements for childcare.

Unlike many cooperatives, Fireside does not have a shared income scheme, but there are various ways in which wealth is redistributed between members. Only adults pay rent, so people without children effectively subsidise those with dependants. Water, internet and insurance bills are shared pro rata according to income, which favours those with lower incomes. " But the real benefit", says Terry, "is the opportunity for flexible and child-friendly living arrangements."

### South Yorkshire Energy Centre

Heeley City Farm grew out of a campaign by local people to develop a piece of urban wasteland into a thriving multifaceted project, which now supports 50 members of staff and hundreds of volunteers. There are training and work experience opportunities for

This refurbished building is home to the South Yorkshire Energy Centre. Photograph: Nick Parsons, South Yorkshire Energy Centre

The South Yorkshire Energy Centre organises regular events for children as well as for adults. Photograph: Nick Parsons, South Yorkshire Energy Centre

socially excluded young people and for adults with learning disabilities. Alongside Elvis the billy goat you'll find courses in basic numeracy and literacy for over-sixteens. You can learn English as a second language and then buy garden plants from the region's only peat-free nursery, feed the ducks and take a course in organic horticulture, woodwork or small animal care. And there are loads of activities for local children.

In 2005 a former bakery on the edge of Heeley City Farm came up for sale and Nick Parsons, who already worked on community energy and sustainable building projects, proposed eco-renovating the solid-walled building and using it as an energy advice and education centre.

Heeley City Farm bought the 1880 building and, with funds from the Lottery and Yorkshire Forward and a lot of help from volunteers, it was refurbished as a working example of energy efficiency, renewable

energy technologies and the range of materials – synthetic as well as natural and recycled insulation – used in refurbishment. With generous discounts from suppliers it was possible to install solar tubes, ground source heat pumps and solar water heating, and much of the work used recycled timber.

As an example of eco-renovation, the South Yorkshire Energy Centre (SYEC) is impressive, but the building itself is only part of the story. Exhibits explain wind and solar energy and demonstrate how a home loses heat and how it is possible to prevent that loss; and there are numerous activities aimed at children. There are school visits and many local people, particularly the retired, use the facilities.

When I visited in October 2009, the Centre coordinator, Vicky Moore, was excited about its successful bid for £83,000 from Scottish Power. The money helps the Centre to take the home energy message out to the community through work with primary schools and by training 'Green Envoys'. Working with young children involves using 'pester power' to change the behaviour of their parents, but it's the innovative 'Green Envoy' scheme that breaks new ground.

SYEC staff work with volunteers, social workers, tenants and residents' groups, community health workers such as district nurses and health visitors, firefighters and the police. All these groups visit people in their homes for reasons other than energy use and are usually respected by the householders they visit. Training through the Green Envoy Programme equips them to offer advice when they see a problem. If a house is cold they can draw attention to grants for insulation; too warm and they may need to explain the correct use of heating controls. This scheme is already operating successfully in Rotherham as the South Yorkshire Hotspots Scheme (see www. nea.org.uk/hotspots).

## The Green Triangle

http://greentriangle.wetpaint.com

Shirebrooke, Albert and Kent are three roads in the Meersbrook area that form a triangle. Starting with just a few friends and growing to around 20 households, the Green Triangle enables people to share their experience of greener living.

Photograph: South Yorkshire Energy Centre

"We also function as a social group," explains Rob Last, "and nothing is too formal. People drop in or out according to the activities that interest them." There are walks, cycle trips and lots of activities around food. Nick Parsons from SYEC spoke at an early meeting and gave advice about internal insulation, but most of the learning comes from within the group.

Naturally there's been a lot of eco-renovation. Many of the houses have solid walls, and Rob and his partner Kevin have installed internal cladding. Details are on the Green Triangle website (http://greentriangle. wetpaint.com/page/Carbon+Reduction), and three other households are planning to follow their example. Others installed triple glazing, solar water heating and photovoltaics, and the triangle arranged a mini eco-tour of the houses involved to share experience.

Izzy Price is one of those inspired by the group. She lives in a solid-walled, end-of-terrace house and, when Rob and I visited her on a chilly October evening, the large house was cold and damp. After learning from others in the group, Izzy negotiated with her neighbours and plans to externally clad the end-terrace wall.

Over a glass of her home-made wine we discuss how she has benefitted from the Green Triangle. "It's great to be in a group of like-minded and supportive people. It's really inspired me," says Izzy. But it's not just the big things such as external cladding and renewables that the group helps with. "Little things like draught-proofing are really important but it's something you often don't get round to." So the group is discussing a 'task force' to tackle these small and unexciting jobs collectively, to overcome the gap between knowing you ought to do something and actually getting round to it.

The Green Triangle seems to have grown spontaneously because people felt the need to take action as part of a group. The disadvantage of this is that the group is relatively isolated. While some members are active within Transition Sheffield they haven't heard about initiatives like Transition Together, from which they could take valuable lessons, and some individuals are pushing ahead with renewables and triple glazing before installing more cost-effective measures such as insulation. This isolation prevents them from tapping into wider networks for advice and contacts, which is common in much smaller towns such as Stroud or Brighton.

But the Green Triangle, for all its limitations, is making real progress, has the capacity to learn from experience and, most important of all, is taking action.

## Solar housing in Sheffield

Paxton Court is a cul-de-sac of 14 homes on a south-facing slope three miles from the city centre. In 1983 13 members of a self-build housing cooperative, supported by the left-wing city council, built their own homes. But these were no ordinary homes. The architect, Cedric Green, used a design that had just won second prize in the European Passive Solar Competition.

Green studied architecture in Lisbon, where the subject was still regarded as an art rather than a science, and already had experience in building solar houses in Suffolk. Although now an artist developing new techniques in etching, Green continues designing solar houses and built a property in France between 2006 and 2009. (See www.greenart.info.)

Paxton Court includes three basic house types, but in each the solar design revolves around an integral conservatory that can be isolated from the main house with insulated shutters during cold weather or at night. These shutters can be moved into a horizontal position during sunny weather, to shade the conservatory and reflect heat away or on to a passive solar collector. Passive heat from the conservatory is used to heat water and air for circulation around the house.

Mike Halsey, a teacher, moved into Paxton Court two years ago. "It took just five minutes to decide I wanted this house and now I'm not moving. I love it." But it's not the passive solar design that appeals to Mike. "The previous owner insulated the conservatory roof with timber cladding and I don't think anybody uses the solar heating in the way Green intended." What Mike loves is the originality of the design. He has lived in a series of uniform boxes in Hampshire, but this house is different. And it's a difference that has a unifying effect on the residents. "We have a shared experience of living somewhere that's a bit different and we like that." Mike also compares Paxton Court to living in a listed home. "I feel an obligation to the original design and would think very carefully about making any changes not in keeping with that design."

Few, if any, of the original cooperative members still live in Paxton Court, and there are stories about disputes and difficulties during the build undermining the community spirit you would expect in a self-build project. Space left on the site for a communal building was eventually used for another house, suggesting that residents had little desire to meet socially. Cedric Green, interviewed by *RIBA Journal* in 1985, suggested the group was too large and should have been limited to six self-builders and a one-year programme.

So what lessons can be drawn from Paxton Court? First, Green's experimental design has not really stood the test of time. Some areas of the houses are too cold while others get too hot, and the passive solar collectors are now rarely used. Second, as with many self-build

groups, the stresses of inexperienced builders working long hours while often coping with another job takes its toll. But there are plusses. The houses in Paxton Court cost between £14,400 and £22,600 – inexpensive even for 1985. And the residents love them. In the words of Mike Halsey, "these houses stand head and shoulders above most architecture from the 1980s".

## Sheffield in a post-oil world

Picture this. An evening in October 2009 and a room packed with senior architects from some of the most prestigious firms in the city, planning officers from Sheffield City Council, researchers, students, the odd professor and a smattering of activists from Transition Sheffield. The theme for the evening, organised by Bond Bryan Architects, is 'The future for Sheffield in a post-oil world'.

Andy Nolan, the council's Director for Sustainable Development, starts with a picture of *Homo petrolensis*, uncannily like Jeremy Clarkson on (or perhaps at)

Speakers at the Sheffield Post Oil meeting, left to right: Ian Ward, Sheffield University, Andy Sheppard, Arup, Jon Bond, Bond Bryan Architects, Andy Nolan, Sheffield City Council and Steve Lewis, Transition Sheffield.
Photograph: Bond Bryan Architects

speed. Other speakers follow and we soon have a comprehensive account of the challenge posed by peak oil and climate change and just what is needed for sustainable housing. Is the government doing enough? Only one person in an audience of over a hundred thinks it is. Have we as individuals made some changes? About half agree. Are we doing enough? No hands.

There are questions about the best way to tackle the problems, but the existence of those problems is never challenged. Climate change and peak oil are accepted as mainstream.

## Conclusions

- Sustainable housing in urban areas is crucial. Half the world's population lives in cities. In the UK 80 per cent of people live in urban areas and over 40 per cent of these live in one of the top ten urban areas, where the average population density is 4,400 people per square kilometre.[6]

- 'Beacon Councils' may be useful but fall far short of what's needed – we should be encouraging them to go much further.

- We can see the potential of community action and protests to shape the response of local councils. Residents in Page Hall prevented the demolition of a neighbourhood, and the outcome is the creation of an 'exemplar' eco-terrace.

- Individuals and small groups can tackle housing issues and at the same time create cohesive communities.

# CHAPTER 13
# MATERIALS AND SKILLS

*"Bah Bah Black Sheep, Have you any wool?*
*Yes Sir, Yes Sir, Three lofts full."*

**With apologies to Anon.**

Sustainable housing is more than a re-hash of existing designs, construction techniques and materials. It calls for a revival of old crafts and, in some cases, new skills. Building without oil means using designs and construction techniques achievable with the minimal use of machinery. Cheap and plentiful fossil fuels enable buildings that won't be possible in a sustainable future unless we plan to reintroduce slavery!

There will be losses, but also opportunities for meaningful new employment in the supply of materials, construction and, most of all, in refurbishment. Farmers have new markets for waste products such as straw and new crops such as hemp. Sustainable forestry has new opportunities, and local supplies of stone and lime will be in demand, as rising fuel prices make it uneconomic to import these products halfway around the planet.

Fortunately, the skills and industries needed for sustainable building have existed for centuries and need only to be revived – and that revival is now under way.

## Cob

### A cob house in Devon

When Jan and Jerry Sharpe decided to build their own house, cob was the obvious choice. "Our business is repairing old buildings and in Devon that frequently means working with cob," explained Jan. The choice of material may have seemed obvious but nobody in Devon had built a new cob house in nearly 80 years.

Cob – subsoil containing clay mixed with straw – is readily available and environmentally friendly, has good insulation properties and thermal mass and, providing you follow certain rules, is a very flexible building material. "Cob houses need a good pair of boots and a hat," says Jerry. He means a stone or concrete wall up to waist height and a good roof to keep out the rain. If cob gets too wet it can turn back into mud and collapse. This also dictates the choice of lime render, which allows moisture to pass through the walls.

In 2000 Jan and Jerry identified a piece of land and persuaded the owner to sell subject to their obtaining planning permission. The next 18 months were spent on persuading the council to grant outline consent. They spoke to their local councillor, who looked at the plans and raised the matter with colleagues. Eventually the elected councillors overruled the planning officers and permission was granted.

The house is a simple design and fits unobtrusively alongside the traditional Devon houses on either side. "We wanted to keep it basic and simple," comments Jerry. "After all, we knew we would have to build it!" It's not quite a Devon Longhouse but is long enough to make full use of passive solar heating on a south-facing slope. The outstanding feature is the spacious, airy and wonderfully light atrium. The huge thermal mass of cob walls rising on either side store the passive solar heat and transmit it through to the kitchen-diner and living room below and the bedrooms above.

From waist up the walls are the most natural building materials on Earth. It *is* the earth. I joined Jan and Jerry on one of their regular cob-and-lime-building courses in the summer of 2004. In the hot sun we mixed subsoil with straw and water at the rate of a bale for every ton. Then we heaved the mix up on to the walls, where it was trodden down by a succession of heavy-booted helpers: hard work but, as the corner of what is now their living room became gradually higher, there was real satisfaction.

By October that year the walls were finished and the roof structure in place. "We didn't want to put too much weight on the cob walls until they'd had a chance to dry out, so we felted the roof but didn't lay the slates," said Jerry. But from the spring of 2005 they worked at full speed to get the house finished by Christmas.

The Glulam (glued laminated timber) staircase and landing in the atrium were particularly challenging. "We had to find a skilled carpenter who could also understand the complex drawings from the structural engineer," explains Jerry. Luckily they found a local craftsman up to the job and the finished work is stunning.

This house is definitely relaxing and comfortable. "I sit down after a stressful day in the office," says Jan, "and after five minutes I feel calm and relaxed."

Jan and Jerry Sharpe's cob house in Devon.
Photograph: JJSharpe

## Build something beautiful

You can't write about the cob revival without talking to Kevin 'The Cob Specialist' McCabe, so I track him down to a £900,000 building plot with a superb view over the Dart estuary. Kevin and his team are finishing the oak roof structure on a new cob house that will cost around £350,000. "It replaces a very ugly bunga-low that would have cost more than that to improve," explains Kevin as we sit down to talk.

## Cob facts

30 per cent of the world's population live in homes built of earth.

In Devon, around half of rural buildings were built in cob until the 1850s, when cheap bricks became available.

Cob can be made from almost any subsoil with 15-25 per cent clay.

Traditionally cattle were used to mix the subsoil with straw. Now mechanical diggers do the hard work.

Cob has been used for houses and barns in Devon for hundreds of years; thousands of these houses remain in use and a few survive from the thirteenth century as testament to its durability. "It's an incredibly strong material and I'm constantly pushing the boundaries of what can be achieved," says Kevin. "A few years ago I wasn't even sure if you could build two stories in one season because it hadn't been done since the nineteenth century. Now I'd happily build a four-storey house if I could start early enough in the year."

Kevin began by repairing a cob wall for English Heritage. Twenty years, 30 buildings and several prestigious awards later, McCabe is the name that crops up whenever people talk about cob. "I am a bit romantic about cob," admits Kevin. "It has a comfortable and flowing form that's aesthetically pleasing and beautiful and that's a big part of the attraction. But I'm also very pragmatic from a building point of view, and local councils know I'm not irrational about it."

## Lime

### Lime basics

There are many situations where lime has advantages over cement as a building material. Less energy is used in its production and, unlike cement, lime sets through a process of carbonation, which absorbs some

Lime rendering. Photographs: Tŷ-Mawr Lime Ltd

of the carbon dioxide released during production. Lime mortars 'breathe', allowing moisture to pass through and evaporate harmlessly, and their flexibility can accommodate slight movements without cracking. Bricks laid with lime mortars are easily recycled, unlike bricks laid with cement mortars, where reclamation is difficult.

There were once thousands of working lime kilns in the UK, but a survey in 1995 found just 450 in Europe and only 26 in Britain.[1] The process of making lime involves heating limestones, including chalk, to 900-1200 Celsius. This releases carbon dioxide and leaves calcium oxide or 'quicklime', also called 'unslaked lime'. Adding water or 'slaking' the lime leads to a reaction producing calcium hydroxide or 'hydrated lime', which can be stored and distributed as a powder or, if excess water is used, as 'lime putty'.

Lime mortars set as they dry and absorb carbon dioxide from the atmosphere. They will not, unlike cement, set under water. However, when limestones containing silica and clay are burnt, they produce a 'hydraulic' lime, which does have this property. Hydraulic lime is therefore an environmentally friendlier alternative to cement: it uses less energy in manufacture, sets almost as quickly, allows a building to breathe and flex, and eliminates the need for expansion joints.

Temporary kilns were sometimes built near construction sites, to avoid having to transport lime. Old kilns and quarries are often found near historic buildings, the limestone providing material for building blocks as well as raw material for the manufacture of lime. With a supply of timber for fuel, the builders had everything they needed to construct magnificent mansions or lowly farm cottages.

Unfortunately lime does have drawbacks. Heat is needed to turn limestone (calcium carbonate) into quicklime (calcium oxide), and this generally comes from burning wood, coal, oil or gas. In addition to carbon dioxide and other greenhouse gases produced by burning these fuels there is also the carbon dioxide released from the limestone itself. While much of this $CO_2$ is reabsorbed, this process can take many years or even decades.

In some countries lime production has resulted in serious deforestation as trees are cut down for fuel, and in the destruction of coral as a source of calcium carbonate. Lime makes less of a contribution to climate change than cement – which is responsible for 8 per cent of global $CO_2$ emissions – but it's not an impact that can be ignored.

## Lime for a living

In 1993 Nigel and Joyce Gervis purchased Tŷ-Mawr, a run-down farm in the heart of the Brecon Beacons National Park. They intended to restore the building sympathetically but couldn't source appropriate lime mortars and plasters. So they made their own. What started as a temporary solution for a renovation project soon germinated into a business plan, and Tŷ-Mawr Lime Ltd was born.

Originally, the focus was on manufacturing lime-based building materials for the conservation of old and historic buildings, but it soon became apparent that, just as lime production had diminished, so too had the necessary skills and knowledge. So Tŷ-Mawr started courses in the use of traditional building materials. This is a common theme and many suppliers of lime and other natural building materials also offer training.

## Collapsing cottages

I first came across lime while repairing a fifteenth-century thatched cob cottage in Devon. The cottage had a serious damp problem. Floorboards on the ground floor, joists, window frames and even some of the massive oak timbers had started to rot. The thatch, although mossy and patchy in places, was not leaking, so I assumed the moisture was coming up through the ground where there was no damp-proof course, as well as from activities such as cooking and using the shower. The solution, a builder told me, was to 'tank' the house with a waterproof membrane. Fortunately I sought advice from an expert on ancient buildings, who pointed out that many of the walls had been rendered in cement and the building couldn't breathe. "Rip off the cement and replace it with lime mortar," said Ollie. "That will solve the problem." And he was right. Many years later there are no signs of damp.

Devon has thousands of cob buildings originally rendered with lime mortar. Over the years many have been repaired with cement renders, which can trap moisture – a particular problem in wealthier areas, where it was seen as 'progress' to replace the lime with cement. The result is cob-collapse 'blackspots' such as the pretty seaside town of Shaldon in South Devon, caused by water building up in the cob, which turns into mud, and the building suddenly collapses.

---

Minimising the impact of buildings on the environment quickly became another focus. This philosophy is behind Tŷ-Mawr's development of a range of environmentally friendly building materials, compatible with 'breathing building' principles. The range includes paints and finishes, building boards including woodfibre boards, wood wool boards, reed mats and reed boards, as well as insulation products made from Welsh sheep's wool, hemp and cellulose (recycled newspaper).

Tŷ-Mawr has won several awards, particularly for its work in developing 'greener' alternatives to main-stream building products. Examples of this are glaster® – a lime plaster made with recycled glass instead of sand; Lime Hemp Plaster, which uses hemp fibres; and Limecrete, an alternative to concrete. In 2009 Tŷ-Mawr was one of 52 sustainable development champions on the first Welsh Green List, which recognises the commitment and contribution of individuals in Wales to the environment.

A course participant learns how to apply lime plaster to wooden laths. Photograph: Tŷ-Mawr Lime Ltd

Students add the finishing touches of lime plaster to a timber-framed structure. Photograph: Tŷ-Mawr Lime Ltd

But didn't this story begin with a restoration project? Yes, and after 15 years it's still going. As well as being the couple's home and business base, the building is also the venue for visitors from all sorts of groups concerned with building and the environment. It incorporates solar thermal water heating, rainwater harvesting and biomass heating, which reduce $CO_2$ emissions by up to 40 tonnes per year. A couple of architects visiting Tŷ-Mawr wrote:

> "it had a big soul . . . with its golden-apricot walls that gleamed proudly in the evening sun . . . Touch, smell and listen to the walls, they are sensual, alive and exude the passion,

respect and great energy that has been invested in them. It's what every building deserves and every owner too."[2]

The lime industry has changed enormously over the last 15 years and lime is now more widely used, not only for traditional buildings but also for new ecological buildings. Tŷ-Mawr now has a purpose-built distribution warehouse and a team of 18 staff.

Nigel and Joyce are fond of saying "you must be the change you want to see in the world". By supplying over 10,000 projects over the last 15 years they've also helped many others to 'be the change'.

Whoever thought that plastering could be fun!
Photograph: Ty-Mawr Lime Ltd

## Zero-carbon cement?

According to the British Cement Association (BCA), manufacturing a tonne of cement produces 853kg of $CO_2$.[3] If global demand for cement continues to rise, that could mean 5 billion tonnes of cement (and almost as much $CO_2$) by 2025 – around ten times the UK's current total $CO_2$ emissions. It also means environmental damage associated with quarrying and transporting raw materials. Meanwhile there are dozens of industries producing waste material, such as slag from blast furnaces, which is stored or sent to landfill.

Cenin Ltd makes cement alternatives from these waste materials, with just 43kg of $CO_2$ emissions per tonne and less need for quarrying and landfill . . . and it gets better. Cenin wants to make the process zero-carbon by using energy from a 1MW combined heat and power plant fuelled with biogas from an anaerobic digester. It is also working with a wind energy partner on the adjacent site. No wonder Martyn Popham, a majority shareholder, and Gary Hunt, the commercial

director, won a sustainability award from the Welsh Assembly and top prize for a presentation at a Global Slag Conference.

The Cenin plant at Bridgend in South Wales is working, profitable, producing 1,000 tonnes of alternative cement every week, and could be replicated anywhere in the country with suitable waste material for processing.

The BCA has just four members, who manufacture over 90 per cent of cement at 14 plants in the UK. This inevitably means transporting raw material and products around the country. Replicating factories like Cenin around the country would reduce transport costs and $CO_2$ emissions and strengthen local economies while providing a far more sustainable construction material.

## Rammed earth

Do you remember that *Grand Designs* episode where they built an eco-house in just seven days? How about the bit where they built an internal rammed-earth wall as a feature? You may not remember, but Michael Thompson does.

"The house itself was primarily timber frame and straw bale," says Michael, "but this feature wall was amazing . . . I had to have a go!" So Michael, a joiner by trade, built an 'eco-shed' in his garden. It actually has a floor area of 66m², a maximum height of 2.8m and a kitchen! The walls are 200mm thick, with a total volume of 60m³ of rammed earth. But the interesting part of this story is what happened next.

Michael was pleased with his shed, and so were a few other people. The building featured in the Green Buildings in Norfolk Open House event sponsored by the Council for the Protection of Rural England, and in 2009 Michael won the Eco-Shed of the Year award – yes, there really is such an award! Anyway, Michael had spent three months on research and many hours designing this building to the last detail, and the whole experience made him think a lot about rammed-earth construction. So he decided to run rammed-earth building courses. The two-day courses are held every month from April through to October and groups travel from as far as Holland. Now Michael has self-published the *DIY Rammed Earth Manual*, with detailed explanations of the technique. What started as another 'man and his shed' story has grown into a sustainable new livelihood.[4]

## Hemp and straw

### The Inedible House

www.renewable-house.co.uk

The National Non-Food Crops Centre (NNFCC) is behind a low-cost, affordable house that meets Code for Sustainable Homes level 4 through materials alone. The house, built at the BRE Innovation Park, cost £75,000 excluding groundworks and can be enhanced with renewables to reach Codes 5 and 6. The key building material, Hemcrete®, was provided by Lime Technology.

In 2007 Rob Hopkins wrote a 'spoof' story for *The Transition Handbook* about a company called 'Hempire Building', which wins an award in the year 2014 for Zero Energy Building. In fact 'Hempire Building Materials Ltd' had been founded in 2005. Truth really is stranger than fiction – or perhaps this is an example of back-dated visioning?

NNFCC "helps to build supply chains for plant-derived renewable materials so that good ideas become products you can buy". It claims to recommend only products that deliver environmental benefits, and its website does talk about life-cycle analysis. Its 'Renewable Building Thematic Working Group' includes members from agriculture, processing and manufacturing, government and large companies, as well as end users and academics.

### The BaleHaus in Bath

www.rbath.ac.uk/features/balehaus

Building with natural materials is usually the preserve of self-builders, but investigations at the BRE Centre for Innovative Construction Materials, part of Bath University, aim to bring these materials into the mainstream.

Professor Peter Walker, who runs the Centre, oversees research into straw, hemp, lime, unfired clay bricks, timber and rammed earth. Most of this work sees the light of day only through publication in academic journals, but in November 2009 the Centre unveiled the BaleHaus, a home constructed with prefabricated load-bearing straw-bale wall panels. The 'ModCell' panels comprise a timber frame infilled with either straw-bale insulation or hemp. The bales are compacted, reinforced and protected with a lime render coat or timber fascia.

Because the straw panels can be prepared off-site in a dry building, there is less chance of their getting wet – a major problem with straw-bale construction, particularly with load-bearing designs, where the walls may be built before a protective roof is in place.

This is a mainstream project with major companies involved. 'ModCell' is the creation of White Design in

# The hemp-building revolution

**Steve Allin, author of *Building with Hemp*[5]**

Hemp has many uses that meet the needs of a society in transition from dependence on cheap fossil fuels to local resilience. Apart from uses in building, for clothing and as a food, growing hemp is also good for improving the soil.

Steve Allin examines the hemp crop. Photograph: Steve Allin

For construction purposes the woody stem is broken down into outer fibres, used for insulation, and 'hurds' or 'shives', which are mixed with a binding agent, usually including lime, to produce what is commonly called hempcrete. Around 10 tonnes of dry matter are produced per hectare – approximately 60 per cent hurds and 40 per cent fibre – enough to build a medium-sized family home with hempcrete walls and hemp-fibre insulation, or retrofit many existing houses.

Hempcrete is a breathable, insulating and heat-storing material that can be cast as a complete envelope around a timber frame in a radical new approach to building: a complete system in its own right, which combines the normally incompatible properties of insulation and thermal mass. With varying ratios of binder to hurd it can be used to enclose the structure, from the floor, up the walls and over the roof, in a seamless blanket. Hempcrete can be either tamped down around the framework manually or sprayed into position using compressed air, depending on how quickly the task needs to be completed. The total $CO_2$ emissions for hempcrete, based on a life-cycle analysis, are between -100 and -130kg/m$^3$. It's a carbon-negative material!

Although most hempcretes are lime-based, containing small amounts of cement, pozzolan or clay-based additives, others use magnesium-based cements and purely clay-based media, depending on what is locally available.

For insulation the fibre is mixed with a small percentage of polypropylene as a durable bonding agent and then made into lagging for water pipes, semi-rigid panels, or rolls to infill timber frameworks in the same way as glass fibre or rockwool, but without dust. This material also provides good soundproofing.

Hemp has advantages for local economies, as production and processing provide sustainable employment from numerous ecological, durable and sometimes high-value products.

Although many of the applications and installation techniques for hemp are quite simple, there needs to be re-skilling before they are taken up by mainstream construction, and training modules are being developed. There's a need to train farmers, architects, builders, decorators, workers in processing plants and even householders, who must learn to live with a very different material.

Hemp is a sustainable and beneficial crop for farmers, a carbon-negative building material with multiple uses, and it provides homes that are healthier to build as well as to live in.

See www.hempbuilding.com

Packing straw bales into the panels used to construct the Balehaus in Bath. Photograph: University of Bath

Bristol and Integral Structural Design in Bath. Other partners are Agrifibre Technologies, Lime Technology, Eurban, Centre for Window & Cladding Technology and Willmott Dixon. The project is part-funded by the Technology Strategy Board.

## The three 'R's

The old mantra – Reduce, Reuse, Recycle – is as important in building as elsewhere, and there are several replicable projects that create new jobs as well as reduce the environmental footprint of our homes. But let's not forget that the mantra has a hierarchy, with reducing consumption being the most important and recycling the least important of the three. Reusing, which in building terms involves reclamation, is in the

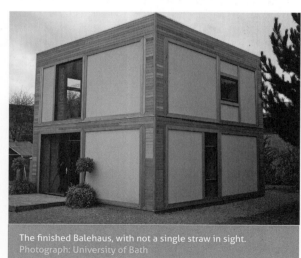

The finished Balehaus, with not a single straw in sight. Photograph: University of Bath

## Making sheep count

When Christine Rowley decided to insulate her home with sheep's wool, her only option was to import a product from New Zealand. So Christine established Second Nature UK Ltd in 2001 and developed Thermafleece from the wool near her Cumbrian home. Ten years later she has a thriving business with 12 staff and a range of insulation products, using fleeces that were previously a waste product and recycled wool from the carpet industry.

Surplus wool from sheep finds a new lease of life in Thermafleece insulation. Photograph: Second Nature UK

middle, although the term is sometimes interchangeable with recycling. Most of the examples described below fall into this category.

Reclaimed building materials are salvaged and reused in their original form. They may be cut to size, adapted, cleaned up or refinished, but they retain their original form, while recycled materials are reprocessed to form part of a new product. Bricks cleaned up and reused rather than crushed for hardcore is an example.

## Brighton & Hove Wood Recycling Project

See www.woodrecycling.org.uk

Every year, hundreds of thousands of tonnes of perfectly usable wood is dumped in landfill, mainly by industries that use wood in construction, packaging and joinery. Brighton & Hove Wood Recycling Project, set up in 1998, tackles this problem by collecting wood from local businesses, selling reusable timber to the public and turning the rest into woodchips for fuel and mulches. Less than 1 per cent of the timber it collects goes back into the waste stream.

The project in Brighton & Hove was soon collecting around 450 tonnes of waste timber a year and generating employment, with seven paid positions and opportunities for volunteer placements. Awards and grants followed and, with assistance from the National Community Wood Recycling Project (NCWRP), this social enterprise business model has been replicated by over 20 projects across the UK.

The model is simple: a financially self-supporting, non-profit-making community business with surpluses invested back into the business. It's a low-capital, low-tech and labour-intensive business. Income is from charges for collection – winning business by being the cheapest form of waste disposal – and selling material back to the community.

## Bristol follows Brighton

www.bwrp.org.uk

In 2003 Ben Moss and Nicola Padden from Bristol met Richard Mehmed, founder of the Brighton & Hove Wood Recycling Project. They knew their city was fertile ground for environmentally and socially progressive ideas, and seized the opportunity. Bristol Wood Recycling Project was born. They begged, borrowed but stopped short of stealing the space, buildings, vehicles and other equipment they needed; they made a logo, registered the company and secured first collection contracts with building companies.

Nicola and Ben volunteered their time, so there was always someone at the yard; other volunteers helped with clearing, building, stacking and painting, and the

## SORDID Sustainability

**Douglas Beal, eco-renovator living in France, with thanks to Sophy Galleymore-Bird**

For 18 years I have been renovating old properties in France. I had some experience of DIY from working on the festival circuit, but no formal training, although I have now completed a Masters in Architecture at the Centre for Alternative Technology's Graduate School of the Environment.

What I've learned can be summed up as 'Spontaneous Organic Resource Driven and Inspired Design' (SORDID) and 'eco-mising'. That is, decide what you need, in terms of its function and material properties, then salvage an alternative. Save money and reduce embodied energy in your project. But strike a balance. Don't drive around in search of a reclaimed nut. Design from and make do with what and who you've got, and let the project go where it needs to with the resources you have. Use offcuts and scraps, delay spending until you are sure there is no alternative, and you will reduce your 'unsustainable' personal debt.

Plan with future upgrades in mind – design so you can go back later and get them right – don't hide pipes and electrics away where you can't reach or change them. In other words, build so you and future generations can take things apart.

Aesthetics are a luxury, but craftsmanship can go a long way to making the interior of your home look good. In terms of the end result I am a little nervous about some of the non-mainstream methods, but our house has a different feel and warms quickly, sometimes with no energy input besides three kids running about.

There's nothing greener than innovative DIY. Labour is the biggest cost factor and professionals have to work to particular codes and practices that often aren't environmentally motivated. Hands-on involvement in providing our own shelter is essential to our nature and best not denied. It can be difficult in the UK but other countries have laxer inspection regimes so there you can get away with doing far more for yourself. With predictions of climate chaos and economic collapse we need to nurture DIY skills!

The MSc didn't enhance my practical skills but it did revive a building philosophy, inspired by my grandfather and the Wombles, of 'making use of the things that everyday folks leave behind'.

Bristol Evening Post did a big article. Pretty soon they started to make money and Ben left a part-time job to work at the project five days a week. BBC Points West did a story and the project soon had a regular crew of volunteers, sheds filling up with timber and contracted collection from clients committed to saving waste and to reducing their waste disposal bills! More people were employed, the council provided a bigger site and more media coverage lead to more growth. Before long the project employed eight people and had recycled over 1,000 tonnes of wood.

The project shrunk with the housing market crash, but there are still six employees and, with consumers hungry for reused, affordable wood and a corporate climate warming to the idea of recycling and social awareness, the future looks rosy for wood recycling.

### Not just wood

Reclaiming building materials has benefits way beyond reducing landfill. Reclamation and reuse mean less extraction of raw materials, less processing and less manufacturing. This saves energy and reduces

Bristol Wood Recycling Project. Photograph: Daniel Oliver

## Reuse it Yourself

www.reiy.net

BioRegional Reclaimed is currently developing a chain of Reuse it Yourself (ReIY) stores as social enterprises that collect excess construction materials and sell them on. Benefits include new jobs and economic regeneration, less waste to landfill, lower landfill costs, less fly tipping and reduced $CO_2$ emissions. The project is run in collaboration with REalliance, representing various recycling initiatives, and with the Waste and Resources Action Programme (WRAP), whose vision is 'a world without waste'. At the time of writing the project is yet to be launched, but there's lots of useful information available, including a detailed generic business plan and resources for developing a site specific plan.

BioRegional Reclaimed has done a lot of work in this area and produced some useful case studies and reports.[7] It also has a link to Salvoweb, a network for architectural salvage and reclaimed building materials.

### Tyres and other rubbish

And it's not just building materials that can have another lease of life in buildings. Earthships (see www.earthship.net) consist largely of what is usually seen as rubbish. 'Garbage Warrior' Mike Reynolds views waste tyres as a valuable and widely available 'natural resource'. Reynolds says: "The very quality of tyres that makes them a problem to society (the fact that they won't go away) makes them an ideal durable building material for earthships."

And not just tyres. The Brighton Earthship (see pages 86-8) includes drinks cans, bottles, reclaimed timber, rubble and stone. Even the Environment Agency recognises the value of reusing these materials rather

environmental impacts such as transport. Comparing the energy impacts of recycled and new materials shows a reduction of 60 per cent for recycled steel and 70 per cent for plastics[6] – a great way to cut costs and carbon, and reclamation gives even larger energy savings.

This house at Findhorn in Scotland had a previous life as a whisky barrel. Photograph: The Findhorn Foundation

ThermoPlan blocks are produced in Germany and imported to the UK, with estimated emissions of nearly 11.5 tonnes of $CO_2$ per home. Producing these blocks regionally would emit almost three times less $CO_2$ and would have significant cost savings. But what would the economic impact be?

The Foundation looked at scenarios ranging from building 300 houses per year up to building 230,000 per year. At the top of the scale an estimated 90,000 new jobs are created, with a boost to local economies

## Skills shortage

In January 2010 a study by the Royal Academy of Engineering warned that the construction sector lacks the skills to produce low-carbon buildings. Doug King, who authored the report, said:

"The sheer pace of change in the regulation of building energy performance has already created problems for the construction industry and the proposed acceleration of this process, aiming to achieve zero-carbon new buildings by 2020, will only widen the gulf between ambitious government policy and the industry's ability to deliver."[9]

King, a founder of King Shaw Associates and visiting professor in building engineering physics at the University of Bath, calls for the introduction of a new discipline: building engineering physics, to investigate the energy performance of buildings.

The report, Engineering a Low Carbon Built Environment, also calls for more reliable information on the actual energy and carbon performance of newly built or refurbished buildings, to validate new designs and establish benchmarks, and urges government to lead by example and to evaluate new public buildings properly.

than disposing of them, often at considerable cost, and has relaxed restrictions under the EU Landfill Directive to allow their use.[8]

### Princes and clay blocks

Can you measure the economic impact of using locally produced and sustainable building products? The Prince's Foundation for the Built Environment used aerated clay blocks to do just that. The clay blocks, sold in the UK as ThermoPlan, are entirely natural, non-toxic, sustainable, durable, easy to use and less expensive than modular building systems. The Foundation's house at the BRE exhibition is constructed using aerated blocks and breathable lime mortars and renders.

## Building the capacity

### Jo Hamilton, Oxfordshire ClimateXchange coordinator

Builders, particularly those involved in home repairs, maintenance and improvements, are vital to delivering sustainable homes. But achieving change in this arena takes time.

The energy-efficiency and eco-renovation market is complex and fragmented, funding is dominated by a small number of large players, while delivery is from a large number of small and medium enterprises.[10] Installing energy efficiency and renewables often crosses traditional trade areas and suffers from a lack of joined-up capacity.[11] This problem is compounded by the lack of independent and trusted suppliers advising on whole-house renovation. Add innovative products and approaches to the mix and we have a recipe for confusion across the supply chain.

Case studies of retrofits show that the 'eco' part of a renovation typically costs just 13-15 per cent of the total.[12] So eco-renovation is far more cost-effective to do alongside other repairs, maintenance and improvements to homes. But making every renovation an opportunity for eco-renovation requires action at many levels, from construction skills and local training providers to local networks and sharing knowledge about non-standard products and techniques.

The Department of Energy and Climate Change publication *Warm Homes, Greener Homes*[13] includes measures to address this fragmentation and the need for quality assurance. These recommendations include home energy advisors, the new single 'quality mark' for products, and the development of a "strong accreditation process for advisers and installers of energy-efficiency measures".

These are welcome, but community-led approaches also increase the capacity of the building sector. Forging links between local builders, suppliers of eco-renovation products and eco-renovation pioneers, shows what is

Builders discuss refurbishment at a breakfast organised by Oxford's ClimateXChange. Photograph: Jo Hamilton, ClimateXChange

possible, answers some of the supply-chain questions, and shares innovation across the sector.

Examples are:

- 'Open Home' events targeted specifically at builders: these events motivate and inspire home owners but can also be an important part of local builder's education by showing what's possible and when the best opportunities are for suggesting improvements.

- Business events / breakfasts: linking up with local builders networks (such as the Federation of Master Builders) to give overviews of home renovations is a great way to encourage learning from existing projects and demonstrate that there is a strong demand for eco-renovation. Linking events to the local Chamber of Commerce, and getting support from organisations such as Business Link, are also useful.

- Suppliers' fairs: showcasing local eco-renovation suppliers increases the profile and demand for eco-renovation. In the current economic climate it's worth making the point that firms who can offer niche skills, particularly eco-renovation, are more resilient in the long term.

These ThermoPlan clay blocks slot together for the easy and accurate construction of thermally efficient walls. The mortar can be laid evenly with this simple device. Photograph: Natural Building Technologies

of £2.6 billion.[14] Natural Building Technology and Ibstock now manufacture the blocks in the East Midlands and the product featured prominently at their Ecobuild 2010 stand.

Nobody is suggesting that all homes in the UK be built from aerated clay blocks, but the study shows considerable social and economic benefits, which can be extrapolated to other local and sustainable materials such as wool insulation, hempcrete, sustainable timber, wood-fibre insulation, local slate and building stone, and a range of recycled products and by-products. The combination of such products in new build and

refurbishment will stimulate local building practice and hence local economies. Encouragement by design codes and planning regulations would promote take-up by the building industry and reduce costs.

The study concludes with recommendations that sound suspiciously like Transition!

"[T]hese benefits suggest that UK housing and planning policy should emphasise the use of locally assembled, ecologically produced, sustainable materials. This would provide jobs and employment, meet the demands of

# Clay works

**Katy Bryce and Adam Weismann, authors of** *Building with Cob* **and** *Using Natural Finishes* **and founders of Clayworks.**

Throughout our journey with cob over the last ten years we have always aimed to make the process more efficient. This was fuelled by a desire to make building with cob accessible to a wider audience and take it beyond its current niche market. We achieved this to some degree but failed to overcome certain limitations to scaling up the process, as follows.

1. Time. In commercial building time is money. Cob takes time to dry between lifts (350mm layer of cob building in one session). Cob walls need time to dry and settle before roofs can be put on and plastering/rendering carried out. Cob building is possible only in the warmer months to allow walls to sufficiently dry.

2. Cost. Cob building is extremely labour-intensive, and in our economy labour is expensive. The extended building period requires a longer building contract, which can be more costly to the client.

3. Variation. Every clay subsoil is unique to its location. This makes it challenging to provide the standard industry statistics required by the building industry.

These limitations gave us the impetus to find ways of capturing the many benefits of building with clay but make it suitable for mainstream building. Our solution is to produce compressed clay bricks and clay plasters using predominantly waste materials. In this form clay speaks a language easily translated into conventional building skills (block laying and plastering). Standardised manufacturing means that each batch of material

Clayworks' stand at the Ecobuild 2010 exhibition in London. Photograph: Clayworks

can be tested and regulated, enabling building warranties and codes to be attained and met. In this form clay can continue to be a relevant solution to creating houses in the contemporary building landscape. By offering up earth in this form, we hope to bridge the gap between art and science whilst retaining the alchemy – the magic that exists within and around buildings made out of mud.

Just as cob buildings of the past tell us a story about the people who made and lived in them, so the ways we utilise and build with this material now can tell future generations about the story of our time – the need to provide homes and buildings that are affordable, efficient to run, healthy to live in and gentle on the planet.

energy-efficient homes for the future, and produce a range of secondary and tertiary benefits . . . It is therefore recommended that policies supporting the production of regional materials, regional and local supply chains, and explicitly local assembly systems be produced, for the benefit of both local communities and the nation as a whole."[15]

## New jobs from old houses

Twenty million homes needing extensive energy-efficiency retrofits is a huge undertaking and will create hundreds of thousands of jobs for decades to come.

### 'One Million Climate Jobs Now'

Climate activists within the trade unions are campaigning for a million new jobs to tackle climate change. In effect they want to see a National Climate Service to deal with climate change in the same way in which the National Health Service deals with health.

Around 300,000 of these new jobs would come from eco-renovation. Insulation, replacing old gas boilers and installing solar thermal heating and photovoltaic panels on over 10 million roofs would keep this workforce busy for at least ten years and create many more jobs in supply chains. There would also be new jobs for housing inspectors, in training and education and in the manufacture of low-energy appliances. Union members can get involved through 'Climate Solidarity', from where you can also obtain *One Million Jobs Now*, a report commissioned by four trade unions.

See www.climatesolidarity.org.uk

## Home improvement and self-improvement in Leeds

www.latch.org.uk

Leeds Action to Create Homes (LATCH) contributes to the regeneration of communities by bringing derelict and disused properties into use as social housing. Central to its work is the belief that the issues of homelessness and disempowerment are closely linked. It tackles these issues by enabling people to do things for themselves such as working on their own property.

Among recent projects is renovation of a Grade II listed derelict coach house in Chapeltown. LATCH minimised environmental impact by using reclaimed, recycled and natural materials. The brick shell is insulated with sheep's wool and plastered with traditional lime plaster, and the building will be heated by a wood stove.

Most of the renovation and refurbishment is undertaken by volunteers who learn practical construction skills such as joinery, insulating, plastering, painting and decorating. Volunteers come for a 12-week placement and have the opportunity to gain construction skills certification and build up a record of achievement.

## Green maintenance

www.greenworkforce.co.uk

Keeping your home in good order is part of being sustainable. It's much better to fix a minor problem, a leaking gutter or dripping tap, than deal with the consequences. But do you have to rely on the services of 'White Van Man'?

In 2008 William Mobsby set up what he claims is a carbon-neutral bicycling handyman service that now covers most of central London.[16] Greenworkforce handymen have a range of basic skills – they can change a light switch or fix that dripping tap but can't rewire the house or fit a new boiler – emphasise energy-efficiency and arrive, complete with necessary tools, on a bike!

Cycling handymen (and women) are particularly suitable for London and other congested cities, where cycling probably saves time as well as money and carbon.

## The Genesis Project

www.genesisproject.com

Genesis delivers education and training in sustainable construction to the mainstream building industry, and where better than in a building that combines the best of traditional and modern building materials and techniques? The Genesis Centre, part of Somerset College, has pavilions constructed of earth, straw, clay and timber, with living roofs. A water pavilion demonstrates the latest water-saving devices and all the buildings showcase energy-saving and renewable technologies.

Construction workers with doubts about the viability of sustainable methods need only look around their classrooms to see that natural materials and crafts work in harmony with modern materials and techniques to create climate-proofed buildings.

And how did it happen? Interestingly, the project grew out of an assignment given to HNC Construction students. The students wanted to promote sustainability within the construction industry and, with support from the Construction Industry Training Board and the Regional Development Agency, the assignment became reality.

## Conclusions

- Vernacular buildings reflect the regional availability of natural materials. We need to relearn the skills associated with these materials.

- Building local resilience and sustainability into building doesn't necessarily mean we can use only the materials we find on our doorsteps. Factories manufacturing low-carbon cements and clay blocks, for example, can be established in many parts of Britain, thus extending the variety of locally available materials.

- Just as CND and campaigners against the arms industry allay fears about job losses with proposals to turn 'swords into ploughshares', so sustainable housing has the potential to revitalise the construction industry.

# CHAPTER 14

# INTERNATIONAL AND GREEN: LESSONS FROM AROUND THE WORLD

With a click of a mouse we can learn from people all over the planet. Almost half the replies to an online survey conducted on sustainable housing through the Transition Network came from outside the UK. So what's happening out there and what can it teach us?

## The USA

There is a long tradition of alternative communities and eco-building in the US, from which we can all learn. You could fill a book – and people have – with lessons from communities such as 'The Farm', cohousing developments and Mike Reynolds' earthships. Here we look at just a few developments in passive housing.

### Passivhaus and Natural House

In Europe, homes built to Passivhaus standard tend to be high-tech and dependent on energy-intense, oil based materials. The end result may be energy-efficient homes, but getting there uses a lot of fossil fuels. Does it have to be that way?

There are only a dozen or so certificated Passivhaus buildings in the US but Americans do have a strong tradition of alternative builders using natural materials. The past few years have seen a new type of eco-build where Passivhaus standards are reached with natural materials to achieve homes that are healthier and have a lower carbon footprint from day one.

### Nauhaus

The Nauhaus is an experimental passive solar house likely to be one of the first dozen homes certified by the Passive House Institute in the US, and is unique in using natural materials (see http://thenauhaus.com).

Nauhaus – the name is a playful nod to the Bauhaus school of design – mixes state-of-the-art building science and technology with natural and local materials such as hempcrete, natural-fibre sealants, compressed earthen blocks for thick tile flooring and interior walls, and natural plaster and paint finishes.

Other key features are similar to those of Passivhaus but go a step further to create a home producing more energy than it uses, to offset carbon emissions resulting from construction.

Nauhaus designs are much smaller than US averages, in recognition of the fact that, whatever performance standard you achieve, the larger the building, the more energy it will use and the more it will cost.

By using local and site-harvested materials wherever possible, Nauhaus reduces the environmental construction footprint of the building. Another component is lifespan – the longer a building lasts, the longer we postpone the energy and carbon investment in constructing a new one. A Nauhaus mantra is 'the 500-year house'.

And beauty too! Features such as thick exterior walls with undulating plaster surfaces, large roof overhangs, ample natural light, smooth transitions between indoor and outdoor rooms, and a variety of edges between outdoor living spaces and the planted and natural environment of the site, all contribute to what the designers believe is a beautiful building.

You can't get huge performance increases without paying more, so how is Nauhaus affordable? Creating customised but repeatable designs is one way to reduce costs. More of the thousands of decisions required to complete a house are defined at the outset, which increases efficiency, reduces confusion, and enables more accurate costing by the contractor.

Increasing the usable area allows a smaller indoor footprint to deliver useful living space equivalent to that of a larger building, and is another way to reduce costs. The Nauhaus Institute calls this 'functional square footage' and achieves it by expanding covered outdoor spaces such as conservatories and porches, which are less expensive to build.

Finally, better efficiency and durability mean lower utility and maintenance costs, so you start saving money when you move in. Nauhaus intends to be part of an educational movement that adjusts the present short-sighted definition of cost to include the financial, environmental and social costs of the entire life cycle of the building.

> "Our goal is not only to design the most beautiful, liveable, energy- and resource-efficient building environments in our region, but to make these designs affordable to a large cross-section of the population. In the process, we'll improve the daily lives of those inhabiting our buildings while doing our part to mitigate climate change."[1]

So how are they making it happen? First, through partnership agreements with green building specialists and suppliers who believe Nauhaus is worth making a reality. Second, with support from Kleiwerks International, a non-profit-making organisation that promotes ecological regeneration and empowers communities through hands-on natural building and education.

## Harvestbuild

www.harvestbuild.com

Mark Hoberecht, who worked as a NASA engineer for nearly 30 years, successfully made the transition from 'rocket scientist' to 'natural building scientist'. He builds 'naturally passive houses', which aspire to Passivhaus standards while using natural materials. Mark uses the principles behind Bau-Biologie to build houses that are healthy for people and the environment – see Table 1, Chapter 1 (page 17).

Design guidelines include the following.

- Maximise the use of unprocessed building materials of natural origin.

- Use materials that allow air diffusion and the self-regulation of humidity.

- Minimise harmful electromagnetic radiation from wiring and appliances.

- Design shapes and proportion in harmonic order.

Materials are scored according to these and other criteria and preference is given to timber, earth and straw, which typically score 2.9 out of a maximum 3.0. Materials such as fibreglass, concrete and plastics all score less than 1.0. (See Table 1, Chapter 1.)

## Natural Design/Build

Ben Graham, an active member of Transition Montpelier in Vermont, USA, established Natural Design/Build to bring natural building up to date with Passivhaus solar designs. Ben also runs regular courses, offers apprenticeships, helps organise a network of natural builders in the region and regularly advocates natural building in the media.

See www.naturaldesignbuild.us

## The Canelo Project

www.caneloproject.com

Athena and Bill Steen founded the Canelo Project in 1989 to explore natural building techniques and sustainable ways of living. Their work has lead to key books on straw-bale building, training courses attended by people from all over the world (Barbara Jones attended a course and subsequently founded Amazonails, see page 121) and outreach work in Mexico, where the project assisted people to build homes for just $500 and a building for Save the Children.

## Australia

Australia's carbon emissions per capita are among the highest in the world, more than double the UK's, and the country is extremely polarised over climate change. Despite this there are some good stories.

### Open Homes down under

Oxford may have held the first Eco Open House event in Britain (see page 54), but Australia was five years ahead of it. Sustainable House Day started in 2001 as an initiative of the Australia and New Zealand Solar Energy Society (ANZSES), and the Australian Govern-ment is a major sponsor. Nearly ten years later the annual event sees around 250 homes open their doors to the public (see www.sustainablehouseday.com).

As in the UK, home visits are free and provide an opportunity for people seeking to make their own homes or rental properties greener to learn from houses designed, built or fitted out with sustainability in mind; to talk to owners; to exchange ideas and to learn from each other.

And there's a financial incentive to get involved. Local community groups across Australia assist in the management of their area's open houses and, in return, receive a donation back to their community. In total some A$100,000 is available.

### Green Loans Program

Australia is also ahead of the UK with 'green loans' for solar, water saving, and energy-efficient products (see www.environment.gov.au/greenloans).

## Transition Tasmania

Sustainable Living Tasmania supports communities making the transition to a low-carbon, resilient future. Glenorchy's Greenhouse Action, funded by a federal government grant under the Low Emissions Technology and Abatement program, with whole-hearted support from Glenorchy City Council, held well-attended community workshops on home energy and climate change. They also provided 50 home energy audits and rebates for home insulation for 67 houses, 17 heat pumps, 18 solar hot water systems and 8 sets of curtains. A major success was recruiting a number of landlords to insulate their rental properties. Hundreds of discounted 'Home Energy Saver Packs' were distributed.

The programme offers free Home Sustainability Assessments of energy and water systems relating to thermal comfort, water heating, lighting, refrigeration, cooking, entertainment, water efficiency and waste management. The assessments give householders a report listing the most effective changes for their homes. Advice ranges from the smallest behaviour change to major investments, such as a solar hot water system or photovoltaic panels. Loans of up to A$10,000, interest-free for up to four years (possible because the Australian Government provides a loan subsidy) help to make the recommended changes.

## Cuba

The inspiring film *Cuba – The Power of Community* outlines how Cubans transformed food production to cope with oil shortages experienced after the collapse of supplies from the Soviet Union. Less well known is how they coped with shortages of building supplies, in particular cement, also caused by the energy crisis.

### From waste to houses

After the Cuban revolution of 1959 housing relied increasingly on the centralised production of building materials in huge state-operated facilities. Prefabricated houses were built all over the country, with supply of building materials to remote places, by road and rail. This system was energy-intensive and dependent on the supply of cheap oil from the Soviet Union.

With the end of Soviet backing during the 1990s energy became scarce, roads were poorly maintained, trucks grew old and the supply of spare parts failed. Portland cement, as well as other materials for house building and repair, became scarce, existing houses deteriorated and fewer new homes were built. Recurring hurricanes aggravated the problem.

In 1999 the Centro de Investigación y Desarrollo de Estructuras y Materiales (Centre for the Investigation and Development of Buildings and Materials – CIDEM) sought alternatives to Portland Cement and came up with a material based on the ash from burning sugar-cane wastes, which replaces up to 40 per cent of the cement in hollow concrete blocks and other materials.

With European funding, the project created a network of building materials' manufacturers. Workshops produce blocks, tiles and alternative cement for sale, mostly to people whose homes were damaged by storms.

As well as hollow concrete blocks and flagstones, the novel cement, called CP-40, is used to manufacture partitions made of bamboo fibre mixed with cement. This innovation makes it possible to build solid walls with local materials.

Ash from sugar cane waste helps replace cement. © CIDEM

CIDEM won the United Nations World Habitat Award, and the techniques are now being rolled out across Cuba. Local authorities set up the workshops and arrange loans for people to buy materials and renovate their homes. By 2010, 25 workshops were producing affordable building materials, thousands of homes had been renovated and 200 jobs created.[2]

## Ireland

### The Village

www.the village.ie

'The Village' began in 1999, when a group of environmentalists held a meeting in Dublin's Central Hotel to plan Ireland's first eco-village. More than 40 sites were considered before Cloughjordan was chosen. The organisers set up a cooperative company to oversee

A group of future residents inspect buildings under construction at The Village in Cloughjordan.
Photograph: Cloughjordan Eco-Village

the project, and everyone who buys a site becomes a member. Outline planning permission was granted without objections, although 32 conditions were attached. The lack of objections was probably thanks to the thorough consultation process the organisers went through with the local community. Brian O'Brien of Solearth Architects, who drew up the masterplan for the 28-hectare site in collaboration with Sally Starbuck of Leech-Gaia Ecotecture and the village members, says that hiring a team of architects, engineers, hydrogeologists, archaeologists and others was key to convincing planners at the early stages.

### Decision-making

Another key to success is the careful thought given to making decisions. The directors, staff and members of The Village use consensus decision-making, a structured approach that allows open debate and leads to clarity and mutual respect. This ensures that everyone takes a share of the rights and responsibilities for making the project work. Only if consensus cannot be reached is a vote called for, and this must be ratified by 75 per cent of those present. The process was developed initially by a sub-group, with help from a skilled facilitator.

Since 2009 The Village has been implementing the Viable Systems Model (VSM), a non-hierarchical way to maximise the freedom of participants while still allowing organisations to fulfil their purpose. Modelled on the central nervous system, VSM creates an adaptive and resilient organisation that preserves the autonomy of members and working groups within a structure of support and accountability. The Village is currently working with two internationally renowned VSM experts, Jon Walker and Angela Espinosa, to study and adopt this model.

Cloughjordan residents prepare a trail through woodland on the site. Photograph: Cloughjordan Eco-Village

## Cloughjordan – building resilient communities

**Davie Philip, Community Resilience Programme Manager and Transition Towns Coordinator**

For ten years I have been involved in developing an eco-village, called simply The Village, in North Tipperary. This blueprint for modern sustainable living includes 130 homes, renewable energy for heating, land for growing food and trees, an enterprise centre and community buildings. A lot more than an eco-housing estate.

We got together in 1999, and the initial plan was to buy a farm and develop around 40 houses with some shared amenities. We soon realised that there are many communities in decline and therefore a better approach was to find land in an existing settlement and act as a model for sustainable regeneration of rural towns and villages.

The Village merges directly into Cloughjordan, a small settlement in the heart of rural Ireland with an attractive mix of houses and diverse businesses. This is rich agricultural land and fine cycling country. Building began in the summer of 2009 and a number of houses are now occupied. There is already a strong sense of community, with over 40 families having already moved into the existing town.

People from all walks of life, young and old, families and single people, are working together to create a beautiful and enriching place to live. In a survey of the 65 households who have bought sites, 80 per cent said a 'sense of community' is what attracted them to the project.

All the homes being built within the eco-village have high ecological standards, combining energy-efficient design with locally sourced natural building materials. There is a wide variety of house styles with examples of timber frame, lime-hemp and cob-built homes. Sites have good south-facing aspect so residents benefit from passive solar heating, and each home has rainwater harvesting and benefits from a community heating system.

Homes are surrounded by an edible landscape of fruit and nut trees, vegetables and herbs. Hundreds of trees are being raised for planting along the pathways and in community gardens. Larger community and personal allotments provide more space for growing food, and remaining land is dedicated to farming and woodland.

Cloughjordan Community Farm has members or subscribers from both the eco-village and residents of the existing community, a fantastic way to link residents of the new community and the old. Local farmers and even the local butcher are involved. Weekly subscriptions pay for seed, livestock, equipment and the wages of a full-time farmer. In return, members pick up vegetables, eggs, meat and milk, and we have been experimenting in growing oats, barley, spelt and wheat for a baker building a micro-bakery in the eco-village.

Renewable energy provides heating and hot water generated by two woodchip boilers, and the biggest array of solar panels in Ireland, pipes water to houses and apartments through insulated underground pipes. The nearby railway and a car-sharing project in the town offer residents the possibility of sustainable transport.

We are committed to creating a vibrant, resilient and sustainable local economy. Already new enterprises have been established in Cloughjordan, including a cosy coffee/bookshop and a thriving bike shop, and existing shops and businesses benefit from new customers moving to the area. The eco-village includes 15 live/work units that combine apartment living with ground-floor office, retail or therapy space, and over €500,000 has been secured for an eco-enterprise centre for new green business. The infrastructure for high-quality cable broadband throughout the eco-village is already in place.

The Village provides a focal point for ecological and sustainable education, a unique opportunity for people to come and learn by immersing themselves in the community. Hands-on courses, workshops and field trips are already popular. Community and enterprise workers have spent time in Cloughjordan and there are plans to involve school students and establish partnerships with third-level colleges such as Tipperary Institute. Cloughjordan is already a Transition Town and plans are progressing to build a state-of-the-art Transition learning centre that focuses on training for leadership, livelihoods and local resilience.

There is an old African proverb, quoted by Al Gore in his Nobel Prize acceptance speech: "If you want to go quickly, go alone. If you want to go far, go together."

# A European perspective

**Kate and Tim Birley, founders of Tim Birley Consultancy, a consultancy specialising in sustainability**

Go by train through much of North Western Europe and the housing doesn't look very different from the UK. Probe below the surface, and the differences are marked. Tim Birley Consultancy helps organisations towards sustainable development.We undertook a study tour in 2009, conducting interviews and site visits, to see sustainable development in ten major cities and projects in the Netherlands, Denmark, Sweden, Germany and Austria. Most of the developments visited were large and either waterfront (HafenCity in Hamburg, Vastra Hammen in Malmo, Älvrummet in Gothenburg and Hammarby Sjostad in Stockholm) or new suburbs (Vathorst in Amersfoort, Kronsberg in Hannover, Vauban and Rieselfeld in Freiburg). This was followed by a visit to study Passivhaus construction in Austria.

When you visit these developments and meet people, you don't feel that these are radically different cultures. Living standards and lifestyles feel familiar to our own, with similar aspirations to more sustainable ways of living, building and tackling climate change. Most effort has been on new build and, as in the UK, only recently is comparable attention to retrofit emerging.

It had not proved easy to identify significant low-carbon developments to visit in the UK – BedZED, Hockerton, OneBrighton, the BRE Innovation Park and the Centre for Alternative Technology formed the basis for a study tour in 2008. There are more, and much larger, examples in mainland Europe, but they are still not commonplace or the normal way of building.

The key differences lie deeper, sometimes literally underground. In many towns and cities in continental Europe, superb integrated public transport and district heating are commonplace. In Copenhagen and Vienna less than 10 per cent of waste goes to landfill, with energy produced from waste-burning combined heat

The tram system was installed at Vauban before building work even began. Photograph: Kate and Tim Birley

and power plants. With the efficiency inherent in district heating, leading to affordable warmth in the home, and when it is easier to use the underground, a tram, bus or bike than use a car, there is less need to advocate radical behaviour change or a hair-shirt approach. Being more sustainable is on the way to becoming the easy option.

While local circumstances vary, there are two major ways in which institutions differ from those in the UK. First, local authorities frequently own development land and the utilities. They have not been through the same regime of nationalisation followed by privatisation as in Britain. Even where major construction companies are engaged (and volume housebuilders are not the norm), steps are taken to ensure variety: for example, in Vathorsteach each architect can design no more than 80 homes. Where public transport goes in during the construction phase, as in Hammarby Sjostad, sustainable travel patterns are established from the outset.

Second, there is a qualitative difference in the skills and attitudes to construction and design.This seems to be a world where district heating pipes don't corrode, mechanical ventilation and heat recovery is reliable and silent, and biomass boilers don't pollute. This commitment to quality is readily apparent in Passivhaus buildings, where high-quality design and construction are vital to building performance.

Progress in the places we visited is step-by-step. This contrasts with Gordon Brown's aspirational, but unrealistic and grandiose, 2006 pledge that "every new home will be a zero-carbon home" by 2016. It is also much easier to assess progress when from Stockholm to Freiburg the common measure is kWh/m²/annum, not the plethora of SAP ratings, BREEAM standards, Codes for Sustainable Homes, Energy Performance Certificates, and Energy Saving Trust and CarbonLite standards we

are saddled with in the UK. To draw an analogy with vehicle performance: we measure this by mpg and g/km, not by getting a consultant to measure cylinder size, then trying to calculate energy losses at every stage of the transmission.

Sustainable development needs many things: leadership, commitment and a willing public are crucial. It also needs the means to deliver and straightforward ways of measuring progress.Unless we empower our local authorities to implement integrated strategies for transport, energy and heat, and re-skill our designers and builders – modern-day craftsmen and women – we will struggle to follow the lead of European emerging best practice.

This low-energy housing at Malmo in Sweden is a car-free development. Photograph: Kate and Tim Birley

## International

A number of sustainable housing projects may have their roots in the USA but are now truly international.

### Global eco-villages

Richard Heinberg, in his foreword to Diane Leafe Christian's *Finding Community*, says: "roughly 99 per cent of our history as a species has been spent in groups of 15 to 50 individuals where each knew all the others, and where resources were shared".[3] In 1800 only 3 per cent of people lived in cities. That figure is now over 50 per cent. We evolved to live in communities but no longer do.

Eco-villages aim to recreate communities of a type that has been lost in the last few centuries. At their heart is the desire to construct human settlements that tread lightly on the Earth and promote a greener way of life. Most reduce dependency on fossil fuels, grow their own food, build from local or green materials and often use ecological technologies for heating and electrical and water systems. Sharing cookers, cars, tools and heating systems saves energy and money. Eco-villages represent a conscious decision to live simply and consume less.

Findhorn, in Scotland (see www.findhorn.org), is undoubtedly the best-known eco-village in the UK. It started as little more than a collection of caravans and an idea for sustainable living. Now Findhorn draws energy from four 225kW wind turbines, ecologically sound buildings have largely replaced the caravans, there's a biological sewage treatment and solar water heating systems, and 70 per cent of fresh food comes from its community supported agriculture scheme, the oldest and largest in the UK.

The Global Ecovillage Network (GEN) was founded in 1991, after a conference organised by the Gaia Trust,

Findhorn was the venue for the first Global Ecovillages Network meeting. Photograph: the Findhorn Foundation

and grew rapidly following its first international conference at Findhorn in 1995. GEN's mission includes "creating a sustainable future by identifying, assisting and coordinating the efforts of communities to acquire, social, spiritual, economic and ecological harmony." Objectives include developing eco-villages around the world, linking eco-villages and projects into a worldwide movement and creating 'Living and Learning Centres' to promote hands-on participatory education in sustainable living. Establishing an eco-village is a difficult task, but GEN helps to give momentum to embryonic developments.

GEN includes large networks such as Sarvodaya (11,000 sustainable villages in Sri Lanka), EcoYoff and Colufifa (350 villages in Senegal) and the Ladakh project; eco-towns such as Auroville in South India,

Damanhur in Italy and Nimbin in Australia; small rural eco-villages such as Gaia Asociación in Argentina and Huehuecoyotl in Mexico; urban rejuvenation projects such as the Los Angeles EcoVillage and Christiania in Copenhagen; permaculture design sites such as Crystal Waters in Australia, Cochabamba in Bolivia and Barus in Brazil; and educational centres such as the Centre for Alternative Technology in Wales and Earthlands in the USA. Its directory lists over 350 affiliated organisations.

## Architecture for humanity

"Design is the ultimate renewable resource", says Cameron Sinclair, Executive Director and CEO (Chief Eternal Optimist!) of Architecture for Humanity. As head of an organisation that taps into a network of over 40,000 professionals to help design a more sustainable future, he is in a good position to know.

Of course, when people are homeless and in desperate need after catastrophes such as Hurricane Katrina or the Haiti earthquake, sustainability may not be as high

> "How do you improve the living standards of five billion people? With100 million solutions."
>
> Cameron Sinclair, CEO, Architecture for Humanity

on their agenda as getting a roof over their heads. Nonetheless, one of the principles of Architecture for Humanity is "Reducing the footprint of the built environment and addressing climate change."

With 80 groups in 25 countries and more than 4,650 volunteer design professionals, this is a big organisation. The scope of projects and training programmes on its website is huge – it has over 15,000 registered users and 50,000 unique visits monthly.

A key feature of the organisation is that everything it designs is freely available under a Creative Commons License through the Open Architecture Network. Since the network was launched, hundreds of organisations and individuals have uploaded humanitarian design solutions. The hope is that sharing will influence other building programmes and leave a legacy of innovative, locally appropriate solutions.

## Conclusion

We are part of a global community. We have friends everywhere, from whom we can learn, and with the click of a mouse we can find out what's happening almost anywhere in the world. Don't neglect this wonderful opportunity.

Maize   Yucca   Tobacco   Beans   Hopi Tea   Juniper   Sage   Pinyon Pine   Squash

This straw bale Hogan was designed for Navajo Indians by Architecture for Humanity. Photograph: Architecture for Humanity

# CHAPTER 15

# A LOOK INTO THE FUTURE: STROUD, BRIGHTON, SHEFFIELD AND TOTNES IN 2030

In 2030, while researching the twelfth edition of *Local Sustainable Homes*, I revisited some of the towns and cities I journeyed to 20 years before. Below are a few extracts from my notes.

## Stroud

Hill Paul still stands beside Stroud station but the red brick facades were clad in hemp insulation and rendered in lime many years ago, the building is now surrounded by allotments and orchards instead of parking spaces, and solar panels cover the roof. I follow the busy canal out to Stonehouse to the reopened brick works, now making compressed clay blocks and clay plasters, where schoolchildren are visiting as part of their GCSE in natural building. It's great to see these buildings alive again and employing nearly a hundred people.

I'm here to meet Ed Budding, developer and resident at Cashes Green eco-village. The village, an exemplary Transition community copied all over Europe, is celebrating its twentieth anniversary by opening a newly refurbished wing in its College for Transitional Skills. We borrow a couple of bikes from the pool and head off on the cycle path. Ed shows me around the clustered homes, shops and workspaces pointing to examples of cob, hempcrete, straw-bale, rammed-earth and clay-block buildings that surround the hospital with its communal kitchens, crèche and workspaces. It's a warm day and many people have left their doors open, some wave or greet us as we pass, children play in green spaces and race along the paths between buildings. "These people have been through some difficult times," explains Ed "and that's created a strong bond. There's a great community spirit here."

Men and women are setting up trestle tables beside the orchard in preparation for the celebrations and a group of teenagers pass with barrows full of vegetables from the community garden. The smell of a spit roasted pig, a rare treat, wafts over us. Ed points out wind turbines on the hills surrounding Stroud and says, "We are lucky to have such a good supply of electricity. Between the solar panels covering the hospital roof, the turbines and four small hydroelectric generators we usually put more power into the local grid than we take out."

## Brighton

Mischa has greyed a little since we last met, but I recognise him waiting for me at the station and we walk down past OneBrighton on our way to a terrace of Victorian homes that Mischa's cooperative has just finished refurbishing. "It has problems," says Mischa "but OneBrighton was groundbreaking for its time and, as one of the last major new builds in Brighton, it's a memorial to the way developments used to be."

Now refurbishment and retrofits outnumber new builds by a thousand to one, and the award-winning 'eco-terrace' Mischa leads me to marks the final stage in bringing Brighton's 'hard to treat' solid-walled properties up to the minimum CarbonLite standard. "All the materials come from farms on the South Downs," explains Mischa. "You probably saw the hemp fields from the train, and sheep have largely replaced beef and dairy herds so we have plenty of wool."

The north-facing windows are now triple-glazed and much smaller than those on the south-facing walls, and insulation and draught-proof doors help to keep the interiors warm in winter. This road was 'greened' soon after Caroline Lucas won the parliamentary seat and the local council radically changed its development framework. Sections of tarmac and pavement on one side of the street were dug up by residents and planted with trees and bushes. Apricots, peaches, almonds and walnuts mingle with apples, pears and plums, and grape vines climb trellises on south-facing walls. "This street has a wine and cider collective and the vines also shade the buildings and prevent overheating," says Mischa.

## Sheffield

The City of Steel had a traumatic few years after the first oil collapse and before the exodus. But life here is better now and the population of 200,000 is settled and confident about the future. It's a short walk up to Park Hill, where the latest round of refurbishment, the third in the last 20 years, is still under way. How much time, materials and energy could have been saved if the work had been done to higher standards in the first place? Wind turbines, mounted above the Park Hill towers, turn lazily in the light breeze. 'Made in Sheffield' could now refer to these turbines or any of a dozen

other renewable energy industries that have sprung up here in the past decade. There are also workshops producing a plant-based foam insulation developed at Sheffield University and first used here to upgrade solid-walled homes.

With so many abandoned homes, Sheffield is a major source for reclaimed building materials. Bricks from older buildings built with lime mortar are easily recovered and transported to rural areas by canal boats, while high-quality timber from older buildings is now used for interiors and furniture. Glazing, pipework and roofing materials are all carefully gleaned as entire neighbourhoods are harvested of construction materials and then rehabilitated for cultivation.

This is now a leading centre for cohousing, with streets and neighbourhoods finding life so much easier when they work together. I'm pleased to see that one of the pioneers for Sheffield's particular brand of urban cohousing is the Green Triangle. Its members followed the logic of neighbourly support all the way to establishing a cohousing community of three entire streets.

## Totnes

The train back to Totnes passes through countryside dotted with newly established eco-hamlets, cohousing clusters and small farms. They blend into their environment partly because they've been designed in harmony with the surroundings, but also because they consist largely of local materials: straw-bale and cob buildings rendered in local clays, rammed-earth walls the same colours as the soils from which they have sprung, and timber buildings carefully locking up tonnes of carbon.

The station now forms part of the Atmos complex, one of the last developments in Totnes built before the first collapse, when oil was still relatively cheap. Construction was heavily weighted towards low-energy materials, but compared to what we are building now this is high-tech. The Code 6 development was built when local materials were still a choice rather than a necessity, and it shows. Still, it was a big step forward at the time and gave the people of Totnes the confidence to redevelop many other parts of the town and to pioneer the refurbishment of heritage buildings.

The town is both familiar and strikingly different. Most of the houses and streets have been here for many decades and even hundreds of years, but all show signs of refurbishment. For the most important listed buildings the signs are subtle – deeper internal window reveals hint at internal cladding, and in winter snow-laden roofs indicate well-insulated lofts. Other buildings have external cladding and timber-framed triple-glazed windows manufactured in one of the new Atmos factories. Most of the timber is local, but in the past few years ships have returned to Baltic Wharf and Totnes is once again an important trading centre for imported timber. We owe a lot to the campaigners who prevented the entire wharf being developed for housing.

Of course, the town is much bigger now the twice-weekly agricultural markets have returned and there are new buildings as well as refurbishments. With all the local expertise in straw-bale and cob, it's not surprising that these materials dominate, particularly in the first two cohousing developments at Baltic Wharf and Follaton House and in the 27 small Transition communities on the outskirts of the town.

But Totnes still has a radical edge and self-build cooperatives have built earthships, timber-frame homes insulated with recycled clothing, hemp and compressed-grass houses and a host of other buildings. Many of the experimental designs started as student projects at the nearby Dartington College of Design and Construction.

The past 20 years have been difficult, but much easier here than for many communities who had less time to prepare. Totnes and other towns have changed, sometimes for the worse, but often for the better. Just like their homes, people and communities are stronger and healthier; have firmer foundations; are more resilient and more natural. People and their homes have both been transformed for the better.

# REFERENCES

## Introduction

1 Alec Clifton-Taylor (1987). *The Pattern of English Building* (4th edn). Faber and Faber.

2 Cited in 'The green house of the future – built c.1550'. *The Guardian*, 8 November 2006.

3 A. Froggatt and G. Lahn (2010). 'Sustainable Energy Security: Strategic risks and opportunities for business'. Lloyds 360° Risk Insight White Paper / Chatham House.

4 Gill Seyfang (in press). 'Community action for sustainable housing: building a low carbon future'. *Energy Policy*. doi: 10.1016/j.enpol.2009.10.027.

## Chapter 1: What is sustainable housing?

1 Figures in the first 3 paragraphs of this chapter are from:

Zero Carbon Britain, http://zcb2030.org.

British Gas. www.britishgas.co.uk/pdf/EnergyEfficiencyReport.pdf.

J. Hacker et al. (2005). 'Beating the Heat: Keeping UK Buildings Cool in a Warming Climate'. UK Climate Impacts Programme Briefing Report.

James Wines (2000). *Green Architecture: The Art of Architecture in the Age of Ecology*. Taschen. p.9.

Adam Weismann and Katy Bryce (2006). *Building with Cob*. Green Books. p.18.

2 Katy Jackson (2007). *The Self-Build Survival Guide*. How To Books Ltd.

3 Paul King. Quoted in *The Guardian*, 31 December 2009.

4 'Most polluting postcodes in Britain identified in heart of middle England'. www.telegraph.co.uk, 18 July 2009.

5 M. Roys et al. (2010). 'The Real Cost of Poor Housing'. Building Research Establishment.

6 James Wines (2000). *Green Architecture: The Art of Architecture in the Age of Ecology*. Taschen. p.9.

7 Ibid. p.14.

8 Quoted in Patrick O'Brian (1976). *Picasso*. Collins.

9 Oliver James (2007). *Affluenza*. Vermilion.

10 Germaine Greer. 'New homes are universally ugly, and eco-homes are the most horrible of the lot'. www.guardian.co.uk, 28 July 2008.

11 Christopher Alexander et al. (1977). *A Pattern Language*. Oxford University Press USA.

12 Christopher Alexander. 'The Nature of Order', quoted in Weismann and Bryce (2006) *Building with Cob*, Green Books.

13 Gill Seyfang (in press). 'Community action for sustainable housing: Building a low carbon future'. *Energy Policy*. doi: 10.1016/j.enpol.2009.10.027.

14 Mayer Hillman, *AECB Yearbook 2006*.

## Chapter 2: Making the case for change

1 Rob Hopkins (2008). *The Transition Handbook*. Green Books.

2 C. DiClemente (2003). *Addiction and Change: How addictions develop and addicted people recover*. The Guildford Press.

3 www.foe-scotland.org.uk/node/169, 28 January 2009.

4 P. Devine-Wright and H. Devine-Wright (2006). 'The Green Doctor Project: A Review'. Groundworks Leicester.

5 www.bristolgreencapital.org/green-capital/energy/peak-oil.

## Chapter 3: Sustainable housing in Totnes

1 Jacqi Hodgson with Rob Hopkins (2010). *Transition in Action: An Energy Descent Action Plan*. Transition Town Totnes. An extended version of the EDAP can be viewed at www.totnesedap.org.uk.

2 www.sustainablebuild.org/documents/jim_carfrae.pdf.

3 Henry David Thoreau (1854). *Walden, or Life in the Woods*. Ticknor and Field.

4 Jacqi Hodgson with Rob Hopkins (2010). *Transition in Action: An Energy Descent Action Plan*. Transition Town Totnes.

## Chapter 4. Refurbishment and retrofit

1 Robert and Brenda Vale (2009). *Time to Eat the Dog? A real guide to sustainable living*. Thames and Hudson.

2 AECB (2010). Comments on consultation document 'Consultation on the Renewable Heat Incentive'. Personal communication.

3 A. Simmonds (2008). 'Radical renovation to CarbonLite standards'. *Green Building*, 18(3), Winter 2008.

4 'Retrofit rethink: Kevin talks to *Inside Housing* magazine'. *Inside Housing*, 3, November 2009.

5 Hannah Solloway (2009). 'Report on Mendip Open Green Homes and Gardens'. www.mendipenvironment.org.uk.

6 Bandura (1977). *Social Learning Theory*. General Learning Press.

7 Jo Hamilton (in press). 'Keeping up with the Joneses in the Great British refurb: the impacts and limits of social learning in eco-renovation'. In Whitmarsh, O'Neill & Lorenzoni (eds). *Engaging the Public with Climate Change: Behaviour change and communication*. Earthscan.

8 A full report on this refurbishment, including how the owners obtained planning consent, was subsequently published. See 'Victorian Passivhaus: A haus in Hackney'. *Building*, 22 January 2010.

9 William Morris (1884). 'How We Live and How We Might Live'. Lecture delivered to the Hammersmith Branch of the Socialist Democratic Federation, 30 November 1884.

10 www.goingcarbonneutral.co.uk/geds-story.

11 Tracey Todhunter (2009) 'Our Earth Village'. *Sustained*, Issue 9.

12 www.innovateuk.org/content/news/17m-government-investment-in-retrofitting-to-pave-.ashx.

13 'Green home makeover will cost up to £15,000, says climate watchdog chief'. *The Guardian*, 11 November 2009.

14 Robert and Brenda Vale (2009). *Time to Eat the Dog? A real guide to sustainable living*. Thames and Hudson.

15 Rob Hopkins. 'What is the payback on your solar panels and should you care?' www.transitionculture.org, 19 June 2008.

16 Geoff Hammond and Craig Jones (2008). 'Inventory of Carbon and Energy'. Available at www.bath.ac.uk/mech-eng/sert/embodied.

17 Vasilis Fthenakis and Erik Alsema (2006). 'Photovoltaics energy payback times, greenhouse gas emissions and external costs'. *Progress in Photovoltaics: Research and Applications*, 14, 275-80. www.clca.columbia.edu/papers/Photovoltaic_Energy_Payback_Times.pdf.

18 C. Bankier and S. Gale (2006). 'Energy payback of roof mounted photovoltaic cells'. *Energy Bulletin*, 16 June 2006. www.energybulletin.net.

## Chapter 5. Building together

1 Simon Fairlie (2009). Foreword to Pickerill and Maxey (eds) *Low Impact Development: The future in our hands*. University of Leicester Department of Geography. p.3.

2 Tony Wrench (2008) *Building a Low Impact Roundhouse*. Permanent Publications.

3 Jenny Pickerill and Larch Maxey (eds) (2008). *Low Impact Development: The future in our hands*. University of Leicester Department of Geography. p.8. Available at www.lowimpactdevelopment.wordpress.com.

4 Ibid.

5 Ibid. p.21.

6 'Communal living: love thy neighbour'. *The Guardian*, 24 October 2009.

7 'A community built on ecological values'. www.lancastercohousing.org.uk.

8 'Living greener, cheaper, friendlier: The policy case for eco-clusters and cohousing'. UK Cohousing Network. www.cohousing.org.uk/node/141.

## Chapter 6: Sustainable housing in Brighton

1 Mischa Hewitt and Kevin Telfer (2007). *Earthships: Building a zero carbon future for homes*. BRE Press. p.1.

2 Ibid. p.113.

3 *Schnews*, Issue 354.

4 Personal communication.

## Chapter 7: New build

1 'Tear down 60s and 70s buildings, says government adviser'. *The Times*, 26 January 2010.

2 www.monbiot.com.

3 'Homes for the Future: More affordable, more sustainable' (2007). Department of Communities and Local Government.

4 transitionculture.org/2009/02/24/a-wander-round-the-wintles.

5 Ibid.

6 www.segalselfbuild.co.uk/about.html.

7 www.nasba.org.

8 Will Anderson (2006). *Diary of an Eco-Builder*. Green Books.

9 www.bioregional.com/news-views/publications/bedzed-seven-years-on.

10 www.designformanufacture.info

11 Jonathan Manns (2008). 'Eco-towns, New Labour and sustainable residential development'. People, Place & Policy Online. http://extra.shu.ac.uk/ppp-online.

## Chapter 8: Social housing

1 www.defendcouncilhousing.org.uk, 'Case against stock transfer'.

2 www.england.shelter.org.uk.

3 Barbara Jones (2010). *Building with Straw Bales*. Green Books.

4 amazonails.org.uk, 'A place for everyone'.

5 www.hse.gov.uk/statistics.

6 Gentoo (2009). 'Code word: A review of traditional and PassivHaus based designs against the Code'. www.gentoohomes.com.

7 www.gentoosunderland.com/?article=8769&track=/355/356/&resizer=.

8 Peter Walls, Chief Executive, Gentoo Group. www.gentoogroup.com.

9 'Thermographic Inspection of the Masonry and Hemp Houses – Haverhill, Suffolk'. http://projects.bre.co.uk/hemphomes/HempThermographicReport.pdf.

10 'Showcasing Excellence Case Study 9: The Honingham Earth Sheltered Social Housing Scheme'. www.publicarchitecture.co.uk/knowledge-base/case-studies.

11 www.dcha.co.uk/green+issues/slp.

12 www.dcha.co.uk/Resources/DCH%20Group/documents/green/DCHA%20Sustainable%20Living%20Report.pdf.

13 www.housingcorp.gov.uk/server/show/nav.13506.

## Chapter 10: New tricks with old bricks

1 www.emptyhomes.com/usefulresources/stats/2009breakdown.htm.

2 www.eci.ox.ac.uk/research/energy/40house/index.php.

3 'New Tricks with Old Bricks' (2009). The Empty Homes Agency. www.emptyhomes.com/documents/publications/reports.

4 'The Role of Historic Buildings in Urban Regeneration' (2004). House of Commons Housing, Planning, Local Government and the Regions Select Committee.

5 'Planning Policy Statement 3: Housing' (2006). Department of Communities and Local Government. paragraph 31.

'Homes for the Future: More affordable, more sustainable' (2007). Department of Communities and Local Government.

6 'East Kent Empty Properties Initiative main report' (2005). www.no-use-empty.org/web/files/FordhamReportEastKent. pdf.

7 'Empty Homes in London 2005-6' (2006). Greater London Authority.

8 'An Assessment of the Housing Potential of Vacant Commercial Space over Shops in Chichester' (2001). Chichester District Council.

9 Robert Neuwirth (2004). *Shadow Cities: A billion squatters.* Routledge.

10 Mark Hines Architects (2008). 'The Rebirth of Toxteth Street – Alternatives to Demolition'. www.savebritainsheritage.org/news/campaign.php?id=7.

11 Ibid.

12 SAVE Britain's Heritage (in press). 'Streets of the Future: Unlocking the Benefits of Terraced Housing'.

13 'Housing Market Renewal: Pathfinders HC106' (2008). House of Commons Committee of Public Accounts. The Stationery Office.

14 Stephen Kingston. 'The fight for Salford's future'. 10 August 2006. www.salfordstar.blogspot.com.

15 Greener Housing Supplement. *The Guardian,* 25 March 2009.

16 'Stock Take: Delivering Improvements in Existing Housing' (2006). Sustainable Development Commission. www.sd-commission.org.uk/publications.php?id=400.

17 Personal communication.

18 'Key Messages and Evidence on the Housing Market Renewal Pathfinder Programme 2003-2009' (2009). Department of Communities and Local Government.

## Chapter 11. Land, planning permission and finance

1 'Want a perfect home? Build it yourself'. *The Independent,* 15 March 2003. www.independent.co.uk.

2 'Homebuilding in the UK' (2007). Office of Fair Trading. www.oft.gov.uk/OFTwork/markets-work/completed/home1.

3 Lloyd Kahn (2004) *Homework: Handbuilt shelters.* Perfect Paperback.

4 www.homesandcommunities.co.uk/Surplus_public_sector_land.

5 Sarah Monk et al. (2006) 'Delivering Affordable Housing through Section 106: Outputs and Outcomes'. Joseph Rowntree Foundation.

6 Quoted in *The Land,* Summer 2008.

7 'Gran in Tesco boss planning war'. www.news.bbc.co.uk, 12 April 2008.

8 www.communities.gov.uk/planningandbuilding.

9 'Cheltenham Borough Local Plan Second Review 1991-2011'. www.cheltenham.gov.uk/downloads/Housing_Background_Paper.pdf.

10 'Planning Policy Statement 7: Sustainable Development in Rural Areas' (2004). Department of Communities and Local Government. paragraph 11.

11 'Code for Sustainable Homes: A step-change in sustainable home building practice' (2006). Department of Communities and Local Government.

12 'Homebuilding Market Study: Annex R – Alternative Development Models' (2008). Office of Fair Trading. www.oft.gov.uk/shared_oft/reports/comp_policy/oft1020r.pdf.

13 Tony Croft, Stonesfield Community Trust. www.stonesfieldcommunitytrust.org.uk.

14 www.highbickington.org.

15 Housing and Regeneration Act (2008) Part 2, Chapter 1, Clause 79. www.opsi.gov.uk/acts/acts2008a.

16 Matthew Taylor MP (2009), 'Living Working Countryside'. www.matthewtaylor.info.

17 'Common Ground – For Mutual Home Ownership'. new economics foundation and CDS Co-ooperatives. http://www.cds.coop/documents/Common Ground leaflet.pdf.

18 Full link is www.bodhi-eco-project.org.uk/Docs/IPSSummaryBodhiRev2.2.20090224.pdf.

## Chapter 12. Sustainable housing in Sheffield

1 J. Ruskin (1884) 'The Storm-Cloud of the Nineteenth Century'. Two lectures delivered at the London Institution, 4 and 11 February 1884.

2 www.beacons.idea.gov.uk.

3 'Learning from the Housing Beacons: Sheffield City Council'. www.idea.gov.uk/idk/core/page.do?page1d=15628499.

4 'Financial crisis forces acclaimed charity's closure'. *The Guardian*, 25 November 2008.

5 www.sheffield.gov.uk.

6 'Focus on People and Migration' (2005). Office for National Statistics.

www.statistics.gov.uk/downloads/theme_compendia/fom2005/03_FOPM_UrbanAreas.pdf.

## Chapter 13. Materials and skills

1 European Lime Association. http://eula.rapportcreative.co.uk.

2 www.lime.org.uk.

3 www.cementindustry.co.uk.

4 http://rammed-earth.org. *DIY Rammed Earth Manual* is available from here.

5 Steve Allin (2005). *Building with Hemp*. Seed Press.

6 'The truth about recycling'. *The Economist*, 7 June 2007.

7 www.bioregional-reclaimed.com.

8 Mischa Hewitt and Kevin Telfer (2007). *Earthships: Building a zero carbon future for homes*. BRE Press. p.82.

9 Doug King (2010). 'Engineering a Low Carbon Built Environment'. Royal Academy of Engineering.

10 UK Green Building Council (2008). 'Low Carbon Existing Homes' report. www.ukgbc.org/site/resources/show-resource-details?id=316.

11 N. Bergman et al. (2009). 'UK microgeneration. Part I: policy and behavioural aspects'. *Energy*, 162, 23-36.

S. Caird et al. (2008). 'Improving the energy performance of UK households: Results from surveys of consumer adoption and use of low- and zero-carbon technologies'. *Energy Efficiency*, 1(2), 149-66. doi: 10.1007/s12053-008-9013-y.

12 Killip, G. (2008). 'Building a Greener Britain: Transforming the UK's Existing Housing Stock'. A report for the Federation of Master Builders by the Environmental Change Institute. www.fmb.org.uk/news/campaigns/building-a-greener-britain.

13 Department of Energy and Climate Change (2010). 'Warm Homes, Greener Homes: a Strategy for Household Energy Management'. www.decc.gov.uk/en/content/cms/what_we_do/consumers/saving_energy/hem/hem.aspx.

14 The Prince's Foundation for the Built Environment (2010). 'Sustainable Supply Chains that Support Local Economic Development'. www.princes-foundation.org/index.php?id=8#reports.

15 Ibid.

16 www.greenworkforce.co.uk.

## Chapter 14. International and green: lessons from around the world

1 www.thenauhaus.com/nauhaus/summary.php.

2 'Increasing the availability of locally produced, ecological building materials'. www.sdc.admin.ch/en/Home/Projects/Production_of_ecological_house_building_materials?userhash=

3 Diana Leafe Christian (2007). *Finding Community*. New Society Publishers.

4 www.ted.com/talks/cameron_sinclair_on_open_source_architecture.html.

# RESOURCES

This section lists resources for sustainable housing. It is not an exhaustive list, which would require a book in itself, but a foot in the door to the wealth of projects, organisations, websites and books available. The four main sections – 'General', 'Building and materials', 'Local organisations and case studies' and 'Community' – are to some extent overlapping. Subsections within these sections make the listings more accessible, e.g. 'Low-impact development' and 'Housing associations' are subsections within 'Community'. Publications are listed at the end of the resources section.

## Contents

## General

### Campaign groups

**Advisory Service for Squatters**
020 3216 0099
www.squatter.org.uk
Provides legal and practical advice to squatters and other homeless people.

**Chapter 7**
01297 561359
www.tlio.org.uk/chapter7/index.html
Magazine and organisation campaigning around land rights.

**Climate Solidarity**
020 7924 2727
www.climatesolidarity.org.uk
Trade union campaign on climate change, which includes a call for a million new jobs to promote low-carbon measures.

**Empty Homes Agency**
020 7022 1870
www.emptyhomes.com
Highlights the waste of empty homes and property.

**Existing Homes Alliance**

www.existinghomesalliance.org

Campaigns for low-carbon improvements to existing UK housing.

**Forum for the Future**

020 7324 3630

www.forumforthefuture.org.uk

UK sustainable development organisation working with leaders from business and the public sector to "create a green, fair and prosperous world".

**Global Commons Institute**

www.gci.org.uk

Founded in 1990 to campaign for a fair way to tackle climate change. Its main focus is 'contraction and convergence'.

**Local Works**

020 7278 4443

www.localworks.org

Campaigns in support of the Sustainable Communities Act

**new economics foundation**

020 7820 6300

www.neweconomics.org

Economics as if people and the planet mattered.

**One Planet Living**

www.oneplanetliving.org

Global initiative developed by BioRegional and WWF, which outlines and promotes ten principles of sustainable living.

**SAVE Britain's Heritage**

020 7253 3500

www.savebritainsheritage.org

Campaigns to preserve our built environment.

**Shelter**

0808 800 4444

www.shelter.org.uk

UK housing and homelessness charity.

## Government

**Beacon Scheme**

See Local Innovation Awards Scheme, below.

**Decent Homes Standard**

www.communities.gov.uk/housing/decenthomes/whatis

Minimum standards for social housing, established by the Department for Communities and Local Government.

**Department of Energy and Climate Change (DECC)**

0300 060 4000

www.decc.gov.uk

Responsible for securing 'clean, safe, affordable energy' and leading the UK response to climate change.

**Homes and Communities Agency**

0300 1234 500

www.homesandcommunities.co.uk

Public body overseeing housing and regeneration, formed in 2008 by the merger of the Housing Corporation and English Partnerships and sponsored by the Department for Communities and Local Government.

**Local Innovation Awards Scheme**

020 7296 6662

www.localinnovation.idea.gov.uk

Government scheme to share best practice around 'homes for the future'. Was the Beacon Scheme prior to April 2010.

**Sustainable Development Commission**

0300 068 6305 (London)

0131 6251880 (Edinburgh)

028 9052 0196 (Belfast)

029 2037 6956 (Cardiff)

www.sd-commission.org.uk

The government's independent adviser on sustainable development; publishes some useful reports.

**Warm Zones**

www.warmzones.co.uk

Originally set up to develop new approaches to fuel poverty, this scheme now includes climate change as a reason for tackling poor fuel energy efficiency.

## Information, advice, education and research

**Carbon calculators**
There are lots of online programmes to help you calculate and reduce your carbon footprint. See, for example: www.carbonfootprint.com/calculator.aspx

**Centre for Alternative Technology**
01654 705989
www.cat.org.uk
Wales-based centre for all things sustainable. Of particular interest is its report 'Zero Carbon Britain 2030'.

**Energy Saving Trust**
0800 512012
www.energysavingtrust.org.uk
Comprehensive source of free advice and information on how to save energy, conserve water and reduce waste.

**Environmental Change Institute**
01865 275848
www.eci.ox.ac.uk
University of Oxford department sponsoring research and outreach.

**Hockerton Housing Project**
01636 816902
www.hockertonhousingproject.org.uk
Earth-sheltered housing project that runs numerous courses and an advisory service.

**Household Energy Service**
01588 630683
www.h-e-s.org
Independent, local energy advice service.

**National Energy Action**
0191 261 5677
www.nea.org.uk
Promotes solutions to the energy needs of low-income households. Has offices in Newcastle, Belfast and Swansea.

**National Energy Foundation**
01908 665555
www.nef.org.uk
Encourages energy efficiency and renewable energy.

**Sustainable Energy Academy**
www.sustainable-energyacademy.org.uk
Promotes education and action to reduce the carbon footprint of buildings and communities. Runs the Old Home Superhome network.

**www.earth.org.uk**
A very informative website going into the fine details of reducing emissions from your home.

**www.greenenergy360.org**
Helps you assess options for renewable energy and lists installers.

**www.greenmoves.co.uk**
Forum for buying, selling or renting 'greener' homes.

**www.lowcarbonlife.net**
Website of Chris Goodall, who wrote *How to Live a Low-carbon Life*, described by *New Scientist* as "the definitive guide to reducing your carbon footprint".

**www.post-carbon-living.com**
Down-to-earth website that includes updates on the refurbishment of a 1980s home.

## The Transition movement

**Transition Network**
www.transitionnetwork.org
The main website of the Transition movement. Provides an introduction to the concepts of Transition and links to Transition initiatives around the world.

**Transition Culture**
www.transitionculture.org
The website of Rob Hopkins. "An evolving exploration into the head, heart and hands of energy descent".

**Transition Books**
www.transitionbooks.net
An imprint of Green Books.

## International

**Architecture for Humanity**
www.architectureforhumanity.org
Promotes architecture and design solutions to global and humanitarian crises.

**Global Ecovillage Network**
http://gen.ecovillage.org
Supports alternative and sustainable communities around the world.

**Post Carbon Institute**
www.postcarbon.org
Campaigns for resilient communities and re-localised economies. Based in the USA.

## Building and materials

### Suppliers of materials and training

**Amazonails**
0845 4582173
www.amazonails.org.uk
Training, consultation and advice on anything to do with straw-bale building.

**Back to Earth**
01363 866999
www.backtoearth.co.uk
Natural building projects and products in Devon.

**Cenin Ltd**
01656 789970
www.cenin.co.uk
Wales-based manufacturers of low-carbon cement replacement products.

**Clayworks**
01326 341339
http://clay-works.com

Cornwall-based cob builders who have developed a system of building with clay blocks and plasters.

**Cornish Lime Company**
01208 79779
www.cornishlime.co.uk
Lime products and courses.

**Elemental Solutions**
01981 540728
www.elementalsolutions.co.uk
Sustainable water management.

**Green Building Store**
01484 461705
www.greenbuildingstore.co.uk
Supplier of 'green' building materials, with links to the construction company that built the Denby Dale Passivhaus.

**The Greenshop**
01452 770629
www.greenshop.co.uk
Wide range of eco-building and household products. Based near Stroud.

**Hemp Technology**
01986 835678
www.hemcore.co.uk
subsidiary of Lime Technology (see page 228); supplies hemp building products.

**Hempire Building Materials Ltd**
+353 (0)47 52049
www.hempirebuilding.net
Ireland-based company supplying sustainable building materials, particularly hemp-based products.

**J&J Sharpe**
01805 603587
www.jjsharpe.co.uk
Builders and material suppliers specialising in cob and lime. Rheir home is a beautiful new-build cob building in Devon.

**Kevin McCabe Cob Buildings Specialists**
01404 814270
www.buildsomethingbeautiful.com
Cob building specialist whose website name says it all.

**Lime Technology**
0845 603 1143
www.limetechnology.co.uk
Suppliers of lime-based building products.

**Modcell**
01179 547325
www.modcell.co.uk
Modular system of straw-bale and hemp panels, used to build the BaleHaus in Bath.

**Natural Building Technologies**
01844 338338
www.natural-building.co.uk
UK supplier of sustainable building materials.

**Refit West**
www.forumforthefuture.org/projects/refit-west
Bristol-based refurbishment project from Forum for the Future

**Second Nature**
017684 86285
www.secondnatureuk.com
Cumbria-based company supplying wool-based insulation materials such as Thermafleece.

**Tŷ-Mawr**
01874 611350
www.lime.org.uk
Welsh company supplying sustainable building materials and running courses in the use of lime-based materials.

**www.greenspec.co.uk**
A directory (and much more) of sustainable construction products available in the UK.

**www.strawbale-building.co.uk**
Includes a directory of straw bale resources in the UK and details of organisations running courses.

## Builders and developers

**BioRegional**
020 8404 4880
www.bioregional.com
Entrepreneurial charity behind developments such as BedZED and OneBrighton.

**Earthwise Construction**
01273 782047
www.earthwiseconstruction.org
Brighton-based 'green' building company established by some of the people responsible for Earthship Brighton.

**Sherwood Energy Village**
01623 860222
www.sev.org.uk
Low-carbon development of a former mining site, promoted by former miners. Offers consultancy.

**Zedfactory**
020 8404 1380
www.zedfactory.com
Design and build company, established by Bill Dunster, behind projects such as BedZED and RuralZED. The ZED stands for 'zero energy development'.

## Reclamation and recycling

**BioRegional Reclaimed**
020 8404 4880
www.bioregional-reclaimed.com
Facilitates the reuse of building materials. Launched **www.reiy.net** (Reuse It Yourself).

**National Community Wood Recycling Project**
01273 203040
www.communitywoodrecycling.org.uk
Rapidly expanding social enterprise establishing wood recycling projects around the UK.

**WRAP**
01295 819900
www.wrap.org.uk
Helps people and businesses to reduce waste, develop

sustainable products and use resources sustainably. WRAP's work includes recycling and reclaiming building materials.

**www.salvoweb.com**
Directory of suppliers of reclaimed building materials and architectural salvage.

## National organisations

### British Earth Sheltering Association
www.besa-uk.org
Non-profit-making organisation encouraging the construction of earth-sheltered buildings in the UK.

### Building Research Establishment (BRE)
01923 664000
www.bre.co.uk
UK-based organisation performing research, testing and certification on building methods and materials around the world. Masses of information, including detailed project reports and evaluation of materials. Also produces a 'Green Guide' to materials: www.thegreenguide.org.uk.

### Hemp Lime Construction Products Association
01420 471618
www.hemplime.org.uk
Promotes the use of hemp lime products by the UK construction industry.

### National Non-Food Crops Centre
01904 435182
www.nnfcc.co.uk
UK centre developing sustainable supply chains for plant-based products, including renewable building materials.

### National Self Build Association
0117 953 0729
www.nasba.org.uk
Campaigns to improve opportunities for self-build across the UK.

### PassivHaus UK
www.passivhaus.org.uk
Home of passivhaus building in the UK.

### Prince's Foundation for the Built Environment
020 7613 8500
www.princes-foundation.org
Promotes "timeless and ecological ways of planning, designing and building".

### Sustainable Building Association (AECB)
0845 456 9773
www.aecb.net
A directory of 'green' builders and architects; provides information about the AECB CarbonLite programme and lots more.

### UK Green Building Council
020 7580 0623
www.ukgbc.org
Building industry umbrella group aiming to "bring clarity, purpose and coordination of sustainability strategy to the sector".

### Walter Segal Self Build Trust
www.segalselfbuild.co.uk
UK charity offering advice on self-build.

## Research and education

### BRE Centre for Innovative Construction Materials
01225 384495
www.bath.ac.uk/bre
Based at the University of Bath, this centre conducts research into sustainable building materials. It developed the BaleHaus in Bath: **www.bath.ac.uk/features/ balehaus**.

### Ecos Trust
01458 254352
www.ecostrust.org.uk
Charity promoting sustainable design and build techniques. Includes Ecos Renew for refurbishment and Ecos Homes for developments.

**Genesis Project**

01823 366528

www.genesisproject.com

Based at Somerset College, this centre offers training in sustainable building in an award-winning building constructed from many natural materials.

**Pesticide Action Network**

020 7065 0905

www.pan-uk.org

Publishes a factsheet on timber treatments.

**Practical Action**

01926 634400

www.practicalaction.org

Development charity that produces lots of excellent 'Technical Briefs' of value to sustainable builders.

**South Yorkshire Energy Centre**

0114 258 4574

www.syec.co.uk

Sheffield-based centre for education on renewable energy and sustainable building.

**www.greenbuilder.co.uk**

Links to hundreds of sustainable building websites.

**www.greenbuildingbible.co.uk**

Supporting website for the popular books of the same name.

**www.ilovecob.com**

The site for cob lovers.

## International organisations

**Building for Social Responsibility**

www.bsr-vt.org

Vermont-based development professionals working to advance environmentally sound technologies and practices.

**The Cob Cottage Company**

www.cobcottage.com

The people behind the beautiful and inspiring 'Hand Sculpted House' and the source for all things cobbish in the US.

**Earthship Biotecture**

http://earthship.com

US-based website of Mike Reynolds; covers earthship building and courses around the world.

**Ecological Builders Network (EBNet)**

www.ecobuildnetwork.org

US-based clearing house for information on building with ecologically friendly materials and energy saving, founded by Bruce King.

**The Canelo Project**

www.caneloproject.com

Natural builders with an emphasis on straw and clay, based in Arizona with projects in Mexico.

**Natural Builders Northeast**

www.nbne.org

A network of building and design professionals in the north-east USA.

**The Natural Building Network**

www.nbnetwork.org

Lists natural builders and events around the world but mainly in the USA.

**Natural Design/Build**

www.naturaldesignbuild.us

Vermont-based natural building company founded by Ben Graham, who also organises a network of natural builders (www.nbne.org).

**The Nauhaus Institute**

http://thenauhaus.com

A US network of designers and builders developing a model of urban sustainable living that combines high-tech with natural and 'green'.

**Pass Net**

www.pass-net.net

A European network of organisations promoting

Passivhaus solutions. The UK partner is the Sustainable Building Association (AECB, see page 229).

### Passivhaus Institut (Germany)
www.passiv.de
An English translation of this website is available.

### Small House Society
www.resourcesforlife.com/small-house-society
US group promoting the environmental and affordability benefits of smaller homes.

## Local organisations and case studies

This section lists those groups, projects and Eco Open House events covered in this book whose contact information is in the public domain.

### Organisations

### Ashton Hayes Going Carbon Neutral
07968 063624
www.goingcarbonneutral.co.uk
A community in Cheshire aiming to become England's first carbon-neutral community.

### Sustainable Blacon
01244 390344
www.sustainableblacon.org.uk
Blacon aims to become a model sustainable community through 'green' approaches to open spaces, energy, transport and social enterprises.

### Totnes Energy Descent Action Plan
01803 867358
http://totnes.transitionnetwork.org/edap/home
A plan for energy descent developed in Totnes. An online version can be accessed from this site.

### Transition Together
01803 867358
www.transitiontogether.org.uk
A programme developed in Totnes showing how to take small, achievable steps to save energy and money.

Transition Streets (www.transitionstreets.org.uk, same phone number) is a related project.

## Case studies

### www.3acorns.co.uk
Upgrade of an 1840s Victorian terrace home to make it one of the most energy efficient homes in the country.
### www.bvt.org.uk/ecohome
A Bourneville eco-home refurbishment.

### www.cropthornehouse.co.uk
A new build in the 'autonomous house' tradition.

### www.ecoterrace.co.uk
Website charting the progress of a Victorian terrace refurbishment.

### www.evelynecoproject.co.uk
Website describing the upgrading of a ordinary semi-detached house to good environmental standards.

### www.barclayscobhouse.blogspot.com
Photographic record of a cob build in Devon.

### www.graylingwellchichester.com
Plans for the redevelopment of the Graylingwell Hospital site in Chichester

### www.greenhouseleeds.co.uk
Low-carbon refurbishment of an old workers' hostel in Leeds.

### www.greeningthebox.co.uk
A collaboration between SEArch Architects and Wherry Housing Association to retrofit an existing dwelling to high energy standards.

### www.renewable-house.co.uk
Hemcrete® house developed by the National Non Food Crops Centre.

### www.msarch.co.uk/ecohome
Retrofit of a Victorian home to a high environmental standard.

**www.rbkc.gov.uk/flagshiphome**
Refurbishment of a Victorian property in Westminster as a model for landlords.

**www.theyellowhouse.org.uk**
The story of how a 1930s ex-council house was turned into an 'environmental dream home'.

**www.tranquilityhouses.com**
Tranquility modestly claims to be 'probably the lowest-energy house ever built'.

**www.treehouseclapham.org.uk**
Will Anderson's 'tree house' – designed around the mature tree on the plot, and to "work like a tree".

## Eco Open House events

### Brighton Eco Open Houses
www.ecoopenhouses.org
The well-funded 2008 event in particular is a superb model of how to run an Eco Open House event – if you have the money!

### Climate Outreach Information Network (COIN)
01865 403334
www.coinet.org.uk
Oxford-based charity using innovative methods to engage the public in action on climate change. Organises the Ecovation Open House events with ClimateXChange.

### ClimateXchange
01865 275856
www.climatex.org
Oxfordshire-based climate action campaign also involved in the Ecovation Open House events.

### Mendip Open Green Homes and Gardens
http://mendip.ourenvironment.org.uk/node/70
Ran an Open Green Homes and Gardens event in 2009.

### Open House London
020 3006 7008
www.londonopenhouse.org
Now renamed Open City. Organises Open House events in London, which include large numbers of eco- and refurbished homes.

### Stroud Eco-Renovation Open Homes
www.stroudopenhomes.org.uk
Very successful Eco Open House event run by Transition Stroud.

### Torridge Action Group 4 Sustainability
01237 477822
www.tag4s.org.uk
Climate campaign based in North Devon which organised the 'Powerhouse Safari', visiting eco-refurbishments and renewable energy installations.

## Community

## Low-impact development

### Diggers & Dreamers
www.diggersanddreamers.org.uk
London-based organisation that provides a guide to communal living in Britain.

### Lammas
www.lammas.org.uk
Eco-village in Wales consisting of nine low-impact eco-smallholdings over 76 acres. Construction began in 2009.

### Landmatters
www.landmatters.org.uk
Low-impact permaculture community near Totnes in Devon.

### Low Impact Living Initiative (LILI)
www.lowimpact.org
Has lots of useful links under the 'Shelter' topic.

### Steward Community Woodland
www.stewardwood.org
A permaculture community in Devon established in 2000.

### www.thatroundhouse.info
Website about a pioneering low-impact roundhouse at the centre of a long battle for planning consent.

## Cohousing, cooperatives and land trusts

### Bodhi Eco-Project
0141 946 8096
www.bodhi-eco-project.org.uk
Glasgow-based group seeking to establish an eco-village. Among the documents on its website is a useful exploration of different legal and financial structures.

### Cohousing Association of America
www.cohousing.org
Website includes a directory of hundreds of cohousing communities and groups in the USA.

### Coin Street Community Builders (CSCB)
020 7021 1600
www.coinstreet.org
Community based organisation behind housing and community facilities in London's regenerated South Bank.

### Community Land Trusts
0161 295 4454
www.communitylandtrusts.org.uk
Supports local groups in 'capturing land value for communities'. Includes a valuable CLT Fund to help groups get started, as well as great resources and links.

### High Bickington Community Property Trust
01769 560161
www.highbickington.org
Pioneered 'community-led planning' and fought a long battle with planning authorities to implement a local plan.

### Lancaster Cohousing
01524 555919
www.lancastercohousing.org.uk
After gaining planning consent in 2010 this group is developing its site at Halton Mill on the River Lune.

### Lilac
www.lilac.coop
Low Impact Living Affordable Community (Lilac) says it all for this group planning straw-bale affordable homes in Leeds.

### Living Village Trust
www.livingvillage.com
Consultancy in the area of energy-efficient building and sustainable living. Developed The Wintles.

### National Association of Housing Cooperatives
www.coophousing.org
Comprehensive website outlining the role of this US organisation and giving details of housing cooperatives in the USA.

### Radical Routes
0845 330 4510
www.radicalroutes.org.uk
A network of cooperatives working for social change. It runs Rootstock as a funding mechanism for cooperatives.

### Springhill Cohousing
www.therightplace.net/coco/public
The first new-build cohousing scheme to be completed in the UK and still a great and all-too-rare example.

### Stonesfield Community Trust
www.stonesfieldcommunitytrust.org.uk
A former mining village. The first Community Land Trust set up in Britain for 100 years.

### The Threshold Centre
01747 821929
www.thresholdcentre.org.uk
Sustainable education centre and cohousing community in Dorset.

### UK Cohousing Network
07545 857366
www.cohousing.org.uk
One-stop shop for cohousing in the UK, with links to all active groups and lots of news and resources.

### The Village
+353 (0)505 42833
www.thevillage.ie
Cloughjordan, Ireland's largest eco-village, with over 100 homes and live/work units on a 67-acre site.

**Westwood Cohousing**
www.westwoodcohousing.com
US cohousing group based on permaculture principles
and sustainable design.

## Housing associations

**Black Country Housing Group**
01202 410500
www.bcha.co.uk
Housing association with a range of eco-projects
including the eco-pod.

**Devon & Cornwall Housing Association**
0300 123 8080
www.dcha.co.uk
Social landlord that has developed sustainability policies
in collaboration with tenants.

**Family Housing Association**
0121 766 1100
www.family-housing.co.uk
Social landlord based in Birmingham with an impressive
range of eco-projects.

**Flagship Housing**
0845 601 3390
www.flagship-housing.co.uk
Parent company for Peddars Way Housing Association,
which developed the first earth-sheltered social housing
in the UK.

**Gentoo Group**
0191 525 5000
www.gentoogroup.com
Sunderland-based property business and social landlord
responsible for a number of innovative 'green' building
projects, including Passivhaus homes.

**National Housing Federation**
020 7067 1010
www.housing.org.uk
Represents 1200 not-for-profit housing associations in
England.

**Penwith Housing Association**
01736 331799
www.penwithha.org.uk
Cornwall-based housing association pioneering the use of
heat pumps.

**Suffolk Housing Society**
01284 767224
www.suffolkhousing.org
Social landlord based in East Anglia pioneering the use of
hemp-based building materials.

## Miscellaneous

**Cambridge Carbon Footprint**
01223 971353
http://cambridgecarbonfootprint.org
The place to find out about 'Carbon Conversations'
(http://cambridgecarbonfootprint.org/action/carbon-
conversations/national-carbon-conversations). Also offers
free energy surveys.

**Community Self Build Agency**
01795 663073
www.communityselfbuildagency.org.uk
Supports groups of people, mainly in London, wanting to
build their own homes.

**Community Solutions**
www.communitysolution.org
US organisation focusing on peak oil and climate change,
with a housing section and some interesting presentations.

**Down to Earth**
01792 346566
www.downtoearthproject.org.uk
Social enterprise based in South Wales that works with
young people and adults on sustainable education and
natural building.

**Green Streets**
www.greenstreets.co.uk
British Gas project 'helping Britain's communities to be
greener'.

### Green Triangle

http://greentriangle.wetpaint.com
A group of neighbours in Sheffield working together for a greener neighbourhood.

### Groundwork

0121 236 8565
www.groundwork.org.uk
Environmental regeneration charity working in partnership with local authorities and business. Created the 'Green Doctor' programme.

### Leeds Action to Create Homes (LATCH)

0113 2374482
www.latch.org.uk
Voluntary sector organisation working with the community to bring derelict and disused properties back into use as social housing.

### Low Carbon Communities Network

http://lowcarboncommunities.net
Network encouraging the adoption of low-carbon and zero-carbon technologies and lifestyles at a community level.

### Low Carbon Trust

07974 122770
www.lowcarbon.co.uk
Brighton-based group running low-carbon construction projects and training. One of its first projects was the Brighton Earthship.

### Hyde Farm CAN

07961 342247
www.hydefarm.org.uk
Climate action network based on the Hyde Farm estate in Balham, London

## Publications

Berge, Bjorn (2009). *The Ecology of Building Materials*. Architectural Press.

Borer, Pat and Harris, Cindy (1998). *The Whole House Book: Ecological building design and materials*. CAT Publications.

Broome, Jon (2007). *The Green Self-build Book: How to design and build your own eco-home*. Green Books. (Inspirational – also worth looking at Jon's other books.)

Dawson, Jonathan (2006). *Ecovillages: New frontiers for sustainability*. Schumacher Briefings, Green Books.

Evans, Ianto; Smith, Michael and Smiley, Linda (2002). *The Hand-Sculpted House: A practical guide to building a cob cottage*. Chelsea Green.

Fairlie, Simon (2009). *Low Impact Development: Planning and people in a sustainable countryside*. Jon Carpenter.

Halliday, Sandy (2008). *Sustainable Construction*. Butterworth-Heinemann.

Laughton, Rebecca (2008). *Surviving and Thriving on the Land: How to use your time and energy to run a successful smallholding*. Green Books.

Mackay, David (2008). *Sustainable Energy – Without the Hot Air*. UIT. Available as a free download from www.withouthotair.com.

Pickerill, Jenny and Maxey, Larch (eds) (2008). *Low Impact Development: The future in our hands*. University of Leicester Department of Geography. Available at www.lowimpactdevelopment.wordpress.com.

Rosen, Nick (2008). *How to Live Off-grid*. Bantam Books. (Associated website is www.off-grid.net.)

Weismann, Adam and Bryce, Katy (2006). *Building with Cob: A step-by-step guide*. Green Books.

Wines, James (2000) *Green Architecture: The art of architecture in the age of ecology*. Taschen.

*Green Building* magazine. www.buildingforafuture.co.uk.

*Permaculture* magazine. www.permaculture-magazine.co.uk.

*Your Home - Technical Manual*. A great guide to retrofitting homes in Australia but still valuable no mater where you live – and it's all free. www.yourhome.gov.au.

# INDEX